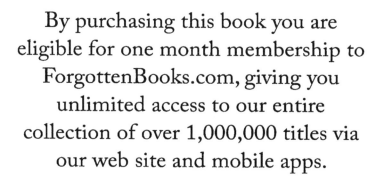

ISBN 978-0-483-41769-4
PIBN 10750270

Vol. 42   SEPTEMBER, 1936   No. 1

THE EDUCATOR

Forward Steps in Handwriting

This new book embodies many improvements and represents new forward steps in handwriting.

Read These Statements by the Authors . . . .

"In order to save time, write rapidly; in order to insure understanding on the part of the reader, write legibly."—JOHN G. KIRK, Director of Commercial Education, Philadelphia, Pa.

"The essentials of learning to write well are:

1. A strong desire to write well.

2. An abundance of good copies and sound methods, both based on correlation.

3. Appropriate practice applied by the student purposively and intelligently to accomplish ends which he recognizes."—

FRANK N. FREEMAN, Professor of Educational Psychology, University of Chicago.

Volume 42   COLUMBUS, OHIO, SEPTEMBER, 1936   No. 1

OVER FOUR DECADES

With this issue we begin our forty-second volume. This will make forty-two years during which time The Educator staff and its host of able contributors have devoted their efforts and money in promoting pen work and the interests of those engaged in it. It has been a pleasant work. Results have been very gratifying. Professional pen work and engrossing in America has developed into a substantial art. The quality of handwriting has advanced in the public schools in spite of many radical methods and the occasional disinterested and unqualified teacher.

Great strides have been made in methods. Out of the extremes of vertical slant, wild muscular movement, excessive movement drills, finger movement, etc., has evolved our modern method of teaching handwriting. An effort is made to interest the child and to train him so that he will become a better and more useful citizen. We no longer teach handwriting as a disconnected, disinteresting, subject but correlate it with other school subjects and activities. Many non-essentials and much drudgery is omitted today. An approximate amount of drill is presented as the student sees the need of it.

Some of the things advocated by this magazine years ago were ridiculed. However, today these same principals are incorporated in modern teaching of handwriting. The Educator was one of the first to advocate the use of the blackboard and the use of large writing for primary pupils. Practically all of the educators today advocate large work for beginners. Some years ago The Educator lead the way in correlating handwriting with other subjects.

While much has been accomplished there still is much to do. School authorities should be urged to demand better handwriting from all pupils and teachers. Many teachers need to be impressed with the importance of the subject and trained in skill and methods. Pupils need to be shown the value of good handwriting.

Penmanship should be given a place on the daily schedule until pupils learn to write well. Hospital classes need to be established in schools not conducting daily classes in handwriting.

Yes, there is work for all, and The Educator is moving forward with the intention of doing its part towards securing greater interest in all kinds of pen work. We earnestly solicit your cooperation. The more support you give The Educator the greater the results of this year's work. From the expressions and support received we are gratified to know that many of the leading men and women in the profession fully appreciate our efforts. We hope The Educator will find its way into more homes this year and be of ever increasing service to the members of our beloved profession.

HANDWRITING DEPARTMENT OF THE N. J. ST. T. ASSN.

New President

At the last meeting of the Handwriting Department of the New Jersey State Teachers' Association, Marjorie Flaacke was selected president. Miss Flaacke has served the department very efficiently for the past three or four years as Publicity Chairman. She teaches handwriting and geography in the State Normal School, Newark, N. J.

Miss Flaacke received her handwriting training in the State Normal School at Newark and the Newark Institute of Arts and Sciences which was then a branch of New York University. For a number of years she has taught handwriting at the State Normal School of Newark and also at the State Normal School of Jersey City. Since graduating from the State Normal School she has continued her work and has received the B. S. and M. A. degrees at New York University.

Miss Flaacke is a very enthusiastic teacher of handwriting and in selecting her the Handwriting Department of the New Jersey Association has secured a very able leader.

HANDWRITING CONTEST

The handwriting department of the New Jersey State Teachers' Association annually holds a handwriting contest which has done much to stimulate interest in handwriting in the state of New Jersey. For a number of years we have had the pleasure of helping to judge the contest. There is some very fine work submitted in this contest. In fact, better work would be hard to find in such large quantities. Following are the results of the contest:

School System	6th G.	8th G.	H.S.	T.P.
Orange	108	177	119	404
Newark	78	82	32	192
Moorestown	62	39	0	101
Plainfield	......	0	84	84
Burlington	......	4	63	67
Irvington	30	......	......	30
Bayonne	0	0	25	25
Margate City	23	0	0	23
Red Bank	9	9	......	18
Bridgeton	15	......	......	15
Maple Shade	......	13	......	13
Boonton	......	......	2	2
Gloucester	......	1	......	1

INCORRECT ENGLISH AND ILLEGIBLE HANDWRITING ARE COSTLY

Because of a grammatical error an indictment against six executives in a large corporation which crashed with a loss of $30,000,000 was dropped. The word "the" was used for an "a".

Many times large losses occur because of the illegibility of handwriting. Some letters are very similarly constructed making words very easily misread. For instance, "on" and "an" look alike when either the "o" or "a" is carelessly made. Also "e's" look like "i's" when made without daylight. "n's" look like "u's" when the turns and angles are not made distinct and in the proper places. There are many letters which if not made carefully cause considerable trouble. We believe that teachers of handwriting can render a very valuable service to their students by making a study of the possibilities of illegibilities in similar letters.

THE EDUCATOR

Published monthly (except July and August)
By THE ZANER-BLOSER CO.,
612 N. Park St., Columbus, O.
E. A. LUPFER..Editor
PARKER ZANER BLOSER..............Business Mgr.

SUBSCRIPTION PRICE. $1.25 A YEAR
(To Canada, 10c more; foreign, 30c more)
Single copy, 15c.
Change of address should be requested promptly in advance, if possible, giving the old as well as the new address.
Advertising rates furnished upon request.

THE EDUCATOR is the best medium through which to reach business college proprietors and managers, commercial teachers and students, and lovers of penmanship. Copy must reach our office by the 10th of the month for the issue of the following month.

Modern Handwriting

By E. A. Lupfer, Zanerian College, Columbus, Ohio

EVERYONE CAN

You can learn to write. You have in you the ability to master the technical skill and knowledge of letter forms necessary to succeed in handwriting. To realize your goal you must have high ideals, aims and ambitions and work intelligently. You yourself must determine the height to which you will climb. Let's start for the goal now.

IT IS IMPORTANT

Good handwriting is more important today than ever to the young man or woman who wishes to succeed in a commercial position. Business and competition are demanding a higher quality of writing. Without a good handwriting it is more difficult to secure a good position. Therefore, if you wish to get a position improve your handwriting.

THE AIM

This course is designed to develop a practical, serviceable handwriting. The important things concerning form and movement will be pointed out. We shall aim to help not only those who wish to improve their handwriting but offer aids to those who are teaching it.

A Few Things to Remember

If you wish to get the most from this course you must have a desire to improve, a love for fine penmanship, and always use good material.

Follow instructions carefully.

Spend an hour or two daily in practice if possible.

Try to concentrate and compare your work with the copies.

Always take a good position when practicing.

Always be careful in all of your writing.

MATERIALS

One cannot do good work without good tools. The Educator will be glad to help you in selecting good materials. You should have a good grade of paper with smooth surface and ruled lines three-eighth of an inch apart. Your ink should be of good quality and flow freely. Use a Zaner-Bloser finger fitting penholder and a medium pointed pen. A good table properly lighted is necessary. Do not go to any extremes, and when in doubt write us.

POSITION

It is very important that you write in the proper way. There is usually one general correct way to do all skillful acts. While no two people write exactly the same, the general position which is recommended for all is as follows:

Sit well back in the chair, leaning forward slightly from the hips. The body should not touch the desk. Rest both arms on the desk evenly. The weight of the arms should rest on the muscles below the elbows. The hand holding the penholder should be directly in front of the body. The wrist should point towards the shoulder. Much of the weight of the body is supported by the other arm. It is important that you use a free hand. That is, that the hand should glide over the paper freely and not go by jerks. If the hand is turned too much on the side crar ped writing is likely to result. Again it is not necessary to have the wrist perfectly flat. Let the weight of the) and rest on the little fingers. Curve the hand in a natural position much as though you were grasping a small ball. The fingers should be doubled under the hand to support the weight of the hand. The heel of the hand should move freely over the paper. The holder should be held lightly between the first and second fingers and thumb. The holder should cross about at the knuckle and should point somewhere between the shoulder and elbow. Always keep the eye of the pen pointing towards the ceiling.

The amount of the skill which you develop will depend upon the kind and quantity of practice you do.

This illustrates the position of the paper for the right-handed writer.

This illustration shows how the left-handed writer should hold the paper.

LEFT-HANDED POSITION

The position for the left-handed pupil is slightly different from the right-handed position in one respect, and that is the way the paper is held. In the right-handed position the top of the paper points to the left. In the left-handed position the top of the paper points to the right. It is very important to left-handed writers to get started with the paper in the proper position. They should never be allowed to twist around and write with the hand above the writing. This manner of writing is a handicap throughout life.

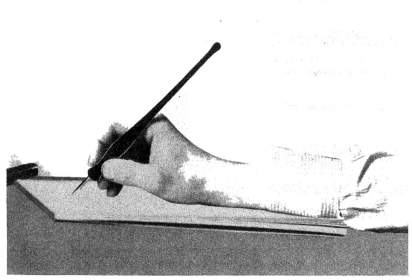

A very good illustration of the proper way to hold the pen, hand and fingers. Notice the graceful, easy curve of the fingers and thumb, the angle at which the pen is held, and the slope of the wrist.

WRITE SPECIMENS

Each pupil is requested to write two specimens containing the capital and small letters and figures, also a sentence as follows:

"This is a specimen of my handwriting at the beginning of the course in September."
Sign and date the specimen. Keep one for future comparison and send one to The Educator.

A B C D E F G H I J K L M
N O P Q R S T U V W X Y Z

1 2 3 4 5 6 7 8 9 0

a b c d e f g h i j k l m
n o p q r s t u v w x y z

This alphabet is known as the standard alphabet and is used in most public schools today. While there are other good styles of letters you will make no mistake by adopting these letter forms.

MOVEMENT

In the position described above roll the arm in an oval direction, resting the weight of the arm on the muscles and the weight of the hand on the little fingers. Circle around freely with a dry pen—feeling, in other words, the movement which is used in making capital letters such as the O. Do not let the pen touch the paper at first. After the position is understood and you are able to roll the arm freely, take ink and roll the arm around making two space oval exercise, etc. This is given mainly to make it clear to beginners the free movement used in writing. In this type of exercises the thumb and fingers should not work to any great extent. If the thumb joint works excessively you are bound to get flat places in your writing. Swing the strokes free enough so that no wabbles appear, and keep the down strokes as light as the up strokes. After you have mastered your position and movement you will be ready to start actual writing in a free, easy manner.

Roll the arm freely on the muscles below the elbow. First go through the motion with the pen in the air, then let the pen touch the paper. See that the pressure is light on the down strokes and that the movement is free. A good speed is to make about two hundred revolutions in a minute. Do not use excessive finger or thumb action.

Pull down on the downward strokes with a regular motion. Study the position of your paper.

Try the oval in a reverse motion, letting the pen travel in the same direction as the hands of a clock. Some good brisk exercises at this stage cannot help but develop a light touch, free motion, and skill. Formal drill is very commendable when properly used. It should be used as a means and not as an end. The exercises are of no particular value if they do not help you to develop better handwriting. Think as you practice.

Be sure that you understand position and that you assume a good writing posture. Study the illustration and ask questions.

Reduce the exercises to one space in height making them direct, indirect, and straight line movements. Do not waste space in making exercises without thought. See if your exercises are properly shaped, properly spaced, and are free and skillful.

In making a letter there is frequently a change in the direction of movement from oval to straight line or reverse. This exercise is given to assist the pupil in making these changes.

This exercise will help to develop freedom and fluency to the right. Let the little finger and hand slide.

Retrace the ovals six times, working for neatness and freedom. Study the slant and make both sides of the ovals equal in roundness.

In this exercise we finish the oval the same as the O. Go around six times finishing with a loop upward.

In order to receive the most benefit from the movement exercises you should combine them with letters. Make the retraced oval, being sure to keep on the track and see that the oval is two-thirds as wide as high. Make the O as freely as the exercise.

This plate is self-explanatory. Take each point illustrated and master it. Practice on each word repeating the word over and over many times—each time trying to improve the execution.

The small o is very similar in form to the capital O except that it is only one-third as tall. Make the o with a quick revolving motion rolling on the little fingers.

Study the similarity between the c, a, and o. Be sure that you finish the o up at the headline, while the a comes down to the base line then swings up. Are your a's and o's distinct? Repeat the words over and over until you have established a uniform free movement.

[handwriting practice exercises: rows of cursive capital O and C letters]

The C is based on the oval. The first exercise will show the similarity. Master this exercise. The second exercise shows the similarity of the loop to a small oval. Retrace the small loop six times, then swing into the body of the C. End the same as the small letter i.

Make page after page of C. First try them a full space high to establish uniform size, then reduce the size so that the letters occupy three-fourth of the space between two blue lines. We suggest that you write words like Columbus, Cincinnati, College, Charles, etc.

[handwriting practice exercises: rows of cursive capital O and E letters]

The E is similar to the C. However, it has a loop in the back. It begins and ends similar to the C. Practice the different exercises.

[handwriting practice: O, E letters and words "Earn Earn Earn. Each Each Each" "E. E. Emerson Emerson Enderson"]

Study the dotted lines. If your name begins with **E** practice it.

[handwriting practice: O, D letters and words "Do Do Do Do Do Don't Don't Don't" "A. C. Evans, D. D. A. C. Evans, D. D."]

The D finishes the same as the O. The D is much the same as the O with the exception of the loop in the base line. It should stand upright to give it strength and firmness. Have the "toe and heel" of the D touch the base line. See how well you can write the words and names.

A B C D E F G H I J K L M
N O P Q R S T U V W X Y Z.

1234567890 1234567890 1234567890 1234567890 12345

Rae Ellen Fose

Rae Ellen Fose is a student of Mr. Oman in Russell, Kansas.

A B C D E F G H I J K L M N

O P Q R S T U V W X Y Z & Co.

I am gaining in my penmanship

Graceful business writing by a student in the Rider College, Trenton, N. J. For many years Rider College has been outstanding for its fine handwriting. Mr. H. W. West is the head of the penmanship work.

These signatures were written by Charles A. Axelsen, who has been a student of the secretarial department of Heald College, Oakland, Calif. The man who is directly responsible for coaching this young man is T. B. Bridges, who is one of the instructors in the school. Mr. Axelsen is to be complimented on the excellent progress he has made in such a short time. We have high hopes of seeing this young man at the top of the penmanship ladder.

Blackboard writing by H. E. Moore.

Mr. H. E. Moore of The Taylor School, Philadelphia, Pa., is an expert blackboard writer. He recently photographed one of his lessons and sent it to us. We asked Mr. Moore to give us a few points regarding this lesson to which he replied as follows:

"We have a 45 minute period for penmanship every day, so I give the students a "warming up" drill in a movement exercise as near as I can to the work planned for that day. In this lesson, the capital L, I have the class practice the push and pull movement two spaces high for 20 counts and alternate with the figure 8 exercise, same height, for 10 counts, keeping the figure 8 exercise quite narrow and starting it with an up curved stroke from the middle of the space. Practice this exercise for 10 minutes. Then the second figure 8 exercise made horizontal and four of them across the page, will make them about the proper length for a good swing in developing the finishing stroke of the L. About 12 of these individual figure 8 exercises is all time will allow for. Then I explain the similarity in the upright figure 8 exercise and the down stroke of the capital L and with that we start making the upright figure 8 exercise again as in the warming up exercise, except I have the class end it with the same kind of finishing stroke as is used on the capital L. I count for them on each exercise they make, counting 1, 2, 3, 4, 5, 6, 7, 8, and finish with the count of nine.

If time will allow, I devote from 8 to 10 minutes to this exercise. Then I have them practice the capital L for four lines on their paper, using the little oval exercise to start it, and after that let them work on the plain capital for the half of the remaining time of that period. The other remaining time I have them practice the word Lanning. I move about the class constantly during the period, giving personal instruction and setting copies for all the students that I can possibly get around to for the duration of the period. For those that I cannot get copies set for that day, I make it a point to get around to them the next day and when it is possible I pick out those papers and mark them in red ink and pass them back for their inspection."

Gems from Penmen of Other Countries

Signatures and cards written by Ramirez Hermanos, Manila, P. I.
We congratulate Mr. Hermanos on his skill in handling the pen.

First Grade Activity
Our Grocery Store
(Its application to Handwriting)

By Florence Burke—Teacher, Madison Avenue School, Atlantic City, N. J.
Miss Olive A. Mellon, Supervisor

I. Introduction

The children had completed a large unit on Homes, and through the above interest, they began to talk about Stores. The Grocery Store being familiar to all of them and since there was a possibility of getting available materials, they set to work making the collection.

Counters, shelves (orange crates and tables), empty jars, cartons, a telephone, toy money, a cash register, pencils, pads, etc., were collected and arranged to their satisfaction, so they were off to a jolly adventure.

They began by waiting on customers, taking orders on the phone or going about the room with pad and pencil, making change and using the cash register.

About this time the figures were to be taught, and some difficult letters and letter combinations needed reviewing. The opportunity was taken to teach them informally, that is, by posting names and prices of food on the blackboard and having posters and labels made to advertise eggs, butter, etc., also by varying prices and grocery signs (after a discussion of what mother paid). It was an honor for a child's sign to be used and the difficulties were soon easily overcome.

Now, for a way to preserve and share their adventure. The bulletin board was one source but a better way was the book. Thus, Our Grocery Store, was the result.

The book as it appeared when completed.

II. Subject Matter

A. AIMS:
1. General
   a. To teach penmanship in connection with "Our Grocery Store" activity.
   b. To stimulate and increase the child's interest in what is to be taught.

c. To encourage cooperation in view of developing desirable group members.

2. Specific
   a. To teach correct formation of figures 1 to 10.

   b. To introduce new letter combinations which appear in the unit of work.

   c. To teach new letter forms.

   d. To introduce short sentences.

   e. To cultivate a desire for neatness and pride.

   f. To establish proper habits of position.

   g. To record best efforts in "Our Grocery Store" book.

B. TO BE TAUGHT:
1. Old Knowledge
   a. Many letter forms and words which were introduced in former activities.

   b. Familiarity with equipment.

   c. Arrangement of writing on paper.

2. New Knowledge
   a. Proper formation of figures.

   b. Certain difficult letter combinations.

   c. Introduction of sentence writing, labels, notices, signs, etc.

   d. The construction of the book used to record best efforts.

C. Types of Activities and their various drill units.

1. Names of Groceries—Word Drill—ham, eggs, milk, lettuce, apples, bacon, butter.

2. Price tags—Figures—

butter - - - 35c	bacon - - - 26c
sugar - - - 8c	bread - - - 10c

3. Money—Denominations showing word and number

cent - - - 1
nickel - - - 5 cents
dime - - - 10 cents
quar er - - 25 cents

4. Signs—sales, announcements.
   Examples: Store Closed, Room 6, Our Grocery Store, Goodbye.

5. Sentences—
   Come to see us.
   Buy at our store.
   We sell ham and eggs.
   The bread is 10c.
   The milk is 14c.
   The lettuce is 9c.
   The eggs are 32c.

6. Introduction of capital letters through word need.
   Capital Letters—Came, We, Room, Our, Store, The, It, Buy.

Atlantic City Public Schools under the supervision of Miss Olive Mellon, have attracted nation wide attention for their outstanding work in handwriting. They have worked out many similar worth-while activities.

III. Materials

blackboard   scissors
pencil   boxes
paper   cartons
crayons   money
The Book   bags

IV. Outcomes

Children learned—

1. To write figures.
2. To write and recognize many new words.
3. To make eight new capital letters.
4. To arrange sentences on paper.
5. The construction of the book.
6. The arrangement of contents.
7. The difference between good and poor writing.
8. A sense of pride.
9. To work with a group.
10. To know money values.

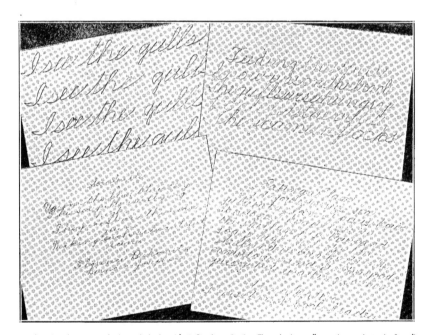

Last winter there was more freezing on the beach at Atlantic City than ordinarily. Thousands of sea gulls were frozen and starved. Sea gulls became a popular topic in the City. It was natural for the pupils to write about gulls.

The above specimens are from a penmanship project on "Sea Gulls". The first specimen was written by a first grade pupil. The second specimen (upper right) is a description by a second grade pupil of feeding the gulls during the deep snow and ice. Naturally when airplanes were used to scatter feed, and restaurants carried garbage out for the gulls, and since the gulls came by thousands to their door steps, the pupils became greatly interested in writing about them. The lower right hand specimen was written by a third grade pupil describing the interesting manner in which the gulls break clams. No. 4 (lower left) is an original poem on gulls composed by Florence Berkowitz and written by Bernard Josephs.

This and many other penmanship projects were carried on under the supervision of Miss Mellon.

Ornamental Penmanship

No. 11   Script by the late A. M. Wonnell

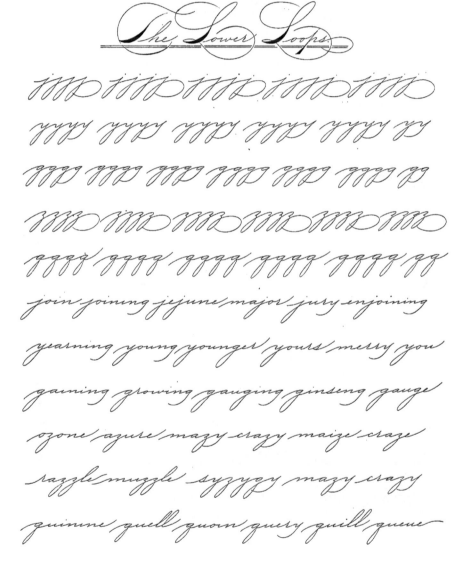

The Lower Loops

join joining jejune major jury enjoining

yearning young younger yours merry you

gaining growing gauging ginseng gauge

ozone azure mazy crazy maize craze

razzle muzzle syzygy mazy crazy

quinine quell quoin query quill queue

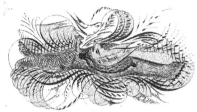

These cards were flourished by M. B. Moore. They were loaned to us by C. W. Jones, Brockton, Mass.

47 YEARS SERVICE

John F. Siple, the handwriting expert of Bellevue, Kentucky, (Suburb of Cincinnati) is doing a very thriving business in the Questioned Handwriting field. He completed normal school training in 1889 and since that time he has followed penmanship, teaching in Cincinnati and Philadelphia. As early as 1892 he gave expert testimony in handwriting cases. Mr. Siple writes a very beautiful hand and is deeply interested in all phases of pen work.

J. R. Pullen, clerk of Logan County Schools, Logan, W. Va., favored us with some very skillfully written signatures. Evidently Mr. Pullen finds good handwriting a valuable asset in his work.

A beautiful original flourish has been received from Shigeo Asao, No. 10 Itchome Kitashimmachi, Higashiku, Osaka, Japan.

Miss Mabel Vogan of Mannington, West Virginia, will teach Business Training in the Elyria High School this year.

Miss Vogan is a Zanerian and an excellent penmanship teacher. The Elyria High School is fortunate in securing the services of Miss Vogan.

Sound Advice

By Prof. J. B. Connatser
Prin. of Sevierville Business College, Sevierville, Tenn.

This is an age for recognition of business ability. The public now demands that a good business man or woman be chosen to fill the important places of trust and responsibility, and naturally so, for we live in the greatest business nation in the world today. Vast fortunes are in evidence on every hand and most of them have been made in business.

Business is attracting the best brains of the universe. The famous Woolworth building in New York is a monument to Frank W. Woolworth and the ten cent store business. The Wrigley building in Chicago is a monument to Wrigley and the chewing gum business. Likewise every large building, every factory, every bank, every insurance company, every business enterprise from the largest manufacturing concern to the corner grocery store, is a monument to the profession of business. Our great inventions have been put into practical use by business brains which have turned the inventor's dream into a reality.

Large corporations throughout the country are constantly on the lookout for competent young men and women to fill important executive positions. Staggering salaries are often paid in order to get a man or woman big enough to fill the position. Andrew Carnegie once said, "Capital is looking everywhere for the right man to direct it, and the men who control capital will pay well for such a man when found. I can recommend a business career as one in which there is abundant room for the exercise of a man's highest power, and of every good quality in human nature. The demand for men of brains and capacity in business is far beyond the supply."

While without question, opportunities in business today are greater, yet more exacting, than ever before. The problem that confronts most young men and women, however, is how to get a start in the business world. Many of them are not willing to pay the price of success, which is hard work, study, and the sacrifice of pleasure until they have sufficient training and experience to earn promotion.

A careful study of the lives of our great business executives reveals the fact that nearly all of them started their careers in minor executive positions, many of them as bookkeepers, stenographers, and office assistants. Hugh Chalmers began as an office boy. Julius Rosenwald made his start toward millions and rose to be President of Sears, Roebuck & Co., from a minor position in the office. Frank A. Vanderlip started as a stenographer. Herbert Hoover started as a typist in the office of a mining engineer. Charles E. Hughes worked his way up from the position of law stenographer and court reporter. James J. Davis took a business course to fit him to hold his job as city clerk in a small town in Indiana. It was by the means of Shorthand that Judge K. M. Landis obtained his knowledge of law. The same thing is true of business and professional men and women everywhere. Business training gave them the proper start and enabled them to secure positions where they came in close contact with the leaders and dictators of great enterprises.

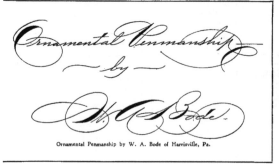

Ornamental Penmanship by W. A. Bode of Harrisville, Pa.

WILL REPRESENT HIGGINS ON THE PACIFIC COAST

James H. Montgomery of Los Angeles, former sales manager and buyer of the stationery division of the Los Angeles News Company, has been appointed representative of Chas. M. Higgins & Co., Inc., makers of Higgins' drawing and writing inks and adhesives, for the Pacific Coast and Mountain States territory. Mr. Montgomery began his work for Higgins in August.

Practical Engrossing

By
E. H. McGhee, McGhee Studio,
143 E. State Street, Trenton, N. J.

No. 10

This style of Text Lettering is used extensively today by engrossers especially for the body of resolutions. It is a style which can be made very legible. It is also very speedy and not quite as exacting as the Old English. However, the more exact you work these letters out the finer your lettering will be. Form your own theory where strokes begin and end, etc. Study the location of the various little points and spurs. Study the balance of letters. Box them up and study them in any way you possibly can to improve your knowledge of form. Memorize them so that you have a good mental picture of each letter when you do not have a copy in front of you.

—————— Commercial Lettering ——————

ABCDEFGHIJKLMNOPQRS
—————— TUVWXYZ ——————

abcdefghhijklmnopqrstuvwxyz

An easily read style of lettering for
using in the body of Resolutions, etc.
Requires very little retouching

INDIANA BUSINESS COLLEGE

An interesting catalog has been received from the Indiana Business College, Marion, Indiana. In the catalog are a large number of photographs of young men and women who are now in positions. It certainly has a very strong appeal for it shows what others have done by preparing in commercial work.

Chancy Taylor, a student of R. C. Haynes, Bliss College, Lewiston, Maine, was recently awarded the Ornamental Penmanship Certificate for his skillful work in ornamental penmanship. This young man has more than average ability in penmanship and has been devoting considerable time to fancy writing.

FROM AUSTRALIA

D. P. Foley, Torwood, 19 The Avenue, Strathfield, N. S. W. Australia, in renewing his subscription to The Educator includes some of his skillful work in ornamental writing, copper plate script, card writing and card carving. It is always a pleasure to see the specimens from our subscribers in other lands.

BEAUTIFULLY ADDRESSED ENVELOPES

by

Examiner of Questioned Documents
Detroit, Michigan

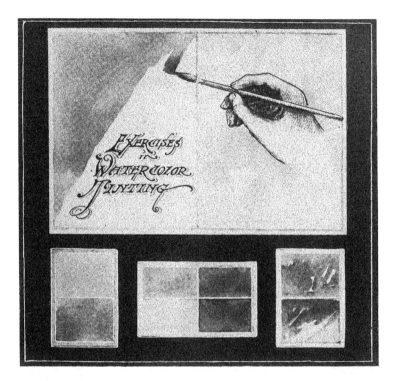

DESIGNING AND ENGROSSING

By E. L. BROWN
Rockland, Maine

Water-color tinting.

The early engrossers in this country did not use brush and color to any great extent. Their work was all made with a pen, so to speak, on white paper or sheepskin. India ink was diluted with water to obtain gray delicate effects. These methods were used by A. R. Dunton, whose skill in producing softness and delicacy in tone values was unexcelled. W. E. Dennis was one of Dunton's pupils and his work equalled that of his teacher in point of execution and general effeet. However, this style required much time and patience and would be impracticable in this day and age of commercialized art, when time means money to an engrosser.

Brush and color tinting is a means of obtaining quick delicate effects, and the exercises given in this connection show several tinted spaces, both light and dark in tone.

Outfit: Saucers for mixing color if you do not own a color box, two sable brushes, numbers 6 and 8, a pan of lamp black, and one of vermilion or blue. Fine effects are obtained by mixing the lamp black with these colors to produce a bluish gray or a reddish gray. A few dabs of red added to lamp black will produce a brownish tone.

The knack of color handling can only be acquired by practice, and here are a few points to be observed:—

Transparency in tone values; a free brush, in other words, a brush well filled with color, always, move puddle of color along with brush over a sur-face slightly moistened; a "dry brush" will produce muddy effects; water color is a difficult medium to handle, but practice and experience will overcome obstacles in the way of direct handling to produce transparent tone values. Next month a practical application of brush tinting will constitute the lesson.

Please bear in mind that we are ever willing to help you in your work, and our criticisms and suggestions will be freely given, to all who send postage for return of specimens.

A resolution of considerable merit executed by P. W. Costello in 1895

BOOK REVIEWS

Our readers are interested in books of merit, but especially in books of interest and value to commercial teachers including books of special educational value and books on business subjects. All such books will be briefly reviewed in these columns, the object being to give sufficient description of each to enable our readers to determine its value.

Present Day Banking, published by BANKING, Journal of the American Bankers Association, New York, N. Y. Cloth cover, 511 pages.

This volume presents in practical working form what is, we think we may fairly say, the very latest and best banking thought on both the current and long-distance problems confronting the banking business. This statement is based on a consideration of the way in which the text was created.

When the present administration of the American Bankers Association came into office at the annual convention held in New Orleans in November, 1935, it was felt that there was a very definite threefold task and opportunity before us. One phase of their task was to make sure that there should come to prevail throughout the banking profession full information and understanding regarding new banking laws and regulations, and the problems resulting from them, which had come so rapidly into operation. A second was to foster through the interchange of advice and experience among bankers, as widely as possible ways and means for improving customer and public relations, which had been inevitably impaired by the events of the depression. Thirdly, it was felt that there was need to enlist bankers in an organized effort to study ways and to take steps, wherever they could soundly do so, to promote the return to chartered banking institutions of many financial functions which were still being performed by the Government.

As a means for exploring these questions and bringing about appropriate measures to meet them, it was decided to hold in various parts of the United States a series of regional conferences on banking service. The first was held in Philadelphia, Pennsylvania, January 23-24. The second was held in Memphis, Tennessee, March 26-27. The third was held in Chicago, Illinois, April 2-3. At each conference there was a number of general sessions at which especially qualified speakers in the banking field were asked to present addresses on subjects of general application to the business of banking. In addition, at each conference there was a series of departmental forums at which specialists were invited to present papers on a number of specific and technical subjects. In all meetings free and open discussions and debate were invited and stimulated.

These three conferences were attended by over 4,000 bankers who gave constant and earnest attention at the day-long and late night sessions which made up the meetings, and it can be said without reservation that no profession ever had the opportunity to listen to more thoughtfully prepared or more practically helpful papers dealing with its operations, functions and duties than were those presented at these three conferences.

For the purpose of making this material available to all members of the banking profession, the American Bankers Association has undertaken the task of reproducing these proceedings in this volume. It is provided with a complete table of contents and cross-reference index, to serve as guides for the use of this volume as a practical working document in connection with the policies of operation and management of any bank.

Workbook for Business-Economic Problems, by H. G. Shields and W. Harmon Wilson. Published by the South-Western Publishing Company, Cincinnati, Ohio. Paper cover, 174 pages.

This workbook is designed to be correlated with the subject matter presented in BUSINESS-ECONOMIC PROBLEMS. The workbook is recommended to provide more efficient instruction and more practical applications of business and economic principles. Many problems and projects are included that could not be satisfactorily included in the textbook.

The purpose of the workbook is to enable the student to apply certain business, economic, and legal principles in terms of his own needs. The problems and the projects have been presented in lifelike situations. They will closely approximate similar situations which the student will confront at some time in his own life. Some of the problems dwelling upon economic principles serve to cause the student to analyze and to interpret certain economic principles and problems of which he might otherwise not be aware.

The workbook provides a sufficient amount of stationery for completing all the problems and the projects. Sheets are perforated to permit their being torn out and submitted to the teacher.

Streamline Your Mind, by James L. Mursell, Ph.D., Teachers College, Columbia University. Published by J. B. Lippincott Company, Philadelphia, Pa. Cloth cover, 254 pages.

The successful man is the man who learns successfully. To "streamline your mind," Mr. Mursell points out, is to learn how to learn. The engineer of today, by eliminating resistance of wind and water through streamlining, has made a ton of coal, a gallon of gasoline and a kilowatt of electricity carry us faster and further than ever before. Mr. Mursell maintains that by eliminating excess mental trappings we can streamline our minds and so get the greatest possible efficiency from our natural equipment. He places particular emphasis on the importance of the will to learn—not the wish to learn, which is diffuse and general, but the will to learn which is concentrated and specific. He speaks of learning as "a process of transformation," and improvement, considered in the truest and most accurate sense, as "a creative process." He offers a new challenge and a new answer to each one of us. With specific suggestions he points the way toward happier and more profitable living. Well qualified to undertake this delicate job of helping others to evaluate their potentialities and use them to the best advantage, James Mursell has made, in this book, a great contribution. Written simply, it is yet challenging, stimulating both to the imagination and to the intellect.

Experimental Pedagogy With Particular Reference to Education Through Activity, by W. A. Lay, Ph.D., translated by Adolf Weil, M.A., and Emmanuel K. Schwartz, B.S.S., M.S., with an introduction by Paul Rankov Radosavljevich, Ph.D., P¹D., Professor of Experimental Education, New York University. Published by Prentice-Hall, Inc., New York. Cloth cover, 371 pages.

The Table of Contents of this book is as follows:
PREFACE TO THE FIRST THREE EDITIONS
TRANSLATORS' NOTE
INTRODUCTION BY DR. PAUL RANKOV RADOSAVLJEVICH
1. INTRODUCTORY STATEMENTS.
2. DOCTOR LAY'S SUMMARY OF THE EDUCATION OF A NATION BASED ON A NEW SCIENCE OF EDUCATION.
3. THE BASIC PEDAGOGICAL PRINCIPLE OF THE TATSCHULE OR LEBENSGEMEINSCHAFTSSCHULE.
4. LAY'S IDEA OF EDUCATIONAL RESEARCH.
5. ILLUSTRATIONS OF LAY'S DIDACTIC EXPERIMENTATION.
6. CONCLUDING REMARKS.
BIBLIOGRAPHY.

EXPERIMENTAL PEDAGOGY, by Dr. W. A. Lay.
A. THE NATURE AND SIGNIFICANCE OF EXPERIMENTAL PEDAGOGY.
1. An Introduction to the Development of Experimental Pedagogy.
2. Methods of Research and the Nature of Experimental Pedagogy.
3. The Nature and the Problems of Education in the Light of Experimental Pedagogy as Universal Pedagogy.
B. RESEARCH IN THE FIELD OF GENERAL PEDAGOGY.
1. Individual Pedagogy.
2. Natural Pedagogy.
3. Social Pedagogy.
C. INVESTIGATIONS IN THE FIELD OF DIDACTICS.
1. The Organic Curriculum.
2. The Unified School System: Co-education.
3. Methods of Teaching.
D. RETROSPECT AND OUTLOOK.
INDEX.

Bookkeepers' Handy Guide, by the Ronald Press Company, New York, N. Y. Cloth cover, 565 pages.

In the preparation of this volume the aim has been to give definite, factual information on bookkeeping practices and procedures in a form to make it quickly available to all who are confronted with specific problems in practical bookkeeping. It is the emphasis on this service aspect of the book— that of giving quick answers to the specific questions that are likely to arise in the practical bookkeeper's daily work—which has motivated all who have collaborated in planning and writing this volume. It is this emphasis which in many respects gives the volume a distinctive character. In organization, in arrangement, in scope and style of presentation the volume differs quite radically from the usual works on bookkeeping intended principally for classroom use.

Every effort has been made to place before the reader information that is accurate and up-to-date, having to do with approved practice. The information is presented in short, self-contained items. Each item treats a specific problem of bookkeeping, or a subject closely allied to bookkeeping and ordinarily falling within the scope of the bookkeeper's work. Where several alternative procedures are in use, these are explained. It has been realized that in bookkeeping some of the seemingly innocent and unimportant practical details are often the cause of much annoyance and embarrassment if not properly attended to at the outset. Accordingly, in preparing this work pains have been taken not to slight such details but to give them the attention which their real practical importance deserves. It has also been the aim to make the explanations full and comprehensive and yet to give them in the briefest possible compass so as to economize the reader's time.

SPECIMENS

The following Japanese penmen desire to exchange signatures or specimens with other penmen:

T. Hashimoto
415 Tazuta-mura
Kume-gun, Okayama

T. Koike
Matsuida, Usuhigun
Gummaken

H. Moriyoshi
No. 24, Showamachi
Sumiyoshiku, Osaka

Y. Kuroda
No. 1 Ebisucho, Naniwa-ku
Osaka-city

J. Onish
Shitsumi-mura
Funai-gun, Kyoto

H. Shima
No. 11 Tamayacho
Minamiku, Osaka

M. Shinada
Yokomachi-Niizu
Niigata-ken

T. Yasuda
Nakai % Karahashi
Rashomoncho, Shimokyo-ku
Kyoto-city

T. Yoshida
Shimonogo, Haruhimura,
Nishikasugai-gun
Aichi-ken

Lessons in Modern Engrosser's Script

Prepared in the office of The Educator

This style of writing is one of the oldest styles in general use. It attained a very high degree of perfection in Europe several hundred years ago. With the exception of a very few letter forms it has been changed very little. Like the Roman Alphabet it is exceedingly difficult to make any appreciable improvement upon it. It is one of the most beautiful styles of writing ever created and because of its beauty it will, no doubt, continue to hold a prominent place in the engrossing field. It can be used appropriately for almost all occasions.

It will pay you financially to master this practical style of writing. It will help you to appreciate other styles of writing and will also help to improve your technique in business writing. Teachers can use it to advantage in inspiring their pupils or in earning money as a side line.

It is a comparatively easy style to master, but requires careful study and intelligent practice.

Use Zanerian 5 lb. Paper, Arnold's Japan Ink, Fine Writer and Gillott's No. 303 Pens, and a Zanerian Oblique Penholder.

In order to get a clear conception of the letter forms, practice on ⅜ inch ruled paper extending your letters between the two blue lines. Practice the individual exercises and letters a full space until you can make them well, then reduce them in size. Rule head lines. See that the pen point slants in the same direction as the shaded down strokes. The shaded down strokes should slant toward the center of the body. Get plenty of slant, watch your spacing and regularity of pen pressure. Study the work in detail getting the turns evenly rounded and the ends cut off straight.

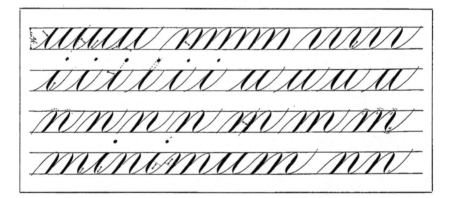

Meet

D. Francis Harrigan, Jr., Pres. N. A. P. T. S.

AFTER 43 YEARS

In 1893, a young man entered the Zanerian to take up pen work. To-day that young man is 74 years of age and writes that he is planning to send a batch of his work to The Educator. He also states that his interests in pen work increase more and more and that he always looks eagerly forward to the arrival of The Educator. This young man is **S. J. Shaw**, of 1332 Locust St., Long Beach, Calif.

There is something about penmanship which sticks to many of those who give it much time and thought. It is an art worthy of the efforts of any one. In too many instances penmanship is not given the prominent place in the educational field which it deserves. If you wish to be thrilled and to have an accomplishment which will stick by you through your entire life study penmanship.

ROANOKE NATIONAL BUSINESS COLLEGE CATALOG

This year marked the fiftieth anniversary of the Roanoke National Business College which has been a pioneer and leader in the field of commercial education. The catalog is full of attractive illustrations, schoolroom scenes and various groups of students. E. M. Coulter is the President and M. A. Smythe is Vice-President and General Manager.

Good penmanship is one of the essential subjects taught in the school. Both Mr. Coulter and Mr. Smythe are nationally known penmen and they consider penmanship a very valuable asset for young men and women going out into business.

A very beautiful ornamental letter and a set of capitals have been received from **Mr. M. Masuda**, Muroran Middle School, Muroran, Hokkaido, Japan.

These skillful signatures were made by C. C. Steed, penman in Bowling Green, Kentucky, Business University.

Mr. Burton A. O'Mealy, Instructor in the High School of Commerce, Portland, Oregon, in an article on penmanship in the Oregon Education Journal, strongly advocates the repetition in columns of words of the same length and with the same beginning or ending letter combinations such as—

halls—calls—pulls—gulls—walls

Mr. O'Mealy lays much stress upon arranging material on the page to produce an attractive appearance. It is rather difficult to acquire skill without repetition of effort. It is necessary to write words and letters over and over many times.

IN choosing the right path, see that it is one which is honorable to thyself and without offence to others. Be as scrupulous about the lightest command as about the weightiest, for no man knoweth the result of his actions. Weigh the present temporal disadvantages of a dutiful course against the reward of the future, and the present desirable fruits of a sinful deed against the injury to thine immortal soul. In general, consider three things and thou will never fall into sin; remember that there is above thee an all-seeing eye, an all-hearing ear, and a record of all thine actions.

Mishna A Tract Aboth - Talmud

This simple, striking lettering was made by Charlton V. Howe, 2312 Girard Trust Bldg., Philadelphia, Pa. Mr. Howe specialized on small, fine work, but this gives one a glimpse of his bold, commercial lettering. Mr. Howe is a very skillful all-round penman and engrosser.

At the commencement exercises of the **Miami-Jacobs College,** Dayton, Ohio, in June, there were 181 graduates. This is a very good class of graduates and indicates that the Miami-Jacobs College is prospering, and we would judge, running as good or better than any time in the past.

We want to congratulate President W. E. Harbottle and his associates for their good work.

Mr. and Mrs. Henry M. Klingensmith announce the marriage of their daughter Anna Walker to Mr. Arthur E. Cole on Wednesday, July the first, nineteen hundred and thirty-six, Tarentum, Pennsylvania.

Mr. A. E. Cole is a high school teacher in Langley High School, Pittsburgh, Pa. He is also one of the finest engrossers in Pittsburgh.

The above letter was written by E. W. Bloser in 1886. It is well worth your careful study and imitation. Notice the strong bold capitals and those long delicate loops. Give special attention to the regularity of slant and spacing. Thousands of beautiful letters were sent out to prospective students by business colleges throughout the country and Mr. Bloser became one of the best at writing page letters. This specimen was loaned to us by C. W. Jones, Brockton, Mass.

A vacation dream by F. B. Courtney, Detroit, Mich.

CARD WRITING

J. R. McAllister, Struthers, Ohio, who wrote the accompanying cards is a government employee, a professional penman, and a radio fan.

COLUMBUS, O.

(Continued from April, May and June)

Correspondence Instruction

In order to accommodate those who cannot attend the Zanerian, we offer correspondence instruction in all branches of penmanship and engrossing. There are courses for beginners, teachers, and professionals who desire to reach a higher degree of skill. Many start the work by correspondence and finish with residence in the Zanerian. Our many years of experience enable us to give courses which are thorough, clear, interesting and profitable.

Business Handwriting Course by Correspondence

This course is intended for those who desire to write a good practical business hand, for professional penmen who desire to improve their skill and for persons who desire to prepare as teachers and supervisors of penmanship.

Pupils are taught correct position, free arm movement, and suggestions are made which are helpful to those who are teaching penmanship. When a lesson is received it is carefully gone over by an experienced teacher and red ink corrections are made and suggestions for improvement are given. With each lesson it is our aim to offer a word of encouragement to keep pupils interested.

The time to complete this course depends upon time spent in practice, the previous training and ability of the pupil. This course should be completed in four to six months by practicing one-half hour a day. Many, of course, by intelligent application complete the course in much less time.

Price of Professional Business Writing
Course $10.00

Supplies for Professional Business Writing Course $2.25

Ornamental Penmanship Course by Correspondence

A course which will train you to write a beautiful ornamental style. It will train you to write cards and flourished penmanship for advertising purposes. By taking this course you will acquire skill with the pen which will greatly improve your plain business penmanship. The work is thoroughly covered from simple principles and letters to difficult combinations and page work.

Teachers can increase their skill and income by learning to write cards, holiday greetings, etc., during spare time. One Zanerian made $300.00 in one year writing cards, while teaching.

Price of Ornamental Penmanship
Course (including text) $12.00

Supplies for Ornamental Penmanship
Course 3.45

Certificates

Upon the satisfactory completion of correspondence courses students are granted certificates. A small fee is charged for engrossing and mailing certificates.

ZANERIAN COLLEGE

612 N. Park St.   Columbus, Ohio

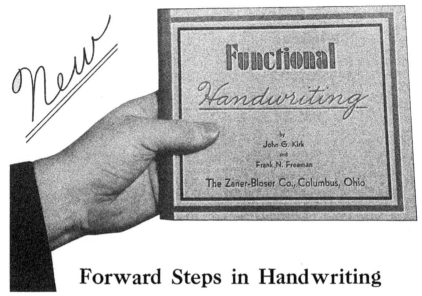

Forward Steps in Handwriting

This new book embodies many improvements and represents new forward steps in handwriting.

Read These Statements by the Authors . . . .

'In order to save time, write rapidly; in order to insure understanding on the part of the reader, write legibly."—JOHN G. KIRK, Director of Commercial Education, Philadelphia, Pa.

"The essentials of learning to write well are:

1. A strong desire to write well.

2. An abundance of good copies and sound methods, both based on correlation.

3. Appropriate practice applied by the student purposively and intelligently to accomplish ends which he recognizes."—

FRANK N. FREEMAN, Professor of Educational Psychology, University of Chicago.

Order a Copy Today

The Zaner-Bloser Co.
Columbus, Ohio.

Please send...
Quantity

Functional Handwriting Books.

Enclosed is...in full payment.
Amount

Name ....

Address ....

City ....

State ....

Title or Position...

Size 6½ x 8 — 132 pages. Price 40c each, net, postpaid. $4.00 per dozen, less 25%, F. O. B. Columbus, Ohio.

Volume 42   COLUMBUS, OHIO, OCTOBER, 1936   No. 2

TRI-STATE COMMERCIAL EDUCATION ASSOCIATION

The fall meeting of the Tri-State Commercial Education Association will be held October 9 and 10 in the Henry Clay Frick Training School, Pittsburgh, Pa. Plans are being completed by the committee under the chairmanship of Mr. Karl M. Maukert, Principal of Duffs-Iron City College, for a gala evening of dancing, cards with prizes, and a general get-together, at the college, 424 Duquesne Way, Pittsburgh, Pa. The general theme for the meetings will be, "Business Education for All?" The Saturday morning sessions will be an inducement for many to attend because of the choice of outstanding speakers for the following sectional meetings:

Vocational Guidance
Administration of Commercial Education
Salesmanship
Business Correspondence
General Business Education
Shorthand
Commercial Law
Economics
Business Arithmetic
Bookkeeping
Penmanship
Typewriting
Extra-Curricular Activities

Luncheon will be served in the cafeteria to all those desiring it.

The afternoon session, typewriting, will have Mr. E. W. Harrison and the students of the John Hay High School, Cleveland, Ohio, who won several events in the International Schools Contest held in Chicago, June 24. The shorthand division, also in the afternoon, will be conducted by Miss Katherine Bracher, Head of the Gregg College, Chicago.

This convention always offers a splendid opportunity for the commercial teachers in the district to establish contacts and to renew friendships with others interested in commercial work and to secure new ideas and methods for the class room work during the year.

Margaret A. Giegerich
Secretary.

HANDWRITING DEPARTMENT NEW JERSEY STATE TEACHERS' ASSOCIATION

On October 14 the Handwriting Department of the New Jersey State Teachers' Association will hold an all day Handwriting Conference at the New Jersey State Teachers' College, Newark, N. J.

The conference will include many phases of teaching handwriting, and will be of interest to all concerned in the handwriting field.

Those desiring a detailed program and information should write to Marjorie Flaacke, New Jersey State Teachers' College, Newark, N. J.

Marjorie Flaacke

New Jersey State Teachers' College, Newark, N. J. President, Handwriting Department, N. J. State Teachers' Association.

E. C. T. A.

We have emerged from the worst depression the world has known and now stand on the threshold of a newer life fraught with implications of deep significance. No period of our national life ever pulsed so violently, no era was confronted with such epoch-making changes, no age was ever so beset with such grave, harassing problems, touching every phase of individual as well as national existence. Our economic, social and governmental viewpoints have been radically changed, and the process of metamorphosis is not yet over. The call for sound, intelligent leadership was never so insistent or urgent.

Readjustment is the order of the day, and in this process every teacher in the land must be prepared to render effective service. Education, now as always must concentrate its efforts and activities upon the development not only of worthy leaders, but also of properly equipped individuals capable of initiating and making any required adjustments. It must blaze the trail in the readjustments involved, not lag in their wake.

As its contribution, the Eastern Commercial Teachers' Association is preparing a series of discussions on the topic "Foundations of Vocational Testing in Business Education." These discussions will take place at the annual Spring Convention of the Association, to be held in Boston, on March 24, 25, 26 and 27, 1937. On that occasion outstanding personalities in the field of business and leaders in the field of commercial education will cooperate. They will bring to the attention of progressive teachers of commercial subjects their views as to what types and degrees of skill, what informational background, and what social understandings, characteristics and practices business must now demand of those seeking entry into its gainful occupations.

The officers of the Eastern Commercial Teachers' Association feel assured of your approval and generous support of the program they are arranging. They take this opportunity to extend to all interested in commercial education their greetings and their best wishes for a school year rich in achievement.

Nathaniel Altholz, President
Eastern Commercial Teachers'
Association

THE EDUCATOR

Published monthly (except July and August)
By THE ZANER-BLOSER CO.
612 N. Park St., Columbus, O.
E. A. LUPFER..Editor
PARKER ZANER BLOSER.............Business Mgr.

SUBSCRIPTION PRICE, $1.25 A YEAR
(To Canada, 10c more; foreign, 30c more)
Single copy, 15c.
Change of address should be requested promptly in advance, if possible, giving the old as well as the new address.
Advertising rates furnished upon request.

THE EDUCATOR is the best medium through which to reach business college proprietors and managers, commercial teachers and students, and lovers of penmanship. Copy must reach our office by the 10th of the month for the issue of the following month.

Modern Handwriting

By E. A. Lupfer, Zanerian College, Columbus, Ohio

No. 2

TO THE TEACHER

See that your pupils become interested in handwriting. They should be made to realize the importance of handwriting. It is a helpful tool in school work, a valuable qualification in securing a position and a valuable asset in business and social life.

There should be a regular time set apart each day for instruction in handwriting. Help every pupil to assume a good healthy writing position and to develop a skillful, free movement. Each pupil should be given individual attention to get started right.

The Blackboard

The blackboard should be used in every lesson. From the blackboard you can demonstrate movement and letter forms. The ability to write well on the blackboard means much towards your success as a teacher, for at the blackboard your pupils can see your writing and are therefore inspired according to the degree of excellence of your writing.

Where blackboard space is available it is advisable to send pupils to the blackboard to practice, or at least part of the class. This is especially true in the lower grades and in the upper grades where pupils are having special difficulties. Primary children should write large on the board. In writing on the board stand well back facing the board. Let the chalk point towards the center of the hand. Students should write at about on a level with their eyes whenever possible.

Where you have special difficulty with a letter practice it on the blackboard. The large movements will help you in getting freer movement on paper.

The teacher should check the position of the paper, hand and body of each pupil each day until correct position is established. Read and reread the instructions regarding position. If you do not have a copy of the September number of The Educator you can secure a copy if you will write immediately. Our supply of the September issue is very low.

Those teachers who desire additional information and help on blackboard writing should write to The Educator.

The other day a young man came into the office of The Educator who had lost a position on account of his poor handwriting. We hope that none of our readers will be so unfortunate but will be wise and industrious and begin now to systematically acquire a handwriting. Let our slogan be LEGIBLE, FREE, BEAUTIFUL HANDWRITING.

W. S. Steele, the skillful penman and high school teacher of handwriting, of Toronto, Ontario, posed for this position illustration when he was in Columbus.

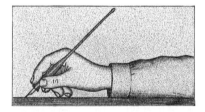

This illustration shows the proper position for primary pupils at the blackboard. Keep the feet apart and swing the body from left to right.

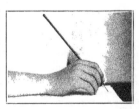
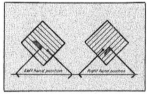

These illustrations show how to hold the pen and paper. Left-handed writers should especially study the position of the paper.

Practice each copy at the blackboard first before attempting it with pen and ink.

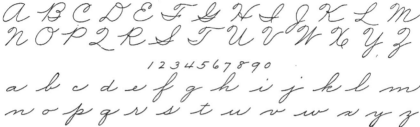

A B C D E F G H I J K L M
N O P Q R S T U V W X Y Z

1 2 3 4 5 6 7 8 9 0

a b c d e f g h i j k l m
n o p q r s t u v w x y z

When time permits a very valuable thing to do is to write the alphabet as given above each day. Preserve these alphabets and note your progress.

If the alphabet cannot be written each day we urge you to write it at least once each week and preserve it for comparison. Each student should get a loose leaf notebook and keep these alphabets and other practice work for future study and comparison.

The capital **A** and small **a** are very similar in construction. The capital is three times the size of the small letter and ends at one-third of its own height. Start the **A** with a swinging motion. The pen should be in motion before it hits the paper. Curve the first stroke more than the other strokes. Get the two turns at the base line even and resting on the base line. Give special attention to the retrace. Avoid looping the retrace. Make about sixty letters a minute. Does your penholder slant towards the shoulder? Are you writing with a free arm movement? Reread the instructions in last month's Educator regarding position.

These exercises aid in making the A. See how well you can trace the first exercise. In the second exercise make the body oval then retrace the straight downward stroke about six times before swinging into the final up finish. Compare your work with the copy. Make the four small a's without raising the pen.

Notice the similarity of movement in A and ll's in All. Slacken the speed as you near the base line.

The letter **a** needs special attention. Always close it and always make the second part down to the base line before making the finishing stroke. Be sure that your a is different from the small o. Write the various combinations and words many times.

The i part of a is made with a movement as in the i.

Write the sentence, and if you have not succeeded in making a good capital **A** review it. We will try to show some of the things to work for in this copy. Study the arrows, size, slant and movement.

ac ai ad al ea ea aeiou aeiou

After mastering the small a see how many different combinations you can write well. Watch beginning, connective and final strokes.

ic ic ic ic care care care care

cinnamon cinnamon cinnamon

can canine canine canine canine

ic ec ci cu ce ca co cr cl ch ck

The c starts with a dot, swings left slowly, then down rather straight to the base line. The hook at the top is very important. In order to strengthen your downward stroke practice the retraced exercise.

Make each group of c's without raising the pen. You should, however, check the motion at the top of the c. Make the individual c's carefully and freely. The words are nice to write. Select other more difficult words. See that your c is no higher than other letters in the words. After practicing on a letter always select some letter combinations to practice. Notice size and slant. Get light down strokes.

Can Can Can Can Can Can Can C

Curve Curve Curve Carve Carve Cu

O. A. Carmine O. A. Carmine Carmine

The C is made with a rolling free motion. The letter contains a large oval with a little loop in the top. Curve the beginning stroke. End the C with an upward curved motion the same as the small i. Study the arrows, as they will help you to become a better student of letter forms.

d d d d d d ddd ddd ddd

hold hold hold hand hand

penholder penholder holders

The small letter d is the same as the small a with the extended top. If you cover the top part of the d it should make a good a. Be careful with the retraced part.

Practice other words containing d.

aa d dd add dad our write

Study closely the similarity between the a and d and practice each combination separately and freely. Are you in a good writing position?

Habit

What we do over and over again becomes a habit. Our habits make up a great part of what we are. Good and bad habits are made in the same way. We may have good habits of writing, speaking and acting by doing these things as well as we can all the time.

Write the entire paragraph. Check especially the letters which you have studied to see that you make them well. The chances are you may have trouble with the capital **H**. Therefore, give special study and drill to the capital **H**.

Exercises like the above help to loosen up the muscles. Do not spend too much time on them, but learn to make them free and uniform in color.

The first exercise is part of an oval. Come down on the right side straight to the base line, stop and repeat.

Retrace the little loop six times. Swing out to the right and down to the base line, stop and raise the pen.

When you have trouble in getting the down strokes at the base line straight, practice on the retraced straight line exercise.

Retrace the entire stem several times, then make individual strokes. Study the shape and slant carefully.

This copy is reduced somewhat in size. Study it carefully and review the different exercises as needed.

Handwriting is used in school

Handwriting is very important in school work and should be mastered by every student. Do not become careless with your writing. Check the slant.

Handwriting Handwriting Hand

H H H H H H H H H H H

H H H H H H H H H H

Repeat the word **Handwriting** many times. Check height of letters, spacing, quality of line, and movement. If you have trouble with the **H** review as suggested in this copy.

hmmmm hhhhh h h h h h h

The small **h** appears about twelve times in the paragraph on habits and therefore is very important. Practice the first exercise to get the top turn rounding. Keep your loop open. Do not raise the pen in making the five connected **h's**.

h h h h h h h h h h h h h h

Be sure that your loops are full and distinct. Watch the slant and make the letters with a free movement.

ch ho th hi ph hy he sch wh

Practice the letter combinations in this copy. Keep in mind that the writing should be free in movement.

Each pupil should keep his paper in front of him.

A COMPOSITE SPECIMEN

We are the penmen of the
Grammar School.
Right proud of our art
are we;
For it has taken a long
time to learn
Where the curved and
straight lines should be
Up lines, curved and down
ones straight
All on uniform slant
One bad letter will
spoil the line.
We have made them
over a thousand times
There's no such word as can't.
We have blotted and
smeared and scratched,
But what care
we, now our goal
we see?
Our pride and our skill
are unmatched.

A Very unique poem prepared by grade school students under the direction of Ella L. Dwyer, Johnstown, N. Y. Each line was written by a different pupil. It shows a Very high aVerage. Very few schools can show so many eXcellent writers in one class. We congratulate the pupils and Miss Dwyer.

Needed Research in Handwriting in Business

John G. Kirk, Author of Functional Handwriting and Director Commercial Education, Philadelphia, Pa.

(An address given at the N. A. P. T. S.)

The alphabet came into new prominence under the new deal. For instance, the R. F. C., N. R. A., C. C. C., C. W. A., and P. W. C. In this connection, it would seem that penmanship teachers should take on renewed strength and zeal and endeavor to secure needed improvement in handwriting. In these days of specialized specialists, of special commissions, of investigations, of surveys, inspections, and inquiries, penmanship must have its share of special studies and researches.

Knight Dunlap in his book entitled "Habits" says: "Useful educational techniques are never the results of guesses or mere 'hunches,' but are laboriously elaborated from the body of psychological knowledge. Scientific innovations are almost always worthless, if not pernicious, unless they are really not innovations, but are evolutionary products of the scientific accomplishments of the predecessors of the apparent innovator."[1] In 1928, Paul V. West, at the N. A. P. T. S. Convention, in his paper, "The Penmanship Supervisor as a Leader of Research,"[2] said: "Until the present time comparatively few supervisors have carried on and published the findings of scientific research." Then again, Doctor West urges: "There are very few research workers among handwriting supervisors. This is most unfortunate for the future development of the subject. Research as emphasized by the local school system is the real basis for recommendations for economy, since it places emphasis upon efficient methods and organization. Even though such research should be concerned merely with collecting valuable information regarding the results of other researches, it will justify itself. When directed to the solving of a local problem, perhaps experimentally, the findings will be worth while, and furthermore the investigation itself will serve as a means of stimulating interest. The scientific supervisor speaks with an authority which gains respect, in contrast to the one who is notable for the expression of biased opinion. The supervisor who writes the results of his researches for the columns of educational journals will receive the local and general recognition which such enterprise merits."[3]

We do not want nor can we afford to teach on mere "hunches." We want and can have definite scientific foundation for our teaching technique.

This paper is to be concerned with keeping the supervisor and the teacher reasonably dissatisfied with the results of the research already attempted in the field of business penmanship, and to try to point the way toward future extensive, needed research by individual supervisors and teachers and by our association. Many investigations in penmanship have been made by such prominent educators as Thorndike, Ayres, Freeman, Downey, Graves, Judd, Starch, West, and others. When we narrow the field, however, to business and vocational penmanship, the number of investigations becomes very few.

In 1915 Frank N. Freeman[4] conducted an investigation to find out the quality of writing which business men regarded as adequate. With infrequent exceptions, the employers responding regarded the qualities 60 and 70 as "essential." This study helped to humanize and to strengthen the thought that a pupil who was able to maintain a quality of 60 in all his correlated work had attained a standard sufficiently high.

Dr. Leonard V. Koos in the February, 1918 number of the Elementary School Journal reported the results of a study called "The Determination of Ultimate Standards of Quality in Handwriting."[5] I quote from the report: "The quality aspect of the vocational need for handwriting was studied by scoring, on the Ayres

Measuring Scale for Adult Handwriting, the writing done by 1,127 employees in a number of occupations. The assumption is that we may use the handwriting done by these employees in establishing vocational standards. If the persons who wrote the specimens used in this study are retained in their positions, this fact is proof that they write well enough for the purpose of their vocation."

Conclusions: "The quality 60 on the Ayres Measuring Scale for Adult Handwriting was set up as the ultimate standard of attainment for all school children for purely social purposes because it is adequate for the needs of most vocations. This standard applies to laborers, skilled and unskilled, as well as to professional men, exclusive of teachers in the elementary schools. For that larger group who will go into commercial work, for telegraphers, and for teachers in the elementary schools, it will be necessary to insist upon the attainment of a somewhat higher quality, but hardly in excess of the quality 70."[5]

Following the general plan of Doctor Koos, we conducted an investigation[6] in Philadelphia to determine the grade standards for Philadelphia schools. From the employees of twenty-one large concerns, two thousand specimens of vocational handwriting were secured. Each specimen was rated by twenty judges; the basis of comparison was the Ayres Measuring Scale for Handwriting, Gettysburg Edition. The rating of each judge was averaged and occupational and general averages determined.

Conclusions: "After considering (1) the judgments of business men as stated in questionnaires, (2) the vocational averages of workers' who wrote specimens, and (3) the average range of scores for those in the non-commercial groups, the investigators concluded that quality 60 is a sufficiently high minimum standard for social correspondence. The results of the rating of specimens reveal that more than 16 per cent of those written by office workers scored 70 or above. In consequence, quality 70 on the Ayres Measuring Scale for Handwriting, Gettysburg Edition, was decided upon as the minimum standard for commercial pupils."

1. Dunlap, Knight—"Habits: Their Making and Unmaking"—1932; Preface, Page ix.

2. West, Paul V.—"The Penmanship Supervisor as a Leader of Research," Report of N. A. P. T. S., 1928. p. 41.

3. West, Paul V.—"Administrative Aspects of Handwriting Supervision," Report of N. A. P. T. S., 1932, p. 13.

4. Freeman, Frank N.—Chap. V. Fourteenth Year Book, National Society for the Study of Education—"Research in Business Writing." 1915.

5. Leonard V. Koos—Elementary School Journal, "The Determination of Ultimate Standards of Quality in Handwriting." February, 1918.

6. Kirk, John G.—Journal of Educational Research, "Handwriting Survey to Determine Grade Standards," March—April, 1926.

Each of the foregoing studies was made for the purpose of determining definite standards for social and vocational writing. Is it not possible that standards determined by these earlier investigators are too low? A reinvestigation of standards at the present time would seem to be most worth while.

We are all quite familiar with the fact that the handwriting of junior and senior high school pupils deteriorates. This deterioration is due to the fact that they have no formal instruction in handwriting beyond the sixth grade. Questions to which we need answers are: (1) What is the amount of deterioration of writing after the termination of handwriting instruction in the sixth grade? (2) Should there be overteaching in the elementary schools to offset this deterioration? (3) Is there an improvement of quality in the senior class of the high school? Some work has already been done in this field, but further research is needed. Miss Ethel Shelley, [7] in an unpublished study, found that while in January, 1928 there were 41.4 per cent of 323 seventh grade pupils whose writing quality scored 70 or above on the Ayres Scale for Measuring Handwriting, in January, 1929, one year later, the number scoring 70 had been reduced to 19.2 per cent of the pupils. Her study shows furthermore that 64.4 per cent of the pupils tested dropped in handwriting quality, 29.1 per cent remained the same, while 6.5 per cent of the pupils raised their scores. The decrease varied from five to forty points; the writing of fifty pupils decreased five points, and that of 90 pupils decreased ten points.

Another study of a similar kind made in the John Paul Jones Junior High School, Philadelphia, shows a loss of a lesser degree than that of Miss Shelley's findings. However, 44.9 per cent or almost half of the pupils wrote at a lower quality at the end of the year. The loss ranged from five to forty points with the greater number from five to fifteen points. Of the entire group, 35.9 per cent had not changed their quality and 19.5 per cent had increased their quality score from five to twenty points with the largest group from five to ten points. If the work of individuals had been studied according to both plans throughout the years of senior high school work, what would the results have shown? Is there not a basis for major research in this problem? A study of it should relate to attainable standards for commercial as well as for non-commercial groups.

Another subject of research relates to the discovery of a standard alphabet. Do pupils in junior and senior high schools and men and women in business use the forms of capitals and small letters which they learned in school? If not, have they discovered speedier and plainer forms? Would a study of samples of business writing reveal that the present standard alphabet needs changing? In a paper entitled, "Making a Handwriting Curriculum," which Henry Marap read in 1930, he said: "It seems to me that the best forms for letters of the alphabet have not yet been objectively determined. There is a challenge in this doubt to someone who may make a major basic investigation. When this investigation has been made, it will do for handwriting what Horn and Thorndike have done for spelling and the reading vocabulary. The investigator should, it seems to me, assemble samples of handwriting from all sources. Since at the age of twelve mastery is attained, specimens should be written by pupils of that age. These

HEARD AT THE CONVENTION

Improvement will be made when we get the school authorities to recognize the importance of plain handwriting and to give it a reasonable amount of time.

specimens should be compared with the handwriting of groups eighteen years of age and also with those of groups thirty years of age. From the study and comparison of such specimens, a series of alphabets may be compiled which would be based on slant, spacing, simplicity, and form. These alphabets should be submitted to handwriting experts and investigators in order that they may suggest modifications in accordance with principles of legibility and speed. The alphabetic forms thus obtained should then be submitted to artists who may suggest way of embellishing them. Finally, handwriting experts may study two or three alphabets under conditions normally found in schools with the idea of selecting the one which has the greatest advantages of legibility and speed."

Definite information has not been gathered concerning the effect of handwriting styles and legibility in

letters of application. The compilation of such information and the study of it should reveal the fact that many employment managers accept or reject applicants because of the style and quality of their handwriting. The questions to which we need answers are:

1. Is angularity a handicap?

2. What is considered the general effect of wide or narrow spacing on the reader?

3. What character traits are conveyed to the prospective employer by
   a. heavy down strokes?
   b. small writing?
   c. large writing?

We might well pause here to consider the splendid research of Shepherd, James, and Morrison [8] on the effect of the Quality of Handwriting on Grading. These studies concern the correlation of handwriting with other subjects and reveal the fact that when writing is poor, the grades on English papers are lower and when writing is legible and easy to read, the grades are correspondingly higher. James found that handwriting affected the grades to the extent of 7 or 8 points and Shepherd reported as high as a 10 per cent difference. If this is so in regard to grading, what effect does writing have on an applicant's chances of securing a position? Would an applicant's chances be 10 per cent better if his handwriting were correspondingly better than another applicant's?

The Industrial Relations Counselor [9] of a large chemical manufacturing company has said: "It is surprising to find such a large number of young applicants for employment who write so illegibly that their applications are either rejected or, if considered, are hired only as a last resort." Again H. T. Hamilton [10] of the New York Trust Company, writes: "Good handwriting should be stressed in all commercial high schools. Handwriting is still fundamental for the young men in the business world: It may be a deciding factor in securing his first position; it is almost indispensable in the early years of his work; and is a good sound asset at all times.".

That business men are interested in legible writing is shown by the results of research begun by this association a couple of years ago. C. P. Gard, in his paper "Questionnaire to Personnel Directors in Various Business Activities" in the 1932 Yearbook of the N. A. P. T. S., reported

---

7. Supervisor of Handwriting, Norristown, Pa.

8. Shepherd, Everett N.—"The Effect of the Quality of Penmanship on Grades," Journal of Educational Research, Vol. XIX, No. 2, February, 1929, p. 102-105.
James, H. W.—"The Effect of Handwriting on Grading," The English Journal, Vol. 16, 1927, pp. 181-185.
Morrison, Henry C.—"The Practice of Teaching in Secondary Schools," P. 10-11.

9. Beck, Cameron—"The Need of Closer Relations Between Commercial Schools and Business," page 11.

10. Beck, Cameron—"The Need of Closer Relations Between Commercial Schools and Business," page 42.

that of a total of 240 replies, 62 per cent answered "Yes" to the questions: "Do you ever reject applications because of poor handwriting?" To the question: "Is attention given to the handwriting of applicants for positions in your firm?"—84 per cent answered "Yes". Miss Myrta L. Ely, in January, 1924, sent a questionnaire to 120 different firms in Saint Paul, Minnesota. To the question, "In passing on applications for stenographic positions, all else being equal, would you consider favorably the one whose penmanship is best?"—110 answered "Yes," while only 8 answered "No." The answers to both of these questionnaires indicate a very definite interest of the employers in the handwriting of future employees. If this is nationally true, what remedies are energetic supervisors and teachers going to use to improve the situation?

Several well-known business men have made a just and well-deserved criticism when they say that the schools make little or no attempt at job analysis. The business man feels that teachers cannot know what to emphasize in teaching unless they know what jobs are open to junior and senior high school pupils and what tasks will be most frequently required of beginners. How true this statement is of handwriting, no one has definitely investigated. In some jobs the employee never uses anything but a pencil, in others he may use ink, and in still others he may use both. In some jobs handwriting involves figure writing only, while in others it involves the writing of names and addresses. Do we know exactly what to stress with any particular group? No! In fact, it is impossible to foretell what any individual or even a group of individuals will need in the future. But some investigator may determine the kinds of work most frequently performed by office workers and thus, on the basis of his findings, we may stress those kinds of skills which fit workers for kinds of employment most often encountered.

Knapp [11] says: "How many habits or styles of writing have you? Do you write differently when applying for a position or when writing to someone on whom you wish to make a good impression? On the other hand, have you another style which is less legible and less attractive to use on occasions which are not so important? And has this poorer style been practiced until it has become easier and therefore preferable to use most of the time? You remember the girl who carried two handkerchiefs, one to show and one to blow. That plan was objectionable because she sometimes showed the wrong one."

Pupils in school are just like us. Most of them have been taught to write legibly, but have practiced slovenly writing so much that it has become most habitual. The age-old question arises, "How can we get the carry-over we want?" Knapp has

11. Knapp, Thad Johnson—"Educational Insurance," pp. 12-21.

Mr. O. E. Hovis, 88 Biltmore St., Springfield, Mass., is the penman who wrote the above.

done some interesting work in this field at the Highland Park High School, Michigan. There the child is rated for satisfactory application of instruction in correlated writing. Speaking of this instruction, in "Educational Insurance," he says: "This method gives worth while results. It is shown by our experience with classes in penmanship in the Highland Park High School (intermediate classes). Two years after an applied marking plan was put into operation, the number of pupils required to take penmanship was reduced approximately fifty per cent, despite a large growth at the same time in the enrollment of the school." Several questions arise involving the need for scientific answers:

1. On what basis should penmanship marks be given?

2. Does the giving of a rating in correlated lessons insure the formation of the habit of a uniform, legible hand at all times?

3. Is the formal drill period necessary when the writing product in correlated lessons is rated?

4. What form should the remedial instruction take?

It is said that in twelve months' time approximately 26 million letters reached the Washington dead letter office. The unclaimed missives contain checks, money orders, and stamps to the value of more than five million dollars. This is a very serious indict-

ment of our slovenly and illegible handwriting. Is anything like this same amount of loss caused in other kinds of business? Is there an actual loss to the business man through errors in writing, figure making, addressing letters, etc.? C. D. Moore, in a paper "Value of Good Penmanship in Business," reported that one business executive told him "of an instance where 6,000 items had to be rechecked in order to locate an error resulting from a carelessly-made figure." How often does this waste of time and energy occur in business?

All speed standards have been set arbitrarily by educators. We teach and attempt to have the pupils attain these standards. Are these speed standards sufficient to enable pupils to keep pace with teachers and business men when they dictate notes and memoranda? Some business men demand rapid writing. What do they mean by rapid writing—100, 125, or 150 letters a minute? Rapid business writing remains undefined. Studies should be made of the speed required in the performance of various kinds of tasks. Higher wages and shorter hours seem inevitable. Hence, the problem of efficient production will enter into the success of persons in business. Unless a pupil is equipped to do a certain amount of work which is acceptable in regard to both quality and quantity, it will be difficult for him to retain a position.

We hear much today about developing social responsibility. The develop-

A gem from the late H. B. Lehman

ment of this social consciousness is certainly not confined to any group, grade, or subject. If handwriting, bookkeeping, or junior business training teachers do not seize every opportunity to develop these social ideals, then they are neglecting one of their greatest opportunities. There is surely no better way to begin than by stressing responsibility for improvement in handwriting. Many questions, however, immediately arise:

1. What is the value of group conferences to individual improvement?

2. What type of incidental instruction is most effective?

3. Can letter forms be improved through self-analysis?

4. What type of textbook is best for vocational instruction?

5. Can improvement be effected by the use of guide or contract sheets? In what form should these sheets be?

6. What effect should the handwriting grade have on a bookkeeping paper?

The business man is willing and eager to employ boys and girls who are well-trained especially in handwriting. Legible writing saves time and money. In 1930 at the National Education Association Convention, Cameron Beck, Personnel Director of the New York Stock Exchange, presented the views of leading business men in a paper, "The Need of Closer Relations between . Commercial Schools and Business." In summarizing his paper he said: "The schools are out of step with business in that:

"(1) little or no provision is made for job analysis;

"(2) no study is made of present or future business needs;

"(3) no advantage is taken of the willingness of business men to cooperate with the schools;

"(4) proper vocational guidance is lacking."

In this paper we have suggested many problems for study. Studies should be made extending over several years. Data should be collected from every state. Only a national association such as the N. A. P. T. S. is organized to collect such information and to outline year by year what has been and is yet to be accomplished. This association is, furthermore, through its publication of the annual proceedings of the convention, best qualified to advertise the results of investigations. Could the association devote its energies to better advantage?

The following problems are suggested for original or further investigation.

(1) **Problem**—Quality of Handwriting Suitable for Business.
Research already done:
Freeman, Frank—1915, Fourteenth Year Book, National Society for the Study of Education, Chapter V.
Kirk, John G.—March—April, 1926, Journal of Educational Research, "Handwriting Survey to Determine Finishing Standards for Philadelphia Public Schools."
Koos, Leonard V.—February, 1918, The Determination of Ultimate Standards of Quality in Handwriting, Elementary School Journal.
Conclusions found:
Quality 60 on Ayres Scale for Measuring Handwriting for non-commercial groups: quality 70 for commercial groups.
Needed Research:
1. To find out if these standards are still satisfactory to the business man.
2. To discover national instead of local standards.

(2) **Problem**—Deterioration of Writing in Junior High School.
Research already done:
Shelley, Ethel—1928—1929.
Philadelphia — John Paul Jones Junior High School.

Conclusions found:
Decrease of 5 to 40 points.
Needed Research:
1. A more intensive study over a longer period.

(3) **Problem**—Effect of Legible Writing on an Applicant's Chances of Securing a Position.
Research already done:
Gard, C. J.—1932 Yearbook of N. A. P. T. S., Questionnaire to Personnel Directors in Various Business Activities.
Ely, Myrta L.—Questionnaire sent to 120 different type firms, January, 1924.
Conclusions found:
Handwriting Counts in securing positions.
Needed Research:
Further national and local verification along the same lines.

(4) **Problem**—What should be the Basis for Rating Handwriting?
Research already done:
Knapp, Thad Johnson—February, 1930. Educational Insurance, pages 12-21.
Conclusions found:
The number of pupils required to take penmanship was reduced approximately 50 per cent in two years.
Research needed:
Study of controlled groups:
1. Formal handwriting instruction —rating given for work done in handwriting period.
2. Formal handwriting instruction —handwriting rating given for correlated work.
3. No handwriting instruction— handwriting rating given for correlated work.

(5) **Problem**—Standard Letter Forms.
Needed Research: ·
1. Study of business and social writing to determine letter forms.

(6) **Problem**—Effect of Handwriting Styles on Applicant's Chances of Securing a Position.
Needed Research:
1. What style of writing is most favored by business men?

(7) **Problem**—Analysis of Jobs which High School Pupils Get to Determine Teaching Needs.
Needed Research:
1. What jobs are open to high and junior high school graduates? · uates? ·
2. What tasks will be most frequently required of them?
3. How many jobs require:
   a. figures?
   b. body writing?
   c. names and addresses?
4. Is pencil, pen, or a combination used?

(8) **Problem**—Definition of Rapid Business Writing.
Needed Research:
1. What speed is needed for notetaking in high school?
2. What speed is required in the various jobs?

(9) **Problem**—To Develop Handwriting Consciousness in Secondary Schools.
Needed Research:
1. Study of various methods with controlled groups.

Ornamental Penmanship

No. 12   Script by the late A. M. Wonnell

Practice the individual letters in the above sentences. Study the graceful **t** crossings and the free oval finish. Give special attention to the T, C and Y.

Lessons in Card Carving

By J. D. Carter, Deerfield, Ill.

Lesson No. 1

In our beginning lesson we should have a good sharp pen knife and 5 or 6 ply white cardboard of the best grade.

For practice work, however, one can get fair results by using white show-card cardboard cut to convenient size to use.

The knife should be of the best steel so it will hold an edge as sharp as a razor. No one can get satisfactory work unless the knife is sharp; for the cutting will appear ragged with a dull knife.

The cutting is done with the point or end of the blade. I always sharpen both front and back of the blade at the point; making the point resemble a rounded spear point. One should sharpen the point giving a shorter or more abrupt bevel to the cutting edge than is on the ordinary knife. When sharpened this way the bevel edge helps to make the cutting raised to a uniform height.

In cutting, hold the knife in hand much the same way as when sharpening a pencil and draw it towards you as you proceed to work from lesson No. 1.

In lesson No. 1, I have given as you see only one form for cutting, the only difference you find is in the varying length of strokes.

I have done this that you may get good results sooner.

You may at the beginning rule lines with pencil as guides and cut carefully each exercise a number of times.

When you have practiced some time, send me a complete copy of lesson No. 1 and I will gladly criticise this lesson and return it to you if you send me the return postage.

The greeting card season will soon be here and let us be ready for it.

I am planning to give something practical along that line in our next lesson.

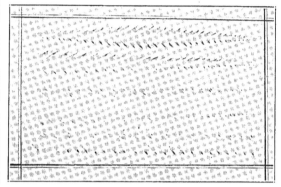

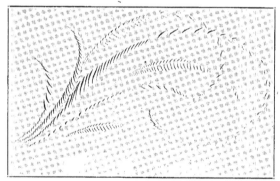

Skill cannot be lost as easily as many investments.

HELP YOUR SCHOOL TO GIVE YOU YOUR MONEY'S WORTH:

In order to get the most out of your course, it is necessary that you do your best at all times and be prompt and regular in attendance. You must make each minute count while you are in school and devote at least two or three hours each day to home study.

It is also essential that you take all of the subjects included in your course. Business English, Spelling, Penmanship, Rapid Calculation, Commercial Law, Salesmanship, etc., are even more important, if anything, than Bookkeeping, Shorthand, and Typewriting; for, unless you are good in all of these fundamentals, you cannot possibly become the best stenographer, bookkeeper, secretary, or accountant.

Incidentally, it should be the ambition of every student to become the very best in his line. Once you get an ambition like that, you will WANT to take all of the subjects in your course and make a good record in each subject. It won't be necessary to urge you to go to school, to be on time, to apply yourself or to chase you to your classes. You will just naturally WANT to make every minute count, and that is exactly the way it should be.

Do not permit yourself to join the lavatory or cloak room "gang".

Spending too much time in those places usually means too much cigarette smoking, which, of course, dulls the mind and should not be indulged in during school hours by anyone. Not only that, but it also means hearing a lot of idle gossip, most of which does not amount to anything at all. It also means getting your mind off your studies and, of course, the waste of much time.

ABOUT SECURING POSITIONS:

It is easier to help some students secure positions than it is others, because some take a broader course, some are neater, more accurate, and more rapid in their work; and some have more energy, or more initiative, or a better personality.

The main thing, is to master, as completely as possible, whatever course you are taking, to have and show plenty of "get-up and hustle", and to be on the job at all times—

While a school is always glad to help every student in every way possible in securing a position, it is to the student's interest to try to help himself, too. He should be able to make a good personal application and have enough initiative to know where to apply, and, above all, he should be able to write a good letter of application—one that will stand out and will help to get him first consideration when the employer sees his letter.

HOBBY SHOW

A very beautiful handmade book has been received from S. J. Shaw, 1376 Locust St., Long Beach, Calif. The book is entitled "The Educator" and is a tribute to The Educator and the Zanerian College of Penmanship. He has pages of ornamental writing, card writing, card carving, color work, pen and ink sketches, birthday and Christmas cards, and other elaborate pieces of pen work. It is bound in stiff cardboard covers upon which Mr. Shaw has designed a very beautiful cover. The book was exhibited at the Hobby Show in Long Beach where 31,000 viewed the collection.

Mr. Shaw attended the Zanerian College of Penmanship in 1893. Today he does pen work for the pleasure he gets out of it. Anyone who wishes to have a real hobby should take up penmanship.

SIGN, NOT PRINT

One of the large investment service corporations in sending out its contracts requests customers to **sign, not print,** their names. This is a step in the right direction. Every one who signs a contract should be able to write his own name legibly. If he does not write it legibly it shows that he has missed some very fundamental education or is very careless and inconsiderate.

The government, in the various reports submitted to it, experienced trouble in deciphering signatures and for some years has requested people to print their names. Evidently the investment company has had trouble in reading printed signatures. Print can be, and frequently is, as illegible as poor cursive writing. It would be interesting to know how many printed signatures on government reports, etc. are illegible.

The slogan everywhere should be "WRITE LEGIBLY".

A flourish by C. A. Romont, 7 Dartmouth Place, Boston, Mass.

Practical Engrossing

By
E. H. McGhee, McGhee Studio,
143 E. State Street, Trenton, N. J.

No. 11

After deciding the size of the page, draw marginal guide lines. Then, locate the different headings and lines and sketch them in roughly but accurately for spacing. In planning a piece of work you will find it an excellent idea to first use a plain piece of wrapping paper.

Letter each line carefully, then retouch with a fine pointed pen. The straight edges of letters should be ruled up. Notice the size of the headings. The important line is the name of the school.

If at first you have difficulty in securing the desired effect compare your work with the copy and keep on studying. It takes years to acquire skill. As someone recently said, "Perfection in all things comes slowly—and never quite arrives." If you have trouble with your pens, write to us. We will be glad to give you any information you desire.

Plainfield High School

Plainfield   New Jersey

This certifies that

_____

has fulfilled the requirements for Graduation as prescribed by the Board of Education and is entitled to this

Diploma

Given this   day of   19

President of Board   Superintendent of Schools

Secretary of Board   Principal of High School

A plain, rich looking diploma made by E. H. McGhee of the McGhee Studio, Trenton, N. J.

Figures from 3 pupils of the Bliss College, Columbus, Ohio, engraved from a penmanship contest held by J. C. Kliewer, the penmanship instructor. The specimens reading from left to right are by Lucile Phelps, Mabel Powelson and Virginia Near.

DESIGNING AND ENGROSSING

By E. L. BROWN
Rockland, Maine

Testimonial Heading

Brush and color work combined with script lettering is quite attractive for engrossing, and the knack obtaining transparency in tone can only be acquired by persistent effort. The previous lesson explains quite fully the procedure for beginners to attain skill in brush handling.

Pencil carefully the name of club, also president and follow with outline in Zanerian water-proof ink. Use dividers for top and base line, and rule all vertical lines with T-square and ruling pen.

After completing the pen work, prepare for the tinting by outlining parts for washes in pencil. Study contrasts. Leave light space at top and left side of letters. Shadow at base of letters ⅜ inch deep—add darker band after first wash is dry. Clear transparent tones are necessary for a satisfactory effect, and in order to obtain this result use a free brush, or in other words, a brush well filled with color. Let it flow freely from the brush to the desired surfaces. Mix lamp black with a small portion of red to produce a brownish tone. Use color with more body for darkest tones. Two

brushes were used for clouded effects. Red sable brushes Nos. 6 and 7 will be needed.

The name "Louis Myers" is rather unique in finish. After the tinting was completed white was used to give a mottled effect. Mix white with generous supply of water to give a very thin wash to allow the under color to show dimly.

This is the class of work which the engrosser will be called upon to do frequently, and the student will find it a practical style to master. Free criticisms and suggestions on all work submitted for this purpose.

of the science which he knew so well and so thoroughly.

From the day he assumed command of the destiny of the Fire Association to the end of his career as its leader, when he retired at a ripe age, his leadership was a triumphant march and many great and disastrous conflagrations that shook to their foundations, and in some instances utterly annihilated, reputable and well established fire insurance companies, were met by him with serene courage, placid faith and unruffled confidence. The ship, at whose helm he stood, weathered these disasters and emerged from these storms sailing on an even keel, with its obligations paid and its high standing unimpaired.

This halftone was made from a photostat and therefore the delicate lines were difficult to reproduce. This beautiful page was written by Charlton V. Howe, 2312 Girard Trust Bldg., Philadelphia, Pa., who for many years has been one of the leading writers of engravers' script. Engravers' script has always been one of the important styles used by engrossers and still maintains that position.

BOOK REVIEWS

Our readers are interested in books of merit, but especially in books of interest and value to commercial teachers including books of special educational value and books on business subjects. All such books will be briefly reviewed in these columns, the object being to give sufficient description of each to enable our readers to determine its value.

Fundamentals of Psychology in Secondary Education, by S. C. Garrison, Dean of the Graduate School of Education and Director of the Senior College, George Peabody College, and K. C. Garrison, Professor of Psychology, North Carolina State College of the University of North Carolina. Published by Prentice-Hall, Inc., New York, N. Y. Cloth cover, 599 pages.

This book is based upon recent scientific, experimental findings, and—a distinguishing feature—it treats the school subjects psychologically. This is not a book of psychological theory; it is a practical application of psychological data and principles to the school problems.

The book is logically and conveniently divided into 3 parts; Thought Problems and Selected References follow each chapter; 66 tables and 18 illustrative figures; the fact that all the data, the problems treated, and the treatment itself are UP TO DATE—in line with modern viewpoints and methods.

Business Organization and Practice, by William B. Cornell, M. E., Professor of Management, Chairman of Department of Business Management, School of Commerce, Accounts and Finance, New York University, and John H. MacDonald, M.C.S., Assistant to the Vice President and Treasurer, National Broadcasting Company, Inc. Published by the American Book Company, Cincinnati, Ohio. Cloth cover, 622 pages.

In this book the authors have brought up to date their earlier text, FUNDAMENTALS OF BUSINESS ORGANIZATION AND MANAGEMENT. In order to make the subject matter abreast of the latest developments in the field of business organization and management they have consulted numerous business men of high standing. Furthermore, they have secured the advice and assistance of many teachers in order that the presentation may meet modern methods of teaching.

With its comprehensive instruction and general business principles the book serves as a senior high school text in business organization and management. Although suited for all commercial students it is of particular interest to pupils in secretarial and bookkeeping courses.

An outstanding feature of this new book is its co-ordinated development. Pupils are given a clear picture of the problems in the business field and the relationship of the different types of business and their departments by means of a logical series of related chapters.

Numerous additions have been made to the practical questions and problems at the ends of the chapters. Many new charts and illustrations stimulate interest and aid pupils in visualizing the points presented.

Many of the chapters have largely been rewritten and expanded. New subjects have been added, treating business as it is today being affected by the changed social, economic, and political conditions.

The chapters in Part VII, From Student to Business Man, are new. They discuss the pupil's vocational interests, the importance of starting right and of adjusting oneself to new situations as they arise, the need of personal budgeting and saving, making investments in substantial securities, and general principles to follow in selecting a business for oneself.

The Table of Contents is as follows:

PART I
Introduction
THE EVOLUTION OF SOCIETY AND BUSINESS

PART II
THE NEW ENTERPRISE
Starting a New Enterprise
Business Ownership
Providing Investment Capital
Providing Working Capital

PART III
PRINCIPLES OF MANAGEMENT
Business Organization
Business Management

PART IV
DEPARTMENT, SERVICES, AND EQUIPMENT
Correspondence and Filing Department
Office Services
Office Equipment
Finance and Accounting Departments
Credit Department
Purchasing Department
Storekeeping and Traffic Departments
The Sales Department
Advertising and Sales Promotion
Manufacturing Department

PART V
THE HUMAN FACTOR IN BUSINESS
Personnel Administration
Training and Protecting Employees

PART VI
TOOLS OF MANAGEMENT
Statistics
Graphic Presentation
Budgeting For Business Control

PART VII
FROM STUDENT TO BUSINESS MAN
The First Job
Holding a Job
Looking Ahead: Personal Money Management
A Business of One's Own

Junior Business Training for Economic Living, by Frederick G. Nichols, Associate Professor of Education, Graduate School of Education, Harvard University. Formerly, State Director of Commercial Education, New York and Pennsylvania; also Chief, Commercial Education Service, Federal Board for Vocational Education. Published by American Book Company, Cincinnati, Ohio. Cloth cover, 678 pages.

In this book the author emphasizes "economic training" that results in right "economic living" for one's immediate personal satisfaction and future economic security. Throughout, he has considered the citizens from the standpoint of a consumer. It is, therefore, basically a "consumer-knowledge" course.

In the following ways the book seeks to present the simple principles of economics which play an important part in satisfactory living in the present and for achieving economic security for the future:

(1) By directing the pupil's attention to economic matters through an abundance of readable material in the text.

(2) By stimulating thinking about economic problems of immediate interest through the use of well-chosen and carefully selected questions and problems.

(3) By an adequate review of economic principles through the introduction of word lists at the conclusion of each unit of instruction.

(4) By placing in each unit of instruction, a series of arithmetical problems in the solution of which an important lesson in personal economic living is taught.

(5) By introducing appropriate pictures and illustrations.

The central theme running throughout the course is "personal economic security." The pupil is shown why he should be concerned about his personal economic affairs. More than 1000 problems dealing with both relative and definite values are given in the text, and these have, as far as possible, been brought within the range of the "potential experience" of the pupil. For example, the family income and budget are within the pupil's potential experience, likewise the father's insurance problem, etc.

Like the principles, the problems are treated from the standpoint of the individual's personal needs and not from the standpoint of business management. Many different types of problems have been included. Some are designed to develop careful thinking, to distinguish between right

and wrong statements. Some require the pupil to check up on factual data, while others seek to find out if the pupil can do something he has been taught to do. Various other kinds of exercises are included. These problems offer a great variety of material and are arranged progressively in the order of their difficulty.

Good handwriting is emphasized. The ability to do arithmetical work quickly and accurately is a primary aim of the course. The development of "figure sense," the faculty of seeing the true relationship between "price" and "value" is stressed even more than is mere calculating ability.

According to present accepted thought in regard to a commercial course, training pupils for office work is a function of business training which is being delayed until the senior high school and college period. Hereafter, commercial training will be based on a cultural-economic foundation and less on technique in the skill subjects. The employment situation has become such that usually boys and girls with a good background of preparation are being given the preference by employers. In his new course, Professor Nichols meets this growing condition.

Fingers that Talk, by Ralph Haefner, Ph. D. Published by Gregg Publishing Company, New York, N. Y. Paper cover, 122 pages.

This typing work book, for children from eight to twelve years of age, opens a new and fascinating field for the child and for our world of education. It records the adventures of Grace and John in learning to typewrite and is adapted for use at home or in school.

The author has been associated with the investigations and development of the use of the typewriter as an influence in elementary education since 1929. Through his connection with Columbia University in a research capacity, he has had a splendid opportunity to investigate and prove the educational values coming from the use of this modern and fascinating business tool—the typewriter—when tied up with elementary education.

The purpose of the book is to: First, provide the child with a large number of typing activities which are educationally valuable; second, to give the child a systematic method of operating the typewriter so he can later develop any degree of skill needed.

The work is divided into four types.

(a) a simple preliminary explanation of the steps in operating a typewriter

(b) lessons for developing systematic finger habits

(c) lessons emphasizing important phases of language and composition

(d) lessons in original composition, such as writing sentences, stories, and letters.

All of the material in the book has been tried out for more than two years with hundreds of children in the third and fourth grades.

Lessons in Modern Engrosser's Script
Prepared in the office of The Educator

No. 2

Use a good grade of ⅜ inch ruled paper and a Fine Writer pen.

Make the **w** the same as the **u**, except the finish. Study the size and location of the dot. Are all of your hair lines curved gracefully and running in same direction? Get ending and beginning strokes parallel. Cut the tops off straight and get turns at base line even. Raise the pen at the base line each time.

The **r** begins like **n**. The finish is slightly different from **w**. It resembles a small **c**. Hair lines should run along the shades, not through them. The second up stroke curves same as the first one.

The **x** is like the last part of **n** with a compound curved crossing. Notice the light suggestion of shades on the ends of the cross stroke. Don't be careless or go too fast. Be sure and firm.

Write each word separately. Watch size. Weight of strokes is also very important.

See that your work has a good general appearance, not spotted or off slant. Uniformity is very important.

Turn the hand well over on the side to get a good firm foundation. The movement, unlike in business writing, is mainly finger.

This is one of the most beautiful styles of writing and is used extensively by engrossers.

Let us see your best efforts.

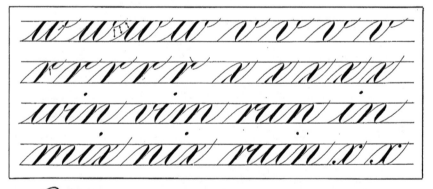

A letter from W. Leroy Brown, 17416 Clifton Blvd., Cleveland, Ohio, states that he is having a good year in the engrossing work. Mr. Brown has been in Cleveland for many years and does very high-class engrossing.

W. J. Hamilton, 176 Western Avenue, Lynn, Mass., writes a beautiful, bold ornamental hand as displayed by an envelope before us.

William Anthony McGuire, a long time associate in the theatre business of Ziegfeld, it is claimed writes all of his plays in longhand. Mr. McGuire, like many authors, is able to think better when writing in longhand.

J. F. Toledo, a student of Enrique Benguria, Habana, Cuba, writes beautiful ornamental cards. He is a subscriber to The Educator following the course of lessons.

Lord Selkirk School
Winnipeg, Man., Canada

A very beautiful pen and ink drawing by David J. Person, Carthage, S. D.

A novel signature by C. O. Ellefson, P. O. Box 1028, Proctor, Minn.

Candor is the seal of a noble man, the ornament and pride of man, the sweetest charm of woman, the scorn of rascal and the rarest virtue of sociability.

To make the world better, nobler and happier is the noblest work of man or woman.

This beautiful business writing was done by Cordelia Esham, a student of H. F. Hudson, Beacom College, Wilmington, Del.

Adjusting the Formal Subject of Handwriting to the Progressive Secondary School Program

By Minnie Knepper

Handwriting is a fundamental school subject. It takes its position along the side of reading, English and mathematics. Morrison clearly expresses its indispensability: "When the pupil arrives at the point at which he can record his thoughts, we have the only picture of his thought life which we can get at . . . We can induce him to write what he means and that is a tangible instrument for clarifying his thought and organizing his thinking in logical coherency."[1]

For the last several decades the demanding importance of handwriting has been disregarded pretty generally. This may be partially attributed to the inability of the majority of teachers to produce results. Administrative people do not understand the procedure and ignore it. Why do not our State Departments of Education make a legible hand and efficient teaching methods of handwriting one of the basic requirements for certification? If this were to prevail, soon we would have a wave of good writing sweep over our schools. Not having been trained in the technique of handwriting, teachers are confronted by a task that they attack blindly. The result is a paralyzing effect on all interest, enthusiasm and desire which a child may possess for this skill. The desire of communicating ideas is inherent; and we can use this curiosity of the child as a motivation. But pure practice is low in stimulation. And writing, like all complex motor activities requires a long period of painstaking practice to overcome the initial diffuse movements and to habituate the writing muscles to swing into the rhythm which differentiates good writing from scribbling.

The necessity of having handwriting as nearly automatic as possible brings the practice period into the field of the adolescent to complete the habituation. For the right kind of practice must be carried on until the pupil is able to withdraw all consciousness from the writing act. "The only kind of practice in writing that will bring, about automatic writing is to have the child think his own thoughts, as he will have to do in later life, and then express these in writing as rapidly and

legibly as possible."[2] It is not sufficient to treat writing as incidental to the other work in the school. The child needs to have his attention called to the requirements of writing itself. If this is done incidentally to the study of some other subject, the child's attention is divided. A skillful teacher, thoroughly in love with this work, appreciating all persevering efforts of a pupil and enthusiastically leading toward the ideals of beauty and legibility engenders in his pupil pride, self-interest and enjoyment in executing smooth rhythmic script. This is the type of penmanship teacher that the adolescent must have in the junior high environment.

Correlation in its completest sense must be carried out with other school subjects in the secondary school. The Freeman writing manuals are based entirely on correlation. In the writing period Freeman places the application on such projects as (1) arrangement of composition on the page, (2) arrangement of arithmetic problems, (3) use of conventional forms of correspondence, (4) practice in writing without lines.[3] Correlation by means of Activity books is one earnestly and joyously entered into by the pupils, and will correlate writing with literature, English, art, health, history and geography. We correlate with music by getting the rhythm with radio music of suitable tempo.

Clubs organized in home rooms, two Clubs per group, having names suitable to the subject, (Scribes and Scriveners were used by two of my clubs) colors to wear during writing exercises, points to win in execution and a corps of officers meet the social needs, create a friendly rivalry and bring marvelous results. The officers have assistants appointed to assist those not up to their grade standard. Each keeps a graph and once a week the teacher grades some of the correlated writing in other subjects and the graph is revised. The graphs especially are enjoyed by pupils and very few would suffer a downward deviation. , The home room Club which wins the highest per cent of certificates for proficiency for the year becomes the proud possessor of the cov-

eted pennant awarded for one year. The pennant is three feet in length, shaped like a steel pen and made of silvery felt with markings of black. It is lettered Best Writers.

A standing committee composed of one representative from each Club elected by his Club has charge of many of the extra writing affairs of the school. They arrange and have beautifully written any needed school resolutions, pen names on attendance certificates, write programs posted by the teachers, and arrange for the writing of invitations needed for any special affairs. They also arrange for an annual display of penmanship work of the school in a large window in the business section of the town taking entire charge of the affair. This committee also appoints sub-committees when needed. One of latter promotes and carries into execution a scrap book of beautiful specimens. This is an activity that is especially liked by pupils and proves to be a coveted honor. The teacher is a supervisory member of the committees. She has the last word on the selection of the worth of specimens for the scrap book.

In the reading room, a sub-committee has one corner fixed up as a Writing Nook. Here is a table for the scrapbook, the activity books when completed, and any interesting books about the art of writing that can be obtained. Many beautiful drills in colors, poems in beautiful writing, lettered poems, and poems written beautifully with illustrated art in outline are displayed on the walls in the Nook.

With such an interesting and attractive program as this, pupils' writing scores far above the grade sixty on the Ayers Scale which Cox suggests is high enough for the maximum. We had this interesting development that less than one per cent graded as low as sixty and very many swung far above Freeman's A grade on his Scale.

1. Henry Morrison, The Practice of Teaching in the Secondary School, p. 11.
2. Mary E. Thompson, Psychology and Pedagogy of Writing, p. 119.
3. Frank N. Freeman, How to Teach Handwriting, p. 34.

There are thousands of young people who are unable to hold desirable positions in business offices or who are deprived of promotion on account of their inability to write a rapid hand.

By F. B. Courtney, Detroit, Mich.

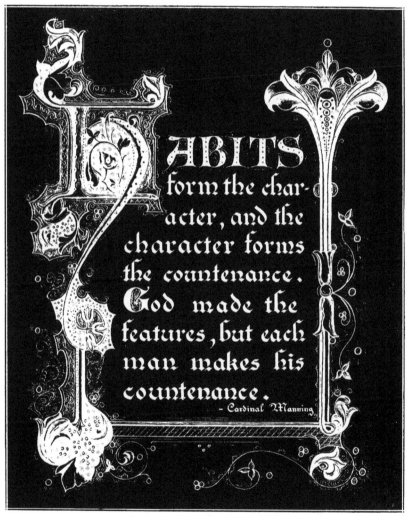

This beautiful piece of illuminating was made by Sister Mary Emmanuel, Felician Sisters of Lodi, N. J., while taking special instruction in the Zanerian College.

A graceful flourish from that well-known penman, H. P. Behrensmeyer, Quincy, Ill.

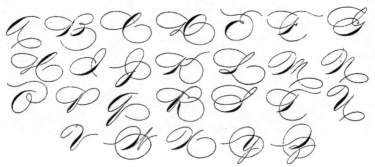

Don't worry if you feel that you are a
Jonah! Remember, he came out all right.

Value a good conscience more than praise

Business writing by G. L. White, Richmond Business College, Richmond, Va.

A skillfully executed alphabet by W. M. Carr, 31st. St., Station P. O., Detroit, Michigan.

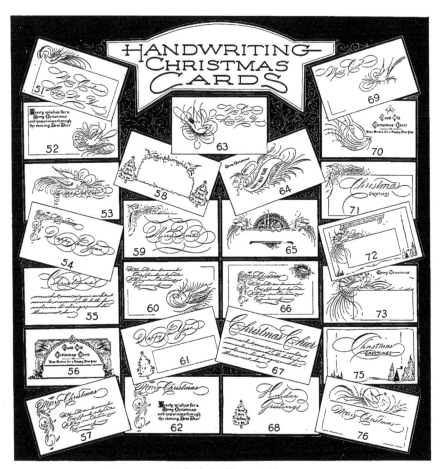

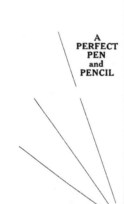

The Educator

VOL. 42   NOVEMBER, 1936   NO. 3.

Penmanship

Education

Engrossing

A
PERFECT
PEN
and
PENCIL

A
PERFECT
GIFT
for
XMAS

ZANER-BLOSER

fountain pen
and pencil

Christmas Special Order Blank for
The Zaner-Bloser Finger Fitting Fountain Pen and Pencil

The Zaner-Bloser Co.,
612 N. Park St., Columbus, Ohio

Please send me................................ ....Zaner-Bloser "finger fitting" Parker-made
(Quantity)
Fountain Pen and Pencil Sets at the especial low price of $5.50 per set, postpaid.

Check color wanted	Check clip or ring wanted	Individual Prices
☐ Mottled Blue & White		
☐ Black	☐ Clip for Men	☐ One Fountain Pen $3.50
☐ Modernistic Blue & White	☐ Ring for Women	☐ One Pencil $2.50

Name ....

☐ Cash enclosed

Address ....

☐ Send C. O. D.

Position ....

Patented in U. S. A. and Canada

Published monthly except July and August at 612 N. Park St., Columbus, O., by the Zaner-Bloser Company. Entered as second-class
matter November 21, 1931, at the post office at Columbus, O., under Act of March 3, 1879. Subscription $1.25 a year.

Volume 42   COLUMBUS, OHIO, NOVEMBER, 1936   No. 3

One of America's Skillful Penmen, S. M. Blue, Passes Away

It is with deep regret that we announce the passing of Stanley Matthews Blue, known to many penmen as "Billy" Blue.

Mr. Blue was one of the outstanding business and ornamental writers. He was born July 12, 1874 at Princeton, Ohio. At the age of 3 he went to live with his grandparents on a farm near Cincinnati where he attended a country school and later high school in Middletown, Ohio. In 1897 he entered Ohio School of Business, Dayton, Ohio. In 1898 he entered The Zanerian College at Columbus, Ohio, working his way through and graduating March 22, 1901 with a handwriting excelled by few penmen. He taught penmanship in Broken Bow Business College, Broken Bow, Nebr.; Grand Island, Nebr. Business College; Beckers Business College, Worcester, Mass.; and worked in the office of The Educator doing office work and skillful writing.

On August 31, 1903 he was married to Miss Maude Jacobs, of New Helena,

Nebr. In 1908 he went to Portland and taught in Armstrong Business College for a number of years. He was employed in the assessor's and auditor's office. For the past 19 years he has been employed by the S. P. &. S. Railroad. His death occurred on September 4, 1936. Besides his wife he is survived by a daughter, Zanerian Leffingwell of Los Angeles, California, and a grandson Richard.

Mr. Blue's skillful penmanship graces the pages of many scrapbooks containing the finest collections of penmanship.

When Mr. Blue worked for the Zaner-Bloser Company he came under the influence of those two masters, Zaner and Bloser. He took a special liking for the work of Mr. Bloser and succeeded in writing a similar style. In fact, it was so similar that experts often found it difficult to distinguish the difference between the two men's work. Some years ago The Educator published a great deal of his work.

Mr. Blue believed in good penmanship and as the above shows was able to write in a superb way. It was his ability in penmanship that secured him his position. The work of S. M. Blue entitles him to be ranked among the master penmen.

THE EDUCATOR

Published monthly (except July and August)
By THE ZANER-BLOSER CO.,
612 N. Park St., Columbus, O.
E. A. LUPFER..Editor
PARKER ZANER BLOSER..............Business Mgr.

SUBSCRIPTION PRICE, $1.25 A YEAR
(To Canada, 10c more; foreign, 30c more)
Single copy, 15c.
Change of address should be requested promptly in advance, if possible, giving the old as well as the new address.
Advertising rates furnished upon request.

THE EDUCATOR is the best medium through which to reach business college proprietors and managers, commercial teachers and students, and lovers of penmanship. Copy must reach our office by the 10th of the month for the issue of the following month.

Modern Handwriting

By E. A. Lupfer, Zanerian College, Columbus, Ohio

No. 3

Every one has to address envelopes. The above is the approved way of arranging the address. Legibility should be the first consideration on an envelope. Thousands of letters go into the dead letter office because of poor writing. Avoid questionable abbreviations.

The N begins the same as a number of other letters like the **M, H, K,** etc. The beginning movement is an indirect oval. Practice the indirect oval, then make the letter N. Notice the change of motion from the indirect to the straight line and finally to the indirect motion. The second part of the N should not be as high as the first part. If necessary stop at the bottom to get a good sharp retrace. Pick out about four or five things to aim for in the letter N. 1. Curve the beginning stroke. 2. Avoid a loop at the base line. 3. Get three turns. 4. Finish like the small letter i.

The first exercise is very good for developing a free movement in the M and N. Let the arm roll along freely, getting a graceful rounding turn at the top and a sharp point at the bottom. If you have trouble getting a loop at the base line we suggest that you stop on the first retrace at the base line. Make enough of these exercises so that you can make them with ease and confidence. Put a ruler along the top of the strokes to see if they grade down gradually.

Be sure that you get three turns at the top of the **M.** Watch the spacing. There are three spaces at the top of the letter which are about equal.

Write the words and abbreviations, working for uniform slant, equal spacing, regular alignment and a free quality of line. If you have difficulty in making a letter, keep on studying and practicing. Quitting will not help you.

M Mmm M mmmm mmmm m

With a dry pen retrace freely the retraced **M.** In retracing your own letters be sure to keep them neat and do not sprawl them out. This copy shows the similarity of form and movement of the capital M and small letter **m.** There is very little difference except the size.

M March Mar. May Monday Mon.

Here are some common words and abbreviations. Master them. Watch the space between the capitals and the following letters. Do you make the capitals and small letters freely? They should be made at about the same rate of speed.

n n n n nnnnn nnnnn
m m m m mmmmm mmmm

Most students can well afford to spend considerable time developing the small letters m and n. So many letters are patterned after these letters that it pays to get them well. Be sure that you get turns and angles where they belong. Roll along on the muscle of the arm. Let the little finger glide on upstrokes and drag on down strokes.

462 W. Fortieth St. T T T T T T
8 8 8 T T T T T T T T T
T T T T Tenn. Thanksgiving

All students should be able to write the word Thanksgiving. Practice the **T** and other exercises. Watch the loop letters above and below the line.

A O A A aauuuuu aaaa a

The secret of good penmanship is intelligent study and repetition. You should review often the letters which you have previously studied. Each time you go over a letter you will discover something which you did not see before. Retrace the capital A six times. It begins with an oval motion and changes to a straight line motion. You should, therefore, work in a little of the oval exercise and also straight line exercise. Make exercises and letters at the same rate of speed. Notice the similarity between the capital letter A and small letter a. Both have a slanting oval body with finish similar to a small i. The two turns at the base line should be equal in width. The upstroke of the body oval is not as curving as the down stroke. Be sure that you get a sharp angle on the retrace at the top of both capital and small letters.

ar at an al ai ac as ay ad am ap
and a are as at all am about any
American Anderson Allen Adams
A.B., A.D., A.G., A.J., A.S.

It takes perseverance to learn a skilled art like penmanship. Practice the combinations and words beginning with A.

This will help you lay a good foundation for writing any word. Watch spacing and movement. Some of these combinations may not be easy, however, you will have to write similar combinations everyday.

O OO O oo ooo o oo ooo o

The **O** is a slanting oval with an upward finish much like in the small letter **i**. Study the slant of the small loop formed at the top of the letter. Both sides of the letter should be curved evenly. The top should also be as rounding as the bottom.

The body of the small **o** is made with a quick rounding motion. Stop at the top and make a quick revolution, glide to the next letter, stop, and make another quick revolution. Study this motion at the blackboard.

on or ou oo ow ol os ot ov ob oc od
of on our one or out order over other
O'Neill O'Brien Owens Oliver Orr
O.A., O.B., O.K., O.L., O.M., O.T.,

Work on these combinations, giving special attention to the gliding stroke joining the **o** to the following letter. This joining should be high. If you drop it too much it will look like a poor **a**.

Practicing capital letter combinations develops freedom.

Writing Writing Writing

Write the word **writing**, then compare it with the copy and see wherein it could be improved.

The chances are you will have trouble with the **W**, especially the retraces and straight lines. Therefore, practice diligently the push-pull exercise.

Make the beginning part of the W, then swing into the push-pull exercise and finally finish like the capital W. Make about six of these groups across the page.

Try mixing the exercise and the letter in order to carry the movement developed in the exercise over into the letter.

In making the W see that the three spaces in the letter are even. Finish the W the same height as you finish the **V** (at two-thirds the height of the letter). If you draw a line across at the top touching the beginning and ending strokes you will find that the **W** should slant down at the same angle as the V, **N**, U and Y. Make from 40 to 45 letters a minute.

It is always a good plan to break the letters up into parts and master the various parts of the letters. This is especially true of the beginning stroke of **W**. Compare the capital W with the small letter. There is a radical difference between the capital and small letter. Both, however, should be finished high. Stop the motion on the small **w** before making the final stroke.

The X is made from the indirect and direct ovals. The first part is made in the same direction as the hands of the clock travel. The last part is made the opposite direction.

Practice the retraced exercises for the **X** and finally work on the letter itself.

Make the letter a full space high. That is, touching the two blue lines. This will help you in getting the letters the same height. Make about twelve letters on a line for correct width. Where letters are made too wide simply try to increase the number of letters on the line and you will improve the proportion.

Reduce the size of the **X** so that there is a little white space between the top of the letter and the blue lines above. Write the word many times and compare your efforts with the copy.

Let us study the **C** more carefully and practice the different exercises given above. The **C** begins with a loop resembling an **O**. These exercises are important and should be mastered. Notice the similarity between the capital **C** and small **c**. In the small letter **c** there is a decided check in the motion on the retrace when written in a word.

The **c** starts with a dot. Keep top as rounding as the bottom turn. There should be no retarding of motion in the capital. We begin with a free start and keep going until the letter is finished. The five joined letters should be made without raising the pen.

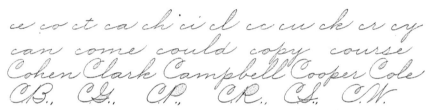

Practice each combination and word separately many times. Be sure that you work intelligently. Compare your work with the copy and try to find places in your work where it can be improved. Have others point out weaknesses.

The **E** begins and ends the same as the **C** but has an extra loop in the center. Do not check the motion at any place on the capital **E**. Glide out of the letter the same as you do in the **C** or small **i**.

The running **e** exercise is a very good one to develop ease and grace. Try to get the exercise uniform in appearance. In making the connected **e** get them spaced evenly and get the downward strokes a little straighter than the upward strokes. Be sure that your **e**'s are open and distinct from the **i**. Watch that the down strokes are light in pressure.

Letter combinations are very important. Stick to them until you have mastered them. Try to get your writing as nearly automatic as possible. The way to do that is to practice on letters alone until you can make them properly. As long as you have to think how letters are made your writing will not be automatic and easy. One of the aims in this course is to write well when thinking of content. We suggest, therefore, that you do considerable actual writing along with practicing these individual copies.

A primary spelling and English lesson written by Betty Luttmann, a student in St. Agnes School, Bond Hill, Cincinnati, Ohio. This shows the splendid correlation of handwriting and other subjects being done by St. Agnes School. Sister Comitilla is the Sister Superior. Specimens were received from Sister Wilma and Sister Amadea. They are to be complimented on the fine free work they are getting in penmanship.

Handwriting in the
Elementary Curriculum

Reprinted from the Chicago Course of Study

"One of the most accurate indices to a teacher's efficiency is the character of the papers and of the blackboard work that his pupils produce. The ability to train pupils to produce accurate written work is a fairly good index to the teacher's general capacity in habit-building."

—Bagley.

Adequate motivation, both for the teacher and the pupil, requires a recognition of the value of handwriting in school and in life. While the use of the typewriter is being extended, both in business and in personal affairs, handwriting is still essential for many purposes, and is used as widely, if not more widely than ever. Legibility and reasonable ease and fluency are, therefore, necessary educational objectives.

Fundamental Principles and Features of Method

The success of a method of teaching handwriting depends largely on securing the right relation between recognition of meaning and skill in execution. Some methods erroneously emphasize skill to the exclusion of meaning; others act on the assumption, that if the child recognizes the meaning of what he writes, the development of skill will take care of itself. Writing should have meaning to the child from the early stages of practice, but appropriate exercises to develop skill must also be employed.

Drill is essential in order that the same exercises may be written over and over again. Such drill, however, should be introduced only as the child recognizes the faults of his writing and his need for special practice.

The types of drill which are used should be as much like actual writing as possible. This means that letter drills should be emphasized more than the more formal types of drills, such as ovals, and push and pull exercises.

Most of the time of the writing period should be spent in practice by the child, and not in talking or in illustrative writing by the teacher. There should be just enough direction to make clear to the child what he should try to attain and the general methods which he should follow.

The work of the successive grades should be adjusted carefully to fit the stages of mental and physical development of the child. The details of this adjustment are brought out in the directions for the various grades.

There should be the closest correlation between the writing in the writing period and in the writing done in other subjects of instruction. Correlation should be carried out by introducing into the writing period practice on the specific problems which are met in the other subjects. The child's writing in the other periods should also be checked up, so that he will take pains to write carefully on every occasion.

Practice will produce improvement only if the child recognizes his faults. This can be brought about by helping him to criticize his own writing. Criticism should be made specific and analytic. This child's attention should be directed toward one aspect at a time. The most important aspects of form are uniformity of alinement, uniformity of slant, letter formation, quality of line, and spacing. In addition, attention may occasionally be directed toward speed.

The most practical and reasonable type of movement to develop is the combined movement. In this movement the hand carries the pen across the page, and contributes to the formation of the longer strokes of the letters, while the fingers complete the details of the letters. Appropriate exercises to develop the sideward movement, and the development of correct position will insure development of this movement.

Ease and coordination, as well as smoothness in letter formation, will be induced by the use of rhythm in writing. Rhythm may be developed by using counting in a limited amount of practice. Various methods of counting may be used, such as numerical counting, descriptive counting, rhymes, and music. Counting should be used only with repetitions of the same letters, or with simple combinations of letters. The speed of counting should be carefully adjusted to the ability of the child of the particular grade.

Careful attention should be given to position from the time the child begins to write at the desk. The fundamentals of good position should be required, but a military type of rigidity should not be expected of the child. The fundamentals of good position are as follows:

The writer should face the desk squarely.

Both forearms should rest about equally on the desk.

The paper should be directly in front of the writer.

The paper should be tilted to the left about thirty degrees.

(In case of the left-handed writer the paper should be tilted to the right.)

The hand should be placed with the palm down so that the wrist does not slope more than forty-five degrees. The hand should rest on the nails, or the first joints of the third and fourth fingers.

The fingers should be comfortably curved and the penholder should be grasped lightly.

The forefingers should rest on the penholder below the thumb.

The pupils should sit in a reasonably erect position.

The instruction in writing should be individualized sufficiently to allow each pupil to progress at his own rate, and to attack the special problems which he finds in his own writing. General instructions and general principles may be given to the pupils according to their ability in handwriting.

There is much controversy concerning the treatment of the left-handed child. The safe procedure is to try to get each pupil to use his right hand in starting to write. If the child is very strongly left-handed in everything else, and appears to have great difficulty in writing with his right hand, and writes very poorly with his right hand, he should be allowed to use his left hand. In such a case, great care should be taken to see that he adopts the position for the left-handed writer, and slants his paper toward the right. The matter should be determined in the first grade, and changes should not be made beyond the second or third grade.

The teacher's writing has great influence on the writing of children. The teacher should take pains to write well on the blackboard, and to use the approved forms which are taught the children. The teacher should also demonstrate on the blackboard the method of making the letters and other features of execution, such as the rhythm of the movement.

Motivation in writing is general and specific. The sight of pleasing forms, such as are furnished by good writing on the part of the teacher and by pleasing copies, is an incitement to the child to write a good form himself. In addition, certain specific motives may be used. The measurement of the individual's progress by means of scales and by comparison of one's writing at successive periods of time, stimulates effort. Individual and group competitions, with or without awards, are also effective, but they should be used in moderation, and care should be taken that they are so employed as to affect the poor writer who needs stimulation the most.

INDIVIDUAL HANDWRITING CHART

Name .... Grade ....

Teacher .... Room ....

The Way I Write

	1	2	3	4	5	6
HEAVINESS:						
Correct Color						
Irregular Color						
Too Light						
Too Heavy						
SIZE:						
Correct Size						
Irregular Size						
Too Small						
Too Large						
LETTER SPACING:						
Correct						
Irregular						
Too Close						
Too Far Apart						
SPACING OF WORDS:						
Correct						
Irregular						
Too Close						
Too Far Apart						
SLANT:						
Correct						
Irregular						
Too Slanting						
Lacking Slant						
ALIGNMENT (Lines):						
Correct						
Irregular						
Above Line						
Below Line						
BEGINNING AND ENDING STROKES:						
Correct						
Irregular						
Too Long						
Too Short						
NEATNESS:						
Usually Neat						
Sometimes Neat						
Not Often Neat						

Writing Rate

Tests		1	2	3	4	5	6	7	8	9	10
	120										
	110										
	100										
	90										
Letters	80										
Per	70										
	60										
Minute	50										
	40										
	30										
	20										
	10										

Writing Quality

		1	2	3	4	5	6	7	8	9	10
	90										
	80										
Points	70										
on	60										
Scale	50										
	40										
	30										
	20										

Letters To Practice

Improve Form:

Joinings:

Prepared by R. T. Neideffer, Director of Elementary Education, Bakersfield, Calif., City Schools author of "ENGLISH, Teachers Guide in Oral and Written Expression, Intermediate Grades."

The above chart is intended as a simple classroom device for motivating and individualizing handwriting problems and to set up immediate goals, and provide for the use of speed and quality records according to standards. Those who desire further information in regard to this chart should write to Mr. Neideffer.

Writing As A Tool of Expression For Primary Children

By Mrs. Delia Petherick, Assistant Supervisor

From the San Francisco Public Schools Monthly Bulletin

The old idea of teaching children to write "beautifully" before they had any real need for writing falls within that philosophy of education that emphasizes the learning of much knowledge and many skills by the child preparatory to living an adult life. The modern philosophy of education, which subscribes to the theory that children are already living a full life as truly as they will be twenty years from now, stresses the teaching of writing as a tool which has use only as it helps to fulfill the need for individual expression. If writing is to be taught as a usable tool and not a detached art, the child must feel a real need for it, and then must have sufficient practice to gain satisfaction from his effort.

In an activity program there are so many motives for writing that children learn the use of the writing tool in natural, practical situations and not in artificially set up ones. Enough real needs can be found so that sufficient practice to fix the learning and to insure satisfaction is the result.

When entering first grade, children need spoken language more than written, so writing in the low first grade should not be forced. Large blackboard writing is suggested for the first lessons in Grade One. Writing of the name seems to be the desire of every beginner. He is going to have a real need for his name for he wishes to identify his drawings, paintings, seat work, or construction work. Other motives for writing in primary grades are: labels for pictures; single words for bulletin board or daily newspaper; single words for weather report, as "warm," "foggy," etc.; days of the week, months, year, seasons, and holidays for newspaper and weather reports; signs to put outside the door to indicate to visitors what unit of study is being carried on, as, "A Study of Jungle Animals"; signs for the room, as, "Painting Studio," "Sewing Corner," "Milk People," "Songs We Know," "Children's Art Gallery"; signs for the library table, as "Handle Carefully," "Speak Quietly"; titles for children's pictures chosen for the "Children's Art Gallery"; names of cooperative stories, borders, posters, etc.; names for place cards at luncheon table; signs used in connection with the unit of study, as advertisements and captions for a play, a puppet show or for a store; invitations to parties or performances; "thank you" notes for favors granted or invitations accepted; simple letters to children ill at home; addressing envelopes for such letters; labels for pictures in scrap books or A-B-C books; spelling words; short compositions or stories; slogans for special weeks and days, as Book Week, Music Week, etc.; thrift and health rules; holiday greetings as for Christmas, Valentine Day, etc. These are a few suggestions for real writing needs in the lower grades. The clever teacher will find many more as the unit of study progresses.

Too great attention to the mechanics of writing, such as the tools and to position at seats and blackboard, in the beginning, interferes with the thought process. It is well to remember, however, that every time a child writes he is emphasizing either a good or a poor writing habit. From the very beginning, children should learn to stand at the blackboard or to sit at their seats in healthful position. Whole arm movement should be emphasized both on the blackboard and on paper to prevent strain. Using the large muscles instead of the small ones is stressed. Letters should be so simply formed as to be easily read.

Desirable principles for primary teachers to remember in teaching writing are: first, that a tool cannot be separated from its use, and the main use of writing is expression; therefore, all writing should have a practical reason for being; secondly, that correct posture at all times is essential to good health; therefore, healthful posture and lack of strain in writing are essential to healthful living; thirdly, writing which cannot be read fails in its purpose, so all writing should be legible. Therefore, purposeful, legible writing at all times in healthful position should be the standard for written expression in the primary grades.

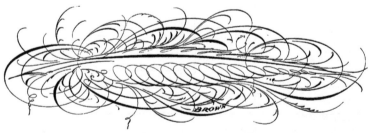

A flourish by our good friend, E. L. Brown; Rockland, Maine.

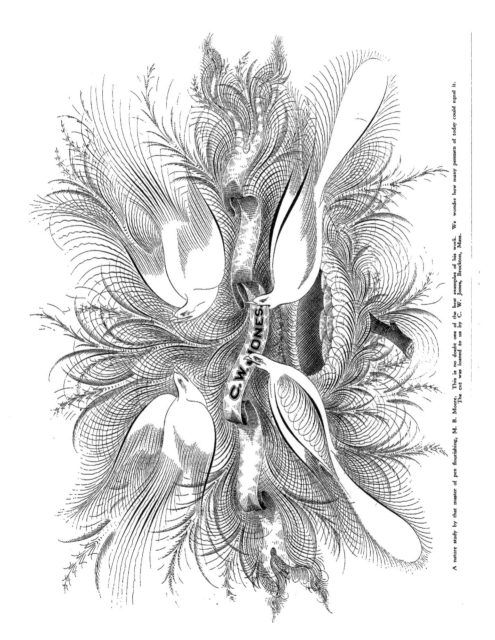

A nature study by that master of pen flourishing, M. B. Moore. This is no doubt one of the best examples of his work. We wonder how many penmen of today could equal it. The cut was loaned to us by C. W. Jones, Brockton, Mass.

Ornamental Penmanship

No. 18   Script by the late A. M. Wonnell

Study the long, graceful loops. See that the small loops are open. Make sharp top t's and d's. Get a light touch and a free movement.

A very beautiful piece of work by J. B. Hague, Haring Studio, New York, N. Y. The grape border was in natural colors. The initial letter was in blue. It is one of the finest pieces of work we have received for some time. You will do well to study the excellent lettering and retouching.

Lessons in Card Carving

By J. D. Carter, Deerfield, Ill.

Lesson No. 2

We are continuing strokes used in Lesson No. 1 in a new design with a knife.

Be sure your knife is sharp. A keen cutting blade gives so much better results in appearance that one feels rewarded for the little time required to put the keen edge on the blade.

In addition to the design cut with a knife for this Lesson, I am including some cutting done with a steel pen, put in the pen holder the reverse way and sharpened.

Very pleasing results can be gotten with a well sharpened pen that cannot be excelled with the sharpest knife.

We make the cutting with the pen by pushing from the body in most strokes; however you can make the strokes in any direction if the cutting is at proper angle.

By this time we are hoping you are beginning to make the cutting strokes of lesson No. 1 very well.

Remember if you get the cutting strokes well, it will be easy to cut elaborate designs to real satisfaction later.

The greeting card design of this lesson is cut partly with knife and partly with pen and is intended to suggest one of many ways to use photo prints for High School, Colleges, Lodges, Societies, etc. Try your hand for best results in this way. You can use the compass to make circles and designs if desired.

When you have worked entire Lesson No. 2, send some of your best work to me and I will gladly look it over for you and return it to you with comment, if you enclose postage.

If you want to know more about the sharpened pen for Card Carving let me know at the time you send in your practice copy.

Otis Sked, Jr., Wilkes-Barre, Pa., who has been following the work in The Educator for some time, sent us this page of engrossing. The scroll and initial letters were in colors and burnished gold.

WHEN MY SHIP COMES IN

"When my ship comes in."

You have heard that expression hundreds of times. You have probably used it yourself.

How can you expect your ship to come in if you never sent one out? It may be necessary for you to go out with it.

Columbus went out with his ship. If he hadn't gone out with it, it would not have come in.

John D. Rockefeller sent out his ship—The Ship of Fortune. It came in laden with oil, which he converted into gold.

He didn't get his fortune through luck or mere accident. He planned, worked, and persevered.

Abraham Lincoln's ship—The Ship of State—finally came in. He studied, labored, and persevered in the face of hardships and discouragement. His ship had a long and perilous voyage, but it eventually arrived safely. He became the nation's greatest "pilot" and one of the "world's six greatest men."

Every successful man and woman, everyone whose ship has come in, sent out a ship. Your ship will come in some day provided you send one out —pay the price of success. The old "Ship Success" demands that you do this. But it's worth it many times.

After all one's ship coming in is nothing more nor less than success arriving. Instead of waiting for it to come in, you must make your preparation in advance—and keep working, persevering, and struggling. Your ship will then come sailing in some day, and, incidentally, you will have "arrived" too—and all will be safe.

It's entirely up to you, young man, young woman, whether your ship shall come in some day. Are you sending one out?

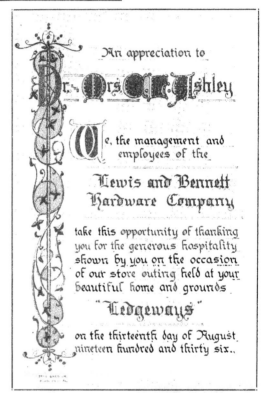

An appreciation to

Dr. & Mrs. A. R. Ashley

We, the management and employees of the

Lewis and Bennett Hardware Company

take this opportunity of thanking you for the generous hospitality shown by you on the occasion of our store outing held at your beautiful home and grounds

"Ledgeways"

on the thirteenth day of August nineteen hundred and thirty six.

Text Lettering »»»

By
F. W. Martin
641 Atlantic Ave., Boston, Mass.

Practice the straight line stroke. Get them parallel. Notice the position of the two strokes. They are both of the same length and the second starts higher than the first. This condition prevails in many of the Old English letters. Slide the pen when beginning a stroke as well as sliding it when you pick up the pen. This makes the end rounding and graceful and the points sharp. Notice the numbers on the strokes. This suggests the order in which the strokes should be made.

After practicing each stroke and letter try your hand at writing words and lettering Christmas Cards.

Practice letters and words over and over again until they are so ingrained in your mind that you will never forget the correct form and that they will be drilled into the muscles and so fastened that the writing becomes automatic. You will never be sorry for the work you have put into study and practice.

Ease of pen movement and lightness of touch are very important essentials in handwriting and one should work untiringly to cultivate them.

The handwriting in other subjects is the real proof of handwriting ability, and success in this depends very largely on your knowledge of letter forms and the skill in movement you have drilled into the arm. Study good writing.

You may recall how difficult it was for you at one time to spell easy words or add 2 and 2, and how in some way you overcame those mountains in time without realizing it. The same thing will happen to your handwriting today. Continue to study and practice and skill is gradually acquired. You may think the progress slow but don't be impatient or too hard on yourself. If you are in earnest to become a good penman you will keep on and will gain satisfaction in seeing your work improve.

Check your own writing with the copy. Perhaps you have missed some punctuation marks. Perhaps you have left some letters open which should be closed or have closed some loops which should be open.

Fong Dong Chu, Kapaa, Kauai, T. H., is practicing from the lessons in The Educator and is doing remarkable work, especially in the ornamental penmanship.

L. W. Heiser is the new head of the Commercial Department of the Gallagher School, Kankakee, Illinois.

Two large, well-made flourishes are hereby acknowledged from **Sam Garner**, Smartt, Tenn.

BEAUTIFULLY ADDRESSED ENVELOPES

by *F. D. Courtney.*

Examiner of Questioned Documents
Detroit, Michigan

E. C. T. A.

We may point with pardonable pride to the objective evidences on all sides of the notable advances made in educational thought and practice during the past fifty years. Administrators, supervisors, educational laboratories, and the teachers themselves, all have contributed their share to bring about the highly improved conditions extant in every sphere of educational activity. The progress they made and the achievements they attained did not however set up permanent goals of accomplishment, for new eras offer new problems for solution.

As the direct agent of contact with these ever changing problems, the teacher must be prepared to adapt his teaching technique to every contingency. His need for assistance in this connection is always an urgent one. To this kind of service the Eastern Commercial Teachers' Association has long dedicated its efforts. Once again, at its next annual convention to be held at the Statler Hotel, in Boston, March 24-27, 1937, it will bring together leaders in business and leaders in business education to discuss a theme of timely import: "Foundations of Vocational Testing in Business Education."

The educational program comprises two general meetings and two sectional meetings. At the general meetings prominent speakers will present their views on the salient aspects of the theme. At the first of the sectional meetings the pragmatic implications of these views will be clearly set forth. The second of these sectional meetings is an informal one in which questions, pertaining to materials of instruction or any phase of classroom procedure, will be answered. This "Question Box Session", whose popularity has always been an outstanding feature, offers you the opportunity of receiving the help and inspiration that only the practical advice of experienced, successful teachers can proffer.

Avail yourself of this unusual opportunity. Prepare your questions and send them in typed form to the President of the Association, Nathaniel Altholz, Director of Commercial Education, 500 Park Avenue, New York, New York. To receive proper attention they should reach him not later than March 10, 1937.

George W. Ahnemann, of Walters, Minnesota, died on September 8, 1936, from the results of an accident.

Mr. Ahnemann became interested in penmanship when taking work under Mr. Frank A. Krupp, of Fargo, North Dakota. In 1923 Mr. Ahnemann came to Columbus to study Engrossing. He followed Engrossing for sometime but was compelled to give it up on account of his health. For the past few years he conducted a turkey farm at Kiester, Minnesota. He was a young man of high ideals and upright character, and attained a high degree of skill in pen work.

STILL FINDS PENMANSHIP HELPFUL

George W. Richards came to Columbus, Ohio, in 1904. While in Columbus he took some work in handwriting and lettering. In later years Mr. Richards moved to New York State where he is now engaged in farming. Recently while on a vacation he dropped in to see his friends at The Zanerian. During his conversation he remarked that he has been doing some pen work every year. He stated that recently after a hard day's work driving a heavy tractor he lettered some school diplomas to the amazement of the school officials. This only proves to us that if one masters any branch of penmanship that he never loses interest in it and that it helps out greatly financially, and is also a magnificent avocation even for a man doing considerable heavy manual work.

COME AGAIN

W. A. Baird, the engrosser of 340-83rd St., Brooklyn, New York, dropped into the office of The Educator recently on a vacation trip. Mr. Baird is enjoying good health and is still as in-terested in all phases of pen work as ever. We wish that all of our readers might have the pleasure of a visit with him. We are sure that all of you would get out your oblique penholder, lettering holder, brushes, etc. and "dig in" to your work with renewed inspiration. Mr. Baird is one of the most capable engrossers in the United States.

J. M. Gardner, the penman of Moose Jaw, Sask., Canada, reports that he was on a two months' vacation away up in Peace River Country. On September 6 they had six inches of snow and mud, with many bushels of wheat yet to be thrashed.

Mr. Gardner states that he is already preparing Christmas cards. Now is a good time for every penman to begin making his Christmas cards.

E. A. Boggs, who is following the work in The Educator, is turning out some especially fine ornamental work. The above has been reproduced from a package of specimens he recently sent us. Mr. Boggs travels but still finds time to work on the lessons in The Educator.

Handwriting Merit Seals

These seals are designed to be used as informal awards to be pasted on papers in handwriting or other subjects. They are printed in two colors on gummed stock, and are die-cut. All are about the size of the sample shown. Some are seasonal in appeal (pumpkin, Santa Claus, Valentine Heart, Washington, etc.) while others may be used equally well at any time throughout the year. Send 10 cents for a complete assortment of 13 seals, or 60 cents for a gross assortment. Address

No. 9

THE A. N. PALMER COMPANY
55 Fifth Avenue, Dept. E, New York, N.Y.

BUSINESS ETIQUETTE

(From The Gist, a school paper published by Goldey College, Wilmington, Delaware)

Each one of us will willingly admit that a knowledge of Shorthand, Typewriting, Accounting, English and other business subjects is essential if one wishes to secure a clerical position. Is securing a position the important thing? Naturally it is. But it is sometimes a perplexing situation to hold the position. Many high school students are graduating. You are not the only person who is qualified to apply. You must compete with other applicants, and you must possess more than mere book knowledge to be considered.

If the Personnel Director or the executive himself is interviewing applicants for a secretarial position, he is very observant. He notices the way you speak. Included in this is your use of everyday sentences and words. If your grammar and pronunciation are incorrect, you are almost immediately excluded. This man knows that it will be your duty to punctuate, and, if your employer is sick or absent from the office, to compose replies to the letters he receives. Will he want to make a bad impression through the carelessness of his secretary? No, he will not.

Your personality will indicate the kind of person you are and the work you do. Are you pleasant, cheerful, considerate, agreeable, willing, honest and ambitious? Are you always courteous even though it hurts? It will always pay to cultivate these traits, for they are essential in whatever vocation you may choose.

Business dress is a very important question for a young woman. Must she be plain and old-maidish? No, that is not the point to be stressed. The secretary has work that is to be completed in the course of a day or week. Her appearance should signify this. Ruffles, frills and laces come into the social program of a girl, but should not be brought into the office. Too much paint and powder on one's face indicate poor taste and a desire to be noticed. A moderate use of cosmetics is not objectionable to most business men.

You may say, "I have friends who are employed in the offices of this city who are this type." No doubt this is true, but they never get any farther than just tickling the keys of a typewriter all day. Do not be included in this class. Practice the rules of good etiquette along with your knowledge, and prove that you are willing and deserving of being advanced to more responsible positions.

Value of Writing Stressed In School Project

Novel Idea Developed at North Fairmount.

(Reprinted from the Cincinnati Times-Star)

A novel project to show the value or writing in life situations is being carried out at North Fairmount School under supervision of Miss Lucille Sanford, special writing teacher. All pupils from the third through the sixth grades are participating. Each class is carrying out the project in its own way.

In Room 3 the activity was initiated by Miss Louise Rau. On many occasions these boys and girls had discussed the importance of writing for school children (for their daily lessons, letters to friends, labels on possessions, etc.) and to various workers whom they had visited (the banker, the post-office worker, salespeople, etc.). The children decided that the value of writing for their parents was a fertile field for conjecture and exploration. They wrote letters to both their mothers and fathers, informing them of their new "study" and asking their help by giving daily use of writing. A large number of parents cooperated. The samples of writing were exhibited and read either by the children or by the teacher, if necessary, at the regular morning class meetings. The class analyzed the types of writing brought in these groups:

1—Book notes.
2—Absence notes.
3—Special notes.
4—Envelopes.
5—Letters.
6—Postal cards.
7—Recipes.
8—Lists of errands.
9—Reports for work.
10—Receipts for rent.
11—Checks.
12—Phone numbers.
13—Radio stations.
14—Budgets.
15—Money order.
16—Invitations.

Betty Ann, who writes very nicely, made a copy of the list. She adds to it when necessary. Each child mounts his own specimen on a large card and puts the card in a long line under the chalk ledge to make it easy to count and compare and so name the best

collector in the class. The boys and girls have maintained an interest in the study and the "writing race" is proving worth while.

The fourth grade, under the guidance of Miss Miriam Stonebraker, divided into two teams. They are carrying on a contest to decide which side can bring in the greatest number of samples of handwriting as it is used in different occupations. Their collection is a large one. They not only have the types mentioned in the collection of Room 3 but also have a telegram and invitation.

> Miss Sanford is to be complimented on her foresightedness in using the newspapers in promoting interest in the teaching of handwriting among the pupils and parents.

The children of the third grade asked not only their parents but also other relatives and friends to help them. They brought in the usual bills, letters, receipts, etc., but they also have some unusual samples. These are a customer's request for investigation, a storeroom credit list, a fireman's inspection list and an inquiry in Spanish for a catalogue and the prices of building supplies. Mrs. Adelaide Blum is the regular teacher of the third grade girls and boys who are cooperating with Miss Sanford.

The pupils of Miss Ruth Kuller's class and those of Miss Clara Albrecht are also collecting many specimens of various uses of writing in the business world.

WRITES AT CLEVELAND EXPOSITION

A very beautiful card came into our possession written by C. A. Barnett of Cleveland, advertising the Spencerian College of Cleveland. The card shows the school building, a beautiful border, and a space upon which Mr. Barnett wrote names. The Spencerian School is finding that good penmanship can be used to advantage in advertising. We are glad to see the Spencerian School use this type of advertising, and hope that other schools will do likewise.

T. B. Cain of Clarksburg, West Virginia, according to a newspaper report, is enjoying an enrollment of more than three hundred students. His enrollment at the present time is larger than it has been at any previous date.

Mrs. Frederick W. Ford has been added to the faculty to teach English. She is the fourth new member of the faculty to be added this year.

COMMERCIAL EDUCATOR CONDUCTS EUROPEAN TOUR

E. F. Burmahln, Director of Business Education, E. C. Glass Senior High School, Lynchburg, Va., with the help of Mrs. Burmahln conducted a very successful "Queen Mary" tour of Europe during July and August.

The party consisted of 65 lawyers, doctors, retired farmers, business men, educators, artists, etc.

The countries covered were England, Holland, Germany, Switzerland, Italy and France with a stop at Cobh (Queenstown), Ireland.

2000 feet of colored film were taken on the trip by Mr. Burmahln.

Mr. Burmahln is one of Virginia's outstanding commercial educators. He has been active in the Virginia Education Association for a number of years. He is a trained penman and a skilled teacher. In 1919 Mr. Burmahln attended the Zanerian to specialize in handwriting.

The above specimen was written by Grace White, a student of C. L. Kress, McKinley School, Parkersburg, W. Va.

BOOK REVIEWS

Our readers are interested in books of merit, but especially in books of interest and value to commercial teachers including books of special educational value and books on business subjects. All such books will be briefly reviewed in these columns, the object being to give sufficient description of each to enable our readers to determine its value.

Constitutional Basis for Judging the New Deal, by Erik McKinley Eriksson and Trent Hewitt Steele. Published by The Rosemead Review Press, Rosemead, Calif.

The authors say that in judging the New Deal attention must be given not only to the Constitution itself, but to "the nine fundamental American constitutional principles, which though not written into the Constitution, are inherent to the document." They demonstrate that almost all of these principles have been violated by the New Dealers.

This book takes up each of the principles and discusses the powers of the various branches of the Federal government in relation to them. Particular stress is placed upon the excesses of power on the part of the Rooseveltians. Their violations of fundamental principles are clearly pointed out.

In view of the numerous delegations of power to the President under the New Deal, special attention was given to the principle of separation of powers. Likewise, because there has been so much abuse of the Supreme Court in recent months, the doctrine of judicial review is examined and defended. The authors hold that it is absurd to refer to judicial review as "an usurped function."

An outstanding feature of the book is a chart showing at a glance the result of the New Deal encounters with the Supreme Court up to date. Seventeen decisions have been handed down thus far, and only three have been favorable to the New Deal. This is the first time that such a chart has been published.

Dr. Eriksson is one of the nation's outstanding authorities on the Constitution, being co-author of *American Constitutional History*, a widely-used university textbook. Mr. Steele has instructed college classes in constitutional history. In the present work they have fortified all of their statements with copious annotations to be found in the back of the book.

STATEMENT OF THE OWNERSHIP, MANAGEMENT, CIRCULATION, ETC., REQUIRED BY THE ACT OF CONGRESS OF AUGUST 24, 1912

Of THE EDUCATOR published monthly except July and August, at Columbus, Ohio, for October 1, 1936.

State of Ohio, County of Franklin, ss.

Before me, a Notary Public in and for the State and county aforesaid, personally appeared Parker Zaner Bloser, who, having been duly sworn according to law, deposes and says that he is the Business Manager of the Educator and that the following is, to the best of his knowledge and belief, a true statement of the ownership, management (and if a daily paper, the circulation), etc., of the aforesaid publication for the date shown in the above caption, required by the Act of August 24, 1912, embodied in section 411, Postal Laws and Regulations, printed on the reverse of this form, to wit:

1. That the names and addresses of the publisher, editor, managing editor, and business managers are:
Publisher, The Zaner-Bloser Co., 612 No. Park St., Columbus, Ohio.
Editor, E. A. Lupfer, 612 No. Park St., Columbus, Ohio.
Managing Editor ....
Business Managers, Parker Zaner Bloser, 612 No. Park St., Columbus, Ohio.

2. That the owner is: (If owned by a corporation, its name and address must be stated and also immediately thereunder the names and addresses of stockholders owning or holding one per cent or more of total amount of stock. If not owned by a corporation, the names and addresses of the individual owners must be given. If owned by a firm, company, or other unincorporated concern, its name and address, as well as those of each individual member, must be given.)

The Zaner-Bloser Co., Columbus, Ohio.
R. E. Bloser, Columbus, Ohio.
Rebecca Bloser, Columbus, Ohio.
Parker Zaner Bloser, Columbus, Ohio.
E. A. Lupfer, Columbus, Ohio.
R. B. Moore, Columbus, Ohio.

3. That the known bondholders, mortgagees, and other security holders owning or holding 1 per cent or more of total amount of bonds, mortgages, or other securities are: (If there are none, so state.) None.

4. That the two paragraphs next above, giving the names of the owners, stockholders, and security holders, if any, contain not only the list of stockholders and security holders as they appear upon the books of the company but also, in cases where the stockholder or security holder appears upon the books of the company as trustee or in any other fiduciary relation, the name of the person or corporation for whom such trustee is acting, is given; also that the said two paragraphs contain statements embracing affiant's full knowledge and belief as to the circumstances and conditions under which stockholders and security holders who do not appear upon the books of the company as trustees, hold stock and securities in a capacity other than that of a bona fide owner; and this affiant has no reason to believe that any other person, association, or corporation has any interest direct or indirect in the said stock, bonds, or other securities than as so stated by him.

5. That the average number of copies of each issue of this publication sold or distributed, through the mails or otherwise, to paid subscribers during the six months preceding the date shown above is.. (This information is required from daily publications only.)

PARKER ZANER BLOSER, Business Manager.

Sworn to and subscribed before me this 18th day of September, 1936.

EARL A. LUPFER
(My commission expires Jan. 11, 1938.)
Seal

SECURES ENGROSSING POSITION

Roger T. Ellzey, Jr., who spent some months in The Zanerian preparing in penmanship and engrossing recently secured a position with the F. W. Tamblyn Studio, Kansas City, Mo.

Mr. Ellzey is a young man of unusual talent and we predict big things from him in the engrossing line.

SCHOOLROOM MEMORIES
By Wilbur LeRoy Newark, Columbus, Ohio.

Teacher—Why don't you write like your father?
Jimmie—You wouldn't like it—
Teacher—Why?
Jimmie—You told me to write so you could read it!

This beautiful signature was written by Mr. Todd and loaned to us by Mr. W. E. Crooks, Keyser, W. Va.

Lessons in Modern Engrosser's Script

Prepared in the office of The Educator

No. 3

Practice the first exercise until you can make all down strokes on the same slant and the same in thickness. Cut the tops off straight and get the turns round at the bottom. Raise the pen at the base line. Let the connecting strokes run into the following letter at about one-half way up. Watch the spacing.

Make **c** exercise similar to **i** exercise. The bottoms should be exactly the same. Get the inside rather straight.

The **c** is similar to **i** with a hook or dot at the top. The bulk of the shade should be slightly below the center. The first part of **e** is the same as the first part of **c**. Study the shape and get a slight shade on the top of the loop.

The **o** is, of course, similar to **c** and **e**. Get tops and bottoms even in roundness. Finish high.

The **a** is a combination of **c** and **i**. Study the top part of the **a**.

Curve the upstrokes of the **r** and **s**. Get a nice bulging shade on the **s**. The dots should be made carefully. Make the dot as thick as the main shade. Study the location of shades. Let the point or top of letter extend slightly above the headline.

This specimen was written by B. H. White, a student of J. D. Rice of the Chillicothe, Missouri, Business College. Mr. Rice has trained some magnificent business writers. In fact, he has trained quite a number who are in the teaching work. We compliment Mr. White on his fine business writing.

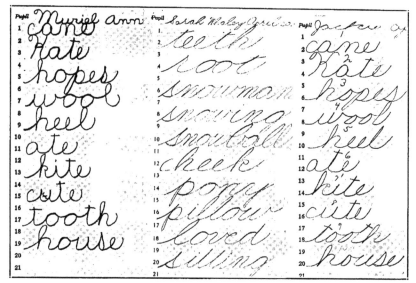

These beautiful specimens were prepared in the regular spelling lesson in the Bexley Elementary School. Miss Ruby Borden is the principal and Miss Beck is the teacher. The first specimen was written by Muriel Ann Ealy, the second by Sarah Whaley, and the third by Jackie Le Mortland.

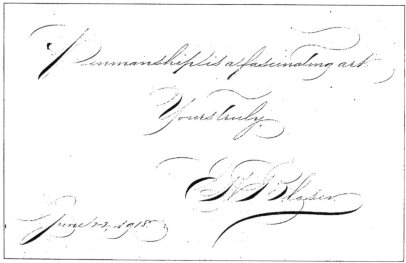

Penmanship fascinated E. W. Bloser to the very last. No one probably ever had a greater love for fine penmanship.

NEW COMMERCIAL SCHOOL

On April 20, 1936, Mr. L. H. Krissler established the Krissler Commercial School, at 395 Main Street, Poughkeepsie, New York.

Mr. Krissler is an honor graduate of the College of Business of Syracuse University, class of 1924. He was associated with the faculty of Rider College, Trenton, N. J., following a term of teaching in the Commercial Geography Department in Syracuse University. Mr. Krissler has had about twelve years experience in private commercial school work.

A. H. Ross

Our friend, A. H. Ross, with whom many of our readers are familiar, has been with the school from the beginning. Mr. Ross is an expert penman and mathematician of national fame. He has been connected with the Eastman School of Business of Poughkeepsie for ten years, and with the Eastman Gaines School of New York City for three years. He has trained thousands of young men and women who are today holding responsible positions in various sections of America. 1322 of his students have won our penmanship certificates. This means that Mr. Ross has done a lot of hard work and has secured unusual high results. He is head of the General Business Department of the Krissler School.

Miss Katherine M. Farrell, who holds a Bachelor of Science degree from the College of New Rochelle, New York, is head of the Secretarial Science department of the School.

The following courses are offered:

The General Business and Banking Course requiring approximately ten or eleven months.

The Secretarial Science Course requiring approximately ten or eleven months.

The Intensive Stenographic, from six to ten months.

The school is furnished with the latest equipment. It is laying a foundation for a fine school with high aims.

Since May 1 the school has grown to the maximum number to which the school is limited, namely fifty.

PENMANSHIP A VALUABLE ASSET

We recently had the pleasure of a visit from A. McB. Colledge, 87 Vernon Drive, Mt. Lebanon, Pittsburgh, Pa., who is connected with a very large corporation where he has plenty of responsibility and chance for advancement. In our conversation Mr. Colledge stated that his letter of application was selected from a large stack of applications and it was his penmanship which secured him the position. Mr. Colledge spent some time in Columbus studying penmanship back in 1907.

Gems from Penmen of Other Countries

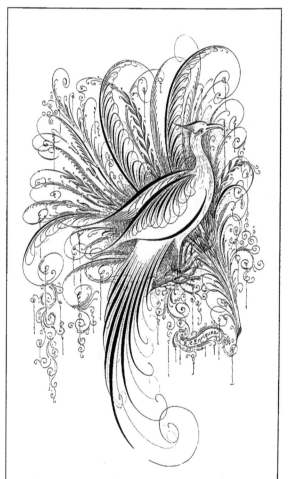

This proud bird is the product of E. C. Enriquez, Pineda, Pasig, Rizal, P. I. Mr. Enriquez is one of the best flourishers of today. His work is very painstaking and beautiful. Flourishing of this kind is as beautiful for framing as any painting.

WHEREAS: In the chronicle of the history of Hotel Casey Company must be permanently recorded the dominant and talented personality of

Patrick J. Casey,

a founder of **Hotel Casey** with his lamented and beloved brother Andrew J. Casey the President and a Director of this organization since its inception in 1913. So his notable leadership of this and allied enterprises, clearness of vision, faultless judgment, and splendid business acumen, we gladly pay deserving and lasting tribute. Todays clamor for high ethical standards in business claimed him as a champion who personified in his family as well as public life the lesson of the Golden Rule. Dauntless of purpose in the achievement of a worthwhile objective, though refreshingly modest, his inborn confidence and courage inspired the allegiance of associates and sub-ordinates, the unstinted admiration and respect of contemporaries whether of high or low station. A true sportsman, he believed in playing the game of business according to the rules, always competing fairly but with keenness, vigor and resourcefulness. A constant student of human character and of a sympathetic and kindly nature, he was always a ready listener and generous helper to those less fortunate in the worldly sense, or seeking the counsel of a friend and business man of wide experience, possessing the rare faculty to advise them for the best. Though his fortitude was tried in the early days of this undertaking, and sorely so in the present disheartening depression years, his wholesome buoyant spirit admonished us in carrying on ever to serve our guests and patrons fairly and with consideration, to keep abreast of the times and trends in the hotel profession and to jealously protect our credit. May his career be an inspiring lesson and a lasting example to his bereaved family and surviving associates in this Company, that the most worthy remembrance of his life and our association may be realized and fulfilled in the further accomplishment of his dearly cherished ambitions; to this end, **Be it Resolved:** the surviving Directors, Associates of Patrick J. Casey in this Company, record their profound sorrow and sense of great loss at his untimely passing from this earthly scene, at an age still promising of many more years of helpful guidance and fruitful endeavor, and, **Be it Further Resolved:** that the original of these sentiments be spread upon the minutes of our meeting and a copy suitably engrossed be forwarded to his bereaved family. We of the Hotel Casey Family, who knew and loved him best shall miss him most.

Anno Domini
February 2, 1935.

Committee.

TRUE CHRISTMAS CHEER . . .

HELP TO MAKE OTHERS HEALTHY

The National, State and Local Tuberculosis Associations of the United States

The top specimen was written by K. Hara. The bottom specimen is
from the pen of Y. Fukuyama, 2-chome, Bingomachi, Higashiku,
Osaka, Japan.

25 Cards for 50c, postpaid

Distinctly Individual - Handwriting Christmas Cards

These cards have a strong penmanship appeal. They are admired by everyone who sees them because of their beauty and dash.

USE THESE CARDS THIS CHRISTMAS

Twenty-five designs to select from. They are different and distinctive. Postal card size, printed in black ink on good heavy cardboard. Price, on blank Christmas cards, 50c per set of 25, postpaid; 100 cards, $1.80; 500 cards, $8.50; 1,000 cards, $15.00. A penman's Christmas Card for 1½ c.

THE ZANER-BLOSER COMPANY

612 NORTH PARK STREET   COLUMBUS, OHIO

Forward Steps in Handwriting

This new book embodies many improvements and represents new forward steps in handwriting.

Read These Statements by the Authors . . . .

"In order to save time, write rapidly; in order to insure understanding on the part of the reader, write legibly."—JOHN G. KIRK, Director of Commercial Education, Philadelphia, Pa.

"The essentials of learning to write well are:

1. A strong desire to write well.

2. An abundance of good copies and sound methods, both based on correlation.

3. Appropriate practice applied by the student purposively and intelligently to accomplish ends which he recognizes."—

FRANK N. FREEMAN, Professor of Educational Psychology, University of Chicago.

Order a Copy Today

The Zaner-Bloser Co.
Columbus, Ohio.

Please send..
                         Quantity

Functional Handwriting Books.

Enclosed is...in full payment.
               Amount

Name ....

Address ....

City ....

State ....

Title or Position..

Size 6½ x 8 — 132 pages. Price 40c each, net, postpaid. $4.00 per dozen, less 25%, F. O. B. Columbus, Ohio.

Published monthly except July and August at 612 N. Park St., Columbus, O., by the Zaner-Bloser Company. Entered as second-class

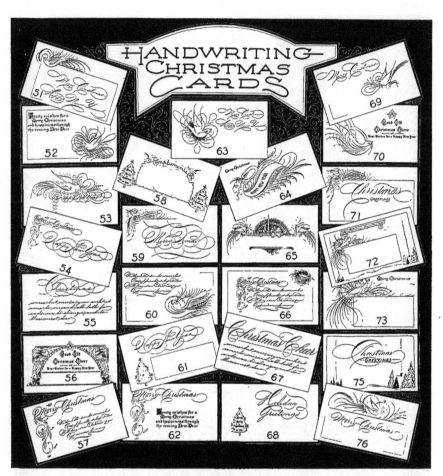

25 Cards for 50c, postpaid

Distinctly Individual - Handwriting Christmas Cards

These cards have a strong penmanship appeal. They are admired by everyone who sees them because of their beauty and dash.

USE THESE CARDS THIS CHRISTMAS

Twenty-five designs to select from. They are different and distinctive. Postal card size, printed in black ink on good heavy cardboard. Price, on blank Christmas cards, 50c per set of 25, postpaid; 100 cards, $1.80; 500 cards, $8.50; 1,000 cards, $15.00. A penman's Christmas Card for 1½c.

THE ZANER-BLOSER COMPANY

612 NORTH PARK STREET   COLUMBUS, OHIO

Volume 42 COLUMBUS, OHIO, DECEMBER, 1936 No. 4

A LARGE COMMUNITY PROJECT LINKED WITH HANDWRITING

It is estimated that about 50,000 students in the Anthracite Coal region of Northeastern Pennsylvania wrote personal letters stating the value of using hard coal to·as many potential Anthracite Coal consumers in New England, New York, ·New Jersey and the non-Anthracite region of Pennsylvania.

The Anthracite region of Pennsylvania extends roughly from Forest City on the North to Pottsville on the South. The southern part of the region extends from about Carbon on the East over to Shamokin on the West. From these two points the field narrows in a triangular direction up towards Nanticoke and then extends through the Wyoming Valley, through Wilkes-Barre, then through the Lackawanna Valley on to Scranton, and runs out at Forest City. This region each year puts on a coal boosting drive. It is anticipated that 60,000,000 tons of coal will be shipped from this region this year.

Since most of the people depend upon the coal industry for a living the children become vitally interested in the coal drive.

This project is quite commendable from a penmanship training standpoint. It correlates handwriting, English and salesmanship. No doubt the Anthracite Coal region will profit immensely by this project. Each city and town in the district was assigned another city with which to exchange letters.

The Educator is interested in all penmanship projects. Tell us about your local projects.

CHRISTMAS is here again with its glamour of cheer and joyous feasting.

It is a time to forget our petty grievances and extend the hand of fellowship to each and every one regardless of race, creed or politics.

Let us be children again for a day and may we all be as happy and contented as the boy who receives his first Christmas gift from his teacher, consisting of a big, juicy orange and bright colored sticks of candy.

May the spirit and sentiment of Christmas be with all of us throughout the· year.

"Whatsoever ye would that men should do to you, do ye even so to them."

—Editor

The above is an H. P. Behrensmeyer flourish.

THE EDUCATOR

Published monthly (except July and August)
By THE ZANER-BLOSER CO.,
612 N. Park St., Columbus, O.
E. A. LUPFER..Editor
PARKER ZANER BLOSER..............Business Mgr.

SUBSCRIPTION PRICE, $1.25 A YEAR
(To Canada, 10c more; foreign, 30c more)
Single copy, 15c.
Change of address should be requested promptly in advance, if possible, giving the old as well as the new address.
Advertising rates furnished upon request.

THE EDUCATOR is the best medium through which to reach business college proprietors and managers, commercial teachers and students, and lovers of penmanship. Copy must reach our office by the 10th of the month for the issue of the following month.

Modern Handwriting

By E. A. Lupfer, Zanerian College, Columbus, Ohio

No. 4

To The Teacher: Teachers of all subjects should help to raise and to maintain the handwriting of pupils up to a passing standard. No poor papers should be accepted in any class, and pupils who have fallen below standard even where they have been excused from handwriting should be shown how important handwriting may be to them in securing positions and diplomatically advised to get into the handwriting class or improve their work.

High schools and business colleges should have regular classes in penmanship. They should at least have hospital classes for poor writers. Scales may be used to determine when pupils fall below the standard and need instruction. Of course all writing must be readable to be of any value.

The U is similar to the **N**. The movement is much the same and the form is the same with the exception that the turns are at the bottom of the U while they are at the top in the **N**. In making **M, U, N** be sure that you get the turns and angles at the right place for legibility sake. Begin the U with a free, curved motion, the same as in the **N**. End U the same as **N**.

Are you using a nice, free arm movement? The first joint in your thumb should not work excessively. Avoid the "gum chewing" motion.

A review copy containing months and abbreviations which you should learn to write well.

Not enough attention is given to small movements. The above exercises are usually slighted by most people. They will help you to make small letters.

These under turn exercises should be made with a free rolling under motion. Watch the space and slant. See if your ending strokes are curved. Study beginning and ending strokes. They are important.

Get the top retraces of the u sharp and the bottom turns rounding. The spaces in the letter should be even.

𝒟 ▥ 𝒪 𝒟 *ddddd* *dddd* *d*

    After you have learned to make a good D spend your time on some of the other letters which you cannot make so well. However, the D is one which usually requires considerable practice. The down stroke is often curved too much. Therefore, practice on straight line exercises has a tendency to strengthen the straight line stroke. Practice each exercise, then practice the letter alone. We suggest that you practice the exercise and letter together, making one exercise, then a letter. The D in the Roman Alphabet is composed of a straight line and a circle. Pattern your D after the Roman letter. Finish like the O.

de da du dc do dd dg dk dr du dy
do day did dear down date dare
Davis Diamond Doyle Dougherty
D.R., D.K., D.B., D.M., D.D., D.E.

    The difficult part of the **d** is the retrace. Special attention is therefore given to the retraced part. The **d** is the same as the **a** except the extended top. Cover up the top of the **d** and see if it makes a good **a**.

    Here are some nice combinations and words to practice. Get them well. In making the large capital combinations write them freely and do not draw them.

𝒲 ▥ 𝒲 𝒲 *uuuuu* *wwww w*

    Select the exercises which you think will do you the most good. We naturally present a good many exercises to cover difficulties experienced by many. Therefore, each one should select and work on the parts which will benefit him most. Notice the similarity of the finish of the small **w** and small **o**.

    The arm should work in and out of the sleeve freely. Watch and study the movement of the arm while making the push-pull exercise.

    Much of the writing of the world is illegible, not because of lack of skill, but for want of observation of turns. Make the down strokes parallel.

    Use precisely the same movements as in **u**, with the exception of the finish, which requires a short pause before making the curved stroke to the right.

iva wc we wh wo wi wn wd wr

we will with was would when

Williams Wilson White Walsh Wolf

W.L., W.E., W.D., W.M., W.O., W.K., W.R.

All can profitably work on these combinations. Pick out your own weak spots and strengthen them. Don't become discouraged. Remember Rome was not built in one day, neither can you master penmanship in one day.

Velma makes neat, accurate figures.

A review copy which is very important. We are likely to get only a vague impression of the letter and after a day or so forget it. For that reason we believe in constantly reviewing letters and where possible introducing new and different exercises to develop the letters as well as combinations of letters to help to "carry over" into words. Much good can be secured by making a comparison of different letters as to form and movement. Study H, V and U.

7 7 H H UMM V V U U United

The V is a beautiful letter and is composed of a loop and two compound curves. It is a very graceful motion when freely and properly made. After all, letters are but pictures of movements. Go to the blackboard and make a large V freely, and notice particularly the movement. You will not find this movement exactly repeated in any other letter. Two other letters contain part of the movement. For instance, the W finishes much the same as the V, and the first parts of the U, V and Y are the same.

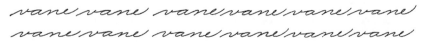

This copy shows how you should repeat a word many times, each time striving for some definite goal.

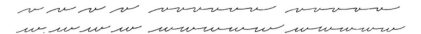

This copy will show you the similarity of the finishing stroke in **v** and **w**. Notice the similarity of the connecting stroke. Both swing across at the headline. Pause on the dot in each letter. Get top turn in v rounding.

Cross practice work has some value in getting freedom and it also trains one in spacing. One thing to watch is to get the work careful and not at any time to become careless.

The part which will be new to you in the Y is the final loop, for the beginning part of the Y is the same as the U. The Y, therefore, is a combination of the U and J. Give special attention to the retraced downward stroke. Practice retracing this part. Watch the arrangement in making a row of Y's.

First make the Y a full space high, then reduce it slightly in size. Cross on the base line. Study size of lower loop.

In writing the sentence see how much real grace and freedom you can get into it. Give special attention to the beginning and ending strokes. Notice where they start and end.

The first exercise is the same as the U exercise with the exception of the J finish. In practicing a sentence, break it up and work on the parts which give you special trouble.

T Tuesday Tues. Thursday Thurs.

F February Feb. Friday Fri. F F

You should write the days of the week and the names of the months well. Try this group containing **T** and **F**.

H H H H H H H H H H

Review the H. See that you curve the top of the second part. The two parts should be connected with a small loop near the center. End at height of small letters gracefully.

We write the letter strokes in time.

This copy is worth your careful study. Notice the uniform slant of the downward strokes. Study the turns and angles and general free swing. Notice that the tall loops are full and open. Spend about half of your time in study, the other half in practice.

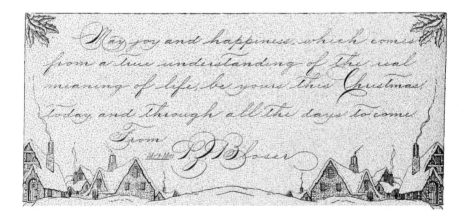

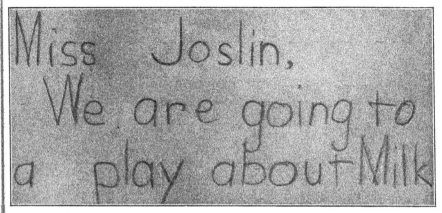

The print writing above shows what has been accomplished by one child in the first grade. The similarity of the print letters to those used in spelling and reading will also be a great help in teaching these subjects. Print writing also subscribes to early expression in the primary grades.

Success " He has achieved success who has lived well, laughed often and loved much; who has gained the respect of intelligent men and the love of little children; who has filled his niche and accomplished his task; who has left the world better than he found it, whether by an improved poppy a perfect poem, or a rescued soul; who has never lacked appreciation of earth's beauty or failed to express it; who has always looked for the best in others and given the best he had; whose life was an inspiration, whose memory a benediction."

A beautiful page of lettering from Tadashi Hashimoto, 415 Tazutamura, Kume-gun, Okayama, Japan.

Getting and Holding a Job

By James J. Hill

(The late James J. Hill was not only a big railroad man, but he was an empire builder)

It is one thing to get a position; it is another thing to keep it. Getting a position requires tact, forcefulness and perspicuity; keeping a position is an art. Getting positions is accomplished by a number of men and women, but the number of those who can keep positions is but small.

Appearance

When one starts to look for a position he must possess the qualities of cleanliness, clearness and perspicuity. So much depends upon the first impression. Lax methods, unkempt hair, soiled fingers, a necktie awry and confused speech are some of the faults that destroy the chances of an applicant. When a man who is conducting a successful business advertises for a janitor or a private secretary he goes to his office and finds several dozen applicants awaiting him. He hears them, one by one, and notices that this young man has failed to polish his shoes, that that young woman talks with a discordant slang that so-and-so is carrying the end of a cigarette in his yellow nicotined fingers, or that Miss This and That is overadorned with cheap jewelry. He finds that the young man is utterly incapable of expressing himself clearly, and that another has a newspaper with a chart of the horse races sticking from his pocket. Each applicant is denied a chance because his outward appearance arouses suspicion. These statements may seem exaggerated, but they are the plain, unvarnished experiences that business men encounter every day. Frequently employers are obliged to engage slovenly, untidy men and women whom they dislike, because the advances of their business demand more workers and the right kind is not to be had; but you may be assured that, when business slackens, such employes are the first to go.

Training

The steady-growing business concerns, the great mercantile houses, and the commercial consolidations of the United States have discovered that the men who will conduct the affairs of the future are the men who have been trained for that purpose. The man who will have worked his way from the lowest rung will be the man who will ultimately determine the destiny of the

business concern. Our vast business enterprises are becoming larger every year. No man can be trusted with the management of one who does not know every fractional part of the working of that concern with which he is connected, and who has not been a part of that working. Hence the importance of giving work to men and women who will keep the best interests of their employers at heart and blend them with their own.

> Training in Handwriting develops such qualities of character as self-control, neatness, accuracy and observation.

Show What You Are

If you seek employment as a stenographer, let your appearance tell that you are a stenographer; if you seek employment as a coal heaver, let your appearance show that you are a coal heaver. I do not mean that the stenographer shall be gay with cheap jewelry or redolent with the lingo of the typewriter, nor do I mean that the coal heaver shall be black, grimy and unwashed. But I do mean, that you must aim straight at your point; that you must show, first of all, by clear expression, by ready answers, by a polite, gentle, yet vigorous, manner, that you are ready to fill the place to the best of your ability.

Having secured your position, how shall you keep it? First, and always by being absolutely and strictly honest, for honor and character are man's greatest promoters. They stimulate energy and promote confidence. Who can deny the great power of energy and confidence? After an employer finds out he has an energetic clerk in whom he can place absolute confidence, that clerk's future is a very promising one.

Personality Acquired

Always remember that, next to honor, the quality that counts the most is personality. While many will tell you that personality is a gift just as surely as is the art of composing music,

let me assure you that nothing else can be acquired as easily as personality, if one has the mind to acquire it. A bad temper, a sour disposition—becoming cross and petulant when denied your way, speaking with sharpness when a kind word can just as easily be uttered, and letting anger have its sway—are faults that may be overcome if one earnestly and persistently tries to do so. They hinder the acquirement of a desirable personality and so lessen one's advancement, and, more than all besides, they shorten life. Personality is nothing if it is not the companion of politeness. No man wants to keep a person in his employ who is not polite. Never let a harsh or impolite personality be the weak link in the chain of your qualities. If it is, you can rest assured that it is the easiest link to strengthen. I do not mean to infer that one should be maudlin and puttylike in order to produce personality, or that he should assume politeness. Such a condition or attempt never exalts a man; it simply makes him appear false in the eyes of his employer. Nature made all of us to act natural. A bad temper can be expurgated, the same as any other vice. Don't confound anger and firmness. We admire a man who can assert his rights and stand by them, and we more than respect a man who can say "no" with vigor and purpose when "No" should be said; but we rightly despise a person who scolds and vociferates.

Always keep your promises. Your employer will never ask you to do more than is possible. Remember that an unfulfilled promise is as bad as a downright untruth. Live within your means. Never let a month pass that you do not put something in the bank. Dress neatly and plainly, for an employer marks a man as a fool who apparels himself with extravagance and glaring colors. Never try to win the favor of your employer by slandering your fellow-worker. Slander always sticks. Resolve slowly and act quickly. Remember, it is better to be alone than in bad company; that you can not give your employer or yourself full value if you try to work after a night of dissipation; that silence, like cleanliness is akin to godliness; that a clear conscience gives sound sleep and good digestion, and clothes one in an impregnable coat of mail.

The Review

Published by the Lawrence, Kansas, Business College.

A very beautiful illuminated piece of work made by Sister Mary Deograce, Felician Sisters, Lodi, N. J., while taking special work in engrossing and illuminating in The Zanerian Summer School. We congratulate Sister Mary Deograce on her skill and artistic ability.

Excerpts From Problems Involved In Professional Relationship Between Handwriting Supervisor and Elementary Teachers

By Mamie Eppler, Supervisor,
Fort Worth, Texas.
(From the N. A. P. T. S. Report)

One of the major problems involved in professional relationship between handwriting supervisor, or indeed any supervisor and the elementary teachers, is the problem of providing **adequate stimuli** which will result in **maximum growth** and the **provision of conditions** which will favor **this growth.**

Difficulties arose between supervisor and principal on account of the lack of the definition of administrative authority, and according to progressive theory the special supervisor should exercise no administrative authority but should have advisory powers only. Supervising the improvement of classroom instruction thus becomes a cooperative undertaking between superintendent, principal, and supervisor, the responsibility of which belongs to the principal.

At the present time supervision is in a state of change. All types exist, but there is a constant tendency toward the professional type of supervision. This method attempts to enlist the teachers in a large constructive program of school improvement. It aims to build up teacher and pupil morale through cooperation and through the spirit of service from the very foundation; pupils help each other, the teacher helps the pupils, the principal helps the teachers, the supervisor helps both principal and teachers—a procedure so necessary for progress.

What are some of the criticisms which teachers have made of supervisors?

1. Failure to provide conditions conducive to cheerfulness, hopefulness, and initiative.

2. Lack of democracy—taxation without representation — too much power, infliction of supervisor's method with no opportunity to use those methods acquired through study.

3. Supervisor's lack of training, personality, and teaching experience.

4. Utter disregard of psychological laws in supervisors' methods of criticism in which they discuss unfavorably the work of the pupils before the class or leave the teachers without courage and self-confidence.

5. Unreliability of judgment of supervisors due to mental and physiological conditions and favoritism.

6. Requirement of teachers to be specialists in all fields.

7. Lack of time sense—in which there is a disregard of the number of demands made on a teacher's time—summer sessions, educational projects, preparation of plans, clerical work which teaching involves, supervisors conferences.

8. Failure to realize that other supervisors make similar demands.

9. Lack of planning and organization of supervisors' meetings and the tendency for them to be too often a clearing house for fault-finding from which teachers leave disheartened and discouraged.

10. Requirement of the knowledge and application of the principles of education and the failure to be guided by the same principles in the demonstration classes which the supervisor gives.

11. Forgetfulness of the fact that the supervisor, too, at one time was in the rank of skillful teachers.

Now many of these criticisms may be unjust, yet they should mean something to you and to me in the study of ourselves and should imbue us with a deep feeling of our responsibility in the great educational program of our land.

In an article by Dr. Hosic of Columbia University in which he discusses **A Balanced Program in Supervision,** he says:

The danger of setting up his subject as a separate kingdom should be of chief concern to the special supervisor. Our efforts must integrate and harmonize with the unity of effort for the school program as a whole. Administrators, supervisors, and teachers must be brought into close relationship. Too often we are unaware of what the others are really doing. It has been said that every supervisor should visit every type of activity in which pupils of the schools are engaged.

In conclusion I would like to mention the human element involved in supervision. Nothing can ever take the place of the sympathetic personal contact of co-workers. Science has its place in educational procedures but it cannot take the place of the supervisor as a "real person."

Dear Sir

We take pleasure in mailing you specimens of our penmanship as ordered. In this you have a fair specimen of our letter writing at the present date.

Hoping to have the pleasure of hearing from you again we are,

Dear Sir,

Your card came to hand. I have mailed you our circulars as requested and hope they will please you.

Hoping to have the pleasure of seeing you with us, I am,

Your card came to hand. I have mailed you our circulars. Please see my special offers in Advocate for time etc.

We have a booming school. I hope to see you with us.

Ornamental Penmanship

No. 14   **Script by the late A. M. Wonnell**

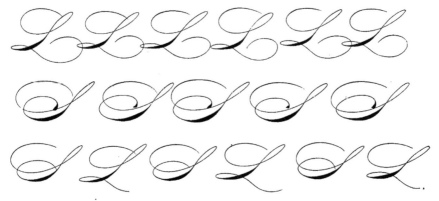

The compound curve or stem is a very important stroke in ornamental penmanship. Practice the compound curve stroke separately as well as practice on the letters. Study the location of the shades and the size of the ovals. Get plenty of snap and grace to your work. The more practice you do the more skillful you should become.

Upon our fields of corn and grain
Made ripe by earth and wind and rain.
The same sun shines that made them glad.
Each little Pilgrim lass and lad.
Long, long ago the Pilgrims bent
Their heads to thank the God who sent
The harvest ripened by the sun.
The evening rest when day was done.

The above beautiful business writing was sent to us by Y. Yashiroda, No. 10 Iwai-Kotobukicho, Okayama-City, Japan.

Lessons in Card Carving

By J. D. Carter, Deerfield, Ill.

Lesson No. 3

In Lesson No. 3 we are presenting some new designs but I have thought it best to use the plain cutting strokes used in Lessons No. 1 and No. 2.

For this Lesson I have arranged a few conventional forms of flowers colored with different colors of ink, then I used a straight cutting stroke on the outer edge of the flower design to the center which gives a pleasing result. It gives a raised effect making the design look much as though it had been cut and pasted on the card.

I suggest in working this lesson that you select one of the more simple designs and make several of them on the card for cutting either with knife or pen as indicated in lesson No. 2. I used pen and knife in cutting the designs of this lesson.

If you have a flower catalogue I suggest you cut out a few of the simple colored flowers—paste them on cardboard and when the paste is dry try cutting with a straight simple stroke from the edge to the center of the flowers. I am sure if you will carefully follow instructions you will soon get pleasing results.

The "Holiday" design of this lesson shows that more elaborate designs can be worked with a few simple carving strokes.

The border work in the two designs of the lesson was cut then retouched with pencil and pen to give a pleasing contrast. Try your skill at this kind of border work.

I will be glad to receive specimens from a number this month. Enclose return postage and I will be glad to give you helpful criticism on the work you are doing.

How May Private School Teachers Improve Themselves and Increase Their Worth to the School

By J. Murray Hill

The subject is all embracing. It recalls the timid teacher who was induced to speak one morning at his school assembly. When he arose (apparently with fear and trembling) his fellow teachers reflected sympathy. But, when he announced his subject, they found that he was at least suffering no territorial inhibitions. He announced he would discuss "The Idiosyncrasies of the Human Race." I feel quite as ambitious as he in addressing myself to the topic of, "How Teachers May Improve Themselves and Increase Their Worth to the School." The dimensions of the subject cannot be fixed, and one hardly knows where to start. I assume, however, that no platitudes concerning the proper use of spare time or the wisdom of personal improvement are indicated or invited.

Few teachers will agree with a prominent educator who said that as a class they have more spare time than is enjoyed in any other profession! Quoting this statement even, may cause me to lose caste with my crowd. However, on one point we can agree: Teachers have all the time there is—so, how best use it?

Any classroom teacher has made a good start toward improving herself and increasing her worth when she determines to do an **increasingly** good job of teaching. The greatest need in America is education, and the greatest need in education is teaching. Not lecturing, reading, or transmitting literally the content of some blindly accepted text—but, original, interesting, and animated teaching—teaching that makes each individual lesson an "adventure for the student."

Every teacher should have, side by side, this simple but beautiful statement from William Lyon Phelps, "I Love to Teach"—

"I LOVE TO TEACH"

"I do not know that I could make entirely clear to an outsider the pleasure I have in teaching. I had rather earn my living by teaching than in any other way. In my mind, teaching is not merely a life work, a profession, an occupation, a struggle; it is a passion. I Love to Teach.

"I love to teach as a painter loves to paint, as a musician loves to play, as a singer loves to sing, as a strong man rejoices to run a race. Teaching is an art—an art so great and so difficult to master that a man or woman can spend a long life at it without realizing much more than his limitations and mistakes, and his distance from the ideal.

"But the main aim of my happy days has been to become a good teacher, just as every architect wishes to be a good architect and every professional poet strives toward perfection."

And this quotation from an editorial, "Shades of Socrates," which appeared some time ago in the college paper of a large University not many miles from Michigan Boulevard.

J. Murray Hill

The accompanying address was delivered by Mr. J. Murray Hill before the private school department of the N. C. T. F. Convention.

Mr. Hill is vice-president of the Bowling Green Business University, Bowling Green, Ky. He has had years of experience teaching accounting, salesmanship and law. In addition to his connection with the N. C. T. F. he has held offices in the Southern Commercial Teachers Association and is a member of the Board of Directors of several firms in Bowling Green and has also held several high positions in the Rotary International.

"SHADES OF SOCRATES"

"One does not expect to dodge the responsibilities of work — but undeniably there are many classes in which the student cannot help knowing without a doubt that he is no more than a name on a yellow class card. His personal interest in the course, his especial difficulties with it, his possibilities of creative work for it—do not exist for the professor.

"To such a teacher, the class members consist of a score or so of nondescript faces and names that swim vaguely without ever hitching. Papers are to be corrected, worse luck, and grades given that allots to a class of twenty-five, one A., two A's—pieces of paper with blue ink marks.

"The students are paying to be taught, and they have a right to demand that their instructors show a gleam of intelligent enthusiasm both for the subject and for the men and women who are enrolled to learn of it."

I repeat—the teacher's first opportunity for personal development is in her own teaching, and while not the only one—it is by far the most potent means, within the reach of the teacher, of increasing his or her worth to the school.

Subsequent suggestions must of course be in some measure a part of the first. Our private school teacher should understand the peculiarly direct responsibility which the private commercial school faces. Patrons who pay direct tuition, expect direct results. It has been said that teachers who have obtained their experience in public schools do not make satisfactory private school instructors. Such a statement is debatable—but the reason given provokes thought. And private school teachers should understand it. It is that the public high school is not held by patrons rigidly accountable for results. Yes, we pay public school tuition, but the process of payment is detached and impersonal. The average citizen may and does resist high taxes, but he wants relief rather than returns. The taxpayer has been told by leading educators, journalists, columnists, business executives, et al., that we are not getting results in our public institutions. It is predicted that America would cast an overwhelming vote to the effect that public education has failed—and yet, within the past six or eight years the taxpayer has poured money into Public Education and continues to do so. Thus, from experience, the public school teacher learns that his income and promotion are not, as a rule, in direct proportion to results obtained. The reverse is true in the experience of the private school teacher. Private business schools know that unless results are obtained, and that within a **given time**, displeased patrons will demand to know why, or worse still, cease to patronize and support.

Therefore, one of the most important things that members of a private school faculty can do to increase their worth is to help to organize and correlate their courses so that students can be equipped as promised, and equally important that it be done within the time limits promised. Patrons of private schools must conclude when courses are not completed within the fixed time limits, that their children are subnormal or that the school has failed. The former—abnormality—may be true but it is a dangerous alibi for the schools.

Teachers should give more study to the content of the courses they are teaching. Too many private schools, being actuated by a desire to keep pace with progress, have added subjects to their courses without increasing the time estimates or time limits originally given to those courses. If such a condition prevails in your school, and I think it does prevail in some of the best private schools in the country, teachers should give thought to the problem.

A member of the staff of a large and well-known business school recently made a study of the records of 900 students, who, over a period of a few years, had filed formal applications for positions in the Employment Department of the school. He found that of this number only 106, or twelve per cent, had fully completed every requirement of the courses taken! Here is both an instructional and administrative problem. If the teachers in that school are able to contribute to its analysis and final solution, they have found a very practical means of "increasing their worth to the school."

Speaking generally, we are the only schools in commercial education who train toward a definite objective—THE JOB. Private schools should hold fast to their original and natural place in education. Some of us—I say us, qualifiedly, have undertaken to disassociate business training from business positions. But that was B. C. (Before the Crash). Now—and probably for years to come, about the biggest thing any kind of education may do is to prepare for and get "bread and butter" jobs! This is our field and the objective takes on a new dignity under present economic conditions. Now is the time for the Private Commercial School to fortify its unique position in the field of education! I recently had a letter from a business school teacher who wanted to change his field "because he did not believe the private business school had any future." He is right so far as his own school is concerned and his attitude is probably a contributing factor. Such a teacher is a liability. Business colleges cannot in these days of stress, carry teachers on their staffs who do not believe in the permanency of good private business schools. For twenty years I have been hearing that the public high school has all but eliminated the private business school and yet after all these gloomy prophesies consider the following: Some time ago I mailed about 325 questionnaires to superintendents of public high schools in

which I sought to determine the Public School Commercial Department objective in the minds of those superintendents.

40% said: They expected their teachers to equip their students to hold positions upon graduation from high school.

20% said: They wanted their teachers to equip commercial students to take similar courses in institutions of higher rank.

31% said: They wanted their commercial teachers to train students in commercial subjects for the sake of education itself. 9% failed to answer the questionnaire—Coming from a goodly number of superintendents in cities of varying sizes from more than thirty states, this is interesting information for private business school people. The attitude of this group of superintendents strongly suggests that leadership in the secondary schools is not inclined to go further with the mistake of converting the public high school into a vocational institution. So far as the policy of these superintendents and principals is concerned, the majority of their graduates are potential business college prospects.

Certainly the public high school has found, speaking generally, that if it goes too far in overloading its curriculum with "tool" subjects, it sacrifices the fundamental equipment of the student, which can never be replaced with a smattering of vocational training. If this assumption is sound, and I think it is with the exception of large city high schools, the average high school then is becoming a growing source of supply and a complement to the standard private business school. Just as a sort of "straw vote" I checked the whereabouts of 421 Kentucky High School Graduates of one class. Eliminating those who have already entered colleges (including a high percentage of business schools) and those who have secured permanent employment, I found there remain 214 or 51% of this number still at home — all potential business school prospects! Regardless of whether this or that business school is failing, viewed from a broad perspective, we must conclude that our field has not been usurped by the public high school and that our place in education is sufficiently secure to insure the perpetuation of good business schools in America. No other kind should survive.

What has all of this to do with the personal development of the teacher? Everything. The private school field needs leadership. We need teachers who will address themselves in thought and action—not only to the problems that are ours—but to the opportunities that are ours. There is no line of demarcation between the interests of the school and the teacher. There never was a time in the history of private school education when business college teachers should be so grateful for their jobs and so encouraged to push forward to the mark of the high calling as now.

HARRY EUGENE BARNES

President of Barnes School of Commerce, Denver, Celebrated his Sixtieth Birthday, October 24, 1936.

At the regular Friday assembly of the faculty and student-body, Mr. Richard J. Triplett, member of the faculty in the Bookkeeping Department, acted as spokesman for the faculty. He said in part:

Mr. Barnes, the faculty wishes to join in this celebration. As we peer into the past—our students and friends view with me some events in the life of a single individual. First we see a young, energetic, school master entering Denver.

We see you, Mr. Barnes, with determination and purpose in your approach to life's problems; toiling with your brother to found this school. We can see you in the classroom; also assuming the duties of president of the school. We see a great army, over 25,000 former students, paying tribute to you as we pay tribute to you today. We see you as President of the Commercial Teachers in the Colorado Education Association; as Vice-President of the National Association of Accredited Commercial Schools; as President of the Central Section of Commercial Teachers in the National Education Association. We see you being made an Honorary Member of the School Masters' Club. We scan thirty years of history, and wherever we find educational leaders, we find you.

We also find you elsewhere. We find you equally active in Business, Social, and Religious circles. We see you becoming a Charter member of the Denver Rotary Club; active in the Advertising Club; and in the Chamber of Commerce. We see you affiliated with the Church, the Sunday School, the Colorado Council for Religious Education; as Superintendent of the Sunday School at Grace Church for twenty-five years; and as President of the Colorado State Sunday School Association.

Without our magic glasses, Mr. Barnes, to open the pages of history, we see you today, a respected, honored, citizen and educator of Sixty.

We all join in wishing you great happiness, joy, and more success in the years to come.

Mr. H. E. Barnes was presented with a flower offering from the students, and with a gift from the faculty.

The Barnes School was founded in 1904. We are indebted to Norman Tower who has been associated with "Barnes" 21 years, for this news item.

A P i o n e e r P e n m a n

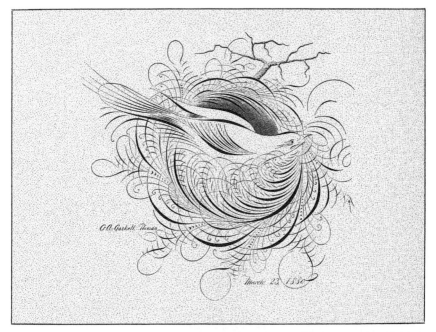

G. A. Gaskell was one of America's most skillful penmen. He was one of the best known penmen because of his national advertising. At the time the above flourish was made in 1880 he was in his prime. He conducted the Bryant and Stratton Business College in Manchester, N. H., where quite a number of America's prominent penmen received some of their early inspiration. Notably among these penmen were L. Madarasz and W. E. Dennis. Gaskell advertised the work of these and other young penmen in magazines throughout the country and was one of the first to promote the "before and after" type of advertising. One of Mr. Gaskell's former associates, L. G. Wilberton, M. D., now of Winona, Minn., writes as follows:

"About the year 1882-83 I accepted a position in the Bryant & Stratton College, Manchester, N. H., and remained with them a year as a teacher of Bookkeeping and other subjects. At that time Prof. G. A. Gaskell was president of that college. He was in the height of his penmanship skill.

Prof. Gaskell was still a young man and of excellent personal appearance. He would be classed as a handsome

G. A. Gaskell

man, about six feet tall. His bearing was erect and pleasing manners. He was a natural orator and speaker as well as a teacher of first rank. He excelled in teaching others. Penmanship was his favorite subject, and he did much to advance the study of good writing; in fact he became a national figure in the penmanship pro-

fession. He evolved a style of writing that was purely his own. He was a real artist and master in describing how each letter should be made, carefully showing the right and wrong way in forming letters and figures. The students soon became interested to learn how to write well. The results were that his students became excellent penmen and teachers.

Shortly after I left Manchester, Prof. Gaskell died. My opinion of him stands high and I am sorry he died so young."

The flourish reproduced above was loaned to us by Capt. F. O. Anderson, Albert Lea, Minn.

H. O. Keesling, President of Pasadena Business College, Pasadena, Calif., celebrated his sixtieth birthday by sending us a package of copies of ornamental penmanship which challenge the ability of the most skillful in the penmanship profession, young or old.

We congratulate Mr. Keesling upon his fine ornamental pen work and hope that we can persuade him to prepare something in black ink which will reproduce for our readers.

E. C. T. A.

A few decades ago the center of interest in educational procedure was transferred from subject matter to its original place—the individual to be educated. With startling rapidity and telling effect, progressive innovations in educational theory and practice immediately followed. To familiarize educators with these progressive theories and practices, teachers' associations used them as theme topics for their conventions and secured eminent educational leaders to discuss them.

Among the first of these organizations to appraise fully and clearly the value of such discussions and the possibilities inherent in them for professional growth and development was the Eastern Commercial Teachers Association, whose annual convention programs have invariably featured as a topic for discussion a paramount and timely educational issue. The interest these discussions aroused, the popularity they attained, and the invaluable services they rendered were soon reflected in an urgent demand that the addresses be preserved in permanent form. In response to this demand, the first Yearbook of the Association made its appearance in 1928. This issue and its successors became an outstanding annual contribution in the field of commercial education.

These are the interesting titles of the Yearbooks already published: Functions of Business Education, Curriculum Making in Business Education, Administration and Supervision of Business Education, Modern Methods of Teaching Business Subjects (Vols. I and II), Teaching Devices and Classroom Equipment, Business Education in a Changing Social and Economic Order, Problems of the Business Teacher, and Guidance in Business Education. All of them have won the well-merited praise of teachers and administrators interested in commercial education, and several of them have been selected in the annual list of the sixty outstanding books in education.

The 1937 Yearbook promises to carry on the tradition established by its predecessors. Under the title, Measuring for Vocational Ability in the Field of Business Education, it will deal fully and significantly with each of the following specific aspects of the general problem: Present Practices and Suggested Improvements in Vocational Ability and Testing; The Test in Fundamentals; The General Background Test; The Personality Rating Schedule; Testing Secretarial Abilities; Testing Bookkeeping and Accounting Abilities; Testing Clerical Abilities; Testing Penmanship Abilities. These are but a few of the topics discussed in this comprehensive and intensely interesting treatment of a subject that has such far-reaching implications for those who seek gainful employment in the business world, as well as for those who train them for such employment.

Signatures by that skillful penman, S. M. Blue, whose obituary appeared in the November number of The Educator. These signatures were loaned to us by M. A. Albin, Portland, Oregon. While they were not prepared for engraving, they show a marvelous command of the pen.

NEW POSITION

Donald M. Glossner, who for some time taught in the Carnegie, Pennsylvania Schools, is now teaching in the Corry High School, Corry, Pa. Before going to Carnegie he specialized in handwriting at Columbus, Ohio. Handwriting has been fundamental in securing good positions for many commercial teachers.

M. Otero Colmenero, San Juan, P.R. and some of his skillful cards.

Mr. Colmenero has been known for many years as Puerto Rico's finest penman. It is with pleasure, therefore, that we present his photograph and some of his work. Notice the graceful curves, the beautiful ovals, and the dashy shades.

Renew Your Subscription

——— PROMPTLY WHEN IT EXPIRES ———

By C. P. Zaner

BOOK REVIEWS

Our readers are interested in books of merit, but especially in books of interest and value to commercial teachers including books of special educational value and books on business subjects. All such books will be briefly reviewed in these columns, the object being to give sufficient description of each to enable our readers to determine its value.

Problem Studies in School Administration, by Ernest C. Witham, Associate Professor of Education, Rutgers University. Published by Prentice-Hall, Inc., New York, N. Y. Paper cover, 186 pages.

The lecture method in graduate courses in education, particularly in the field of school administration, is not satisfactory to either students or instructors. Consequently, whenever a class is made up of students who have had valuable years of experience behind them, ample opportunity should be provided for a full utilization of such background. Unquestionably, wide reading is necessary and a good textbook is important, but in order to capitalize on the experience of the class it is necessary to have a set of real problems that have been drawn from actual experience.

There is not a single fictitious problem in this book. So real are the experiences presented here, that regarding nearly every problem some person might say: "I recognize the school system where this took place." As a matter of fact, although the exact school system referred to in the problem may not be known, like situations may be recalled.

As a guide for the student, a sample problem, "General Supervision," has been presented, together with a solution. The solution offered here should not be considered as the only one possible; its purpose is rather to serve as an illustration. All the other problems have been presented without solutions, and with every problem pertinent questions and a selected bibliography have been given.

The best method of using the exercises will depend upon the size and make-up of the class. Sometimes a general assignment of two to four problems to all members of the group may be found desirable; at other times more effective results may be obtained if special assignments are given to individual students.

Key-Driven Calculator Course, by Raymond C. Goodfellow, Director of Commercial Education, Newark, New Jersey, Rosann School, Burroughs Adding Machine Company, New York, New York, and Albert Stern, Manager, School Department, New York Burroughs Adding Machine Company and Instructor, College of the City of New York. Published by South-Western Publishing Company, Cincinnati, Ohio. Paper cover, 182 pages.

The key-driven calculator is recognized as one of the essential office machines upon which modern business depends. This type of calculator, because of its wide use in business offices throughout the country, has become a definite unit of instruction in many schools on the secondary and university levels. It is essential that proper instruction be given if satisfactory standards are to be attained by students who enter business offices as calculator operators.

The authors have studied all phases that enter into a suitable course of study for students who contemplate the use of the key-driven calculator. The following factors are considered essential in a satisfactory course of study for this type of machine:

1. The type of material used must be within the mental range of the average student.

2. A complete knowledge of the calculator should be possible of attainment within a reasonable length of time.

3. The teaching materials should be carefully planned and convenient for practice and for checking results.

This workbook has been written with the idea of providing material that is arranged in proper sequence and that includes the types of work that are usually required in business situations. The course has, therefore, the following characteristics:

1. It can be completed within a school semester.

2. It is possible of accomplishment by, and within the capabilities of, the average student.

3. It teaches the principles and operations required in the use of the calculator.

4. It teaches the exercise of correct techniques.

5. Its content is practical because it has been selected from standard business practice material.

6. It introduces business forms at the earliest possible moment so that the student can gain actual experience from their use.

The course consists of sixty assignments. Fifty-four of these assignments are bound in the workbook. An additional six assignments, Assignments Nos. 10, 20, 30, 40, 50 and 60, are provided separately for use as tests. Each assignment in the workbook has been planned so that the average student is able to complete it within a forty-five minute period. Each of the six tests may be given in fifteen minutes. The material in the assignments is cumulative, that is, once a certain operation or skill is taught, it is put into use in succeeding lessons.

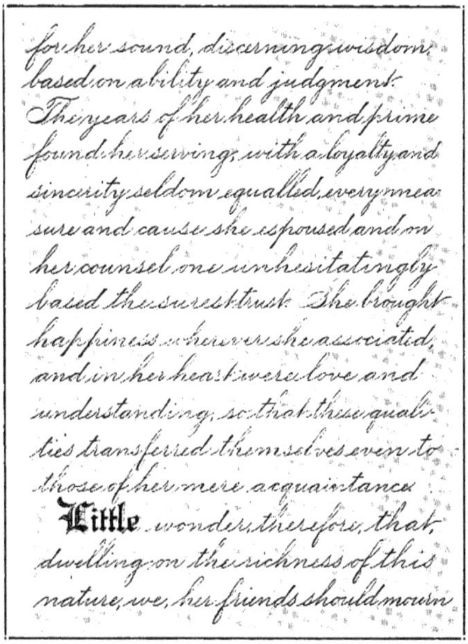

This illustrates how accurate script may be appropriately used in engrossing resolutions. It represents a page from an album prepared by Charlton V. Howe, 2312 Girard Trust Bldg., Philadelphia, Pa. While Mr. Howe has been noted for his superb engravers' script he is equally as skillful in plain Spencerian style of penmanship. The delicate shades give the work an artistic effect which is very pleasing in resolution work. Penmen should be able to do all classes of pen work.

Lessons in Modern Engrosser's Script

Prepared in the office of The Educator

No. 4

Half the battle in learning to write script is study, the other half is practice. Before writing any of the copies in this lesson study them. Get a good mental picture of each letter. Know exactly where the strokes should go. There are so many things to speak of and to watch in these few words. However, we would suggest that you watch **slant, spacing, height, uniform thick down strokes,** and be sure to get a light touch.

Send your work to The Educator for a few free suggestions. Be sure to enclose return postage.

cue cure in one or am coarse us success owes can common across

╬─────────────────────╬
DESIGNING AND
ENGROSSING
By E. L. BROWN
Rockland, Maine
╬─────────────────────╬

Pen drawing:

The design herewith has a seasonable effect and also impresses the fact that The Educator is the door of opportunity. It is well to cultivate originality in making commercial designs, and often a design that tells its story convincingly is more successful than one better artistically, although good art is highly desirable.

Lay off a rough sketch first, developing the idea to be expressed in smaller form than the proposed drawing, giving especial attention to balance and arrangement. Next make a careful pencil drawing enlarged to desired size, (7 x 13½) inches is size of original pen work. Suggest tone values and aim for the icy effect.

Zanerian ink is best for pen drawing and lettering. Coarse and fine pointed pens will be necessary. Note quality and direction of lines in treating the different values. Short parallel lines give ice effect; thicken lines to produce contrast between background and lettering. Use a fine pen for holly wreath and a coarse one for the background. The ground of the words "The Educator" may be laid in solid black and afterward stippled with Chinese white in a clean pen, or stippled in the usual way.

We are glad to note a renewed interest in these lessons, and many have sent in work, and very good work too, for criticism. Shall be glad to hear from others, as we are always pleased to be of service to all faithful workers.

By the late H. B. Lehman

MISTAKES

(With apologies to somebody.)

By Leewin B. Williams

When a lawyer makes a mistake—he tries it all over again.

When a judge makes a mistake—he hangs it.

When a doctor makes a mistake—he buries it.

When a preacher makes a mistake—nobody knows the difference.

When a plumber makes a mistake—he charges twice for it.

When a professor makes a mistake—everybody laughs.

When an engrosser makes a mistake —GOOD NIGHT!

At the diploma season the work frequently comes in a rush. Engrossers must work rapidly and long hours. Mistakes are expensive—to somebody. Spoilage should be reduced to the minimum. Corrections are never nice and are difficult to make, especially on sheepskin diplomas. Engrossers, no doubt, would save much annoyance, time and expense by advising schools to furnish correct data according to the following suggestions:

1. Typewrite all names exactly as they are to appear on the diplomas.

2. Do not place titles (Mr., Mrs., Rev., etc.) before names, or degrees and orders after names unless it is intended that these are to appear on the diplomas. The engrosser is supposed to follow copy exactly.

3. Carefully check back all names and accompanying data for possible errors.

4. DO NOT furnish engrossers with carbon copies of names.

5. DO NOT type names ALL CAPS. If so written, names like LEROY, DE SALES, etc., do not indicate whether they should be written Le Roy, Leroy; Desales or De Sales.

6. Underscore all names with unusual spelling; e. g. Elisabeth, Soloman, Mary Francis Jones. This middle name, if underscored, would indicate to the engrosser that Francis is a family name and not an oversight in spelling. Frequently a special date is to be placed on certain diplomas, or some extra or unusual wording, these should all be underscored, preferably with a red pencil.

7. If "he" or "she" is to be inserted, indicate the sex, unless the name clearly indicates the sex.

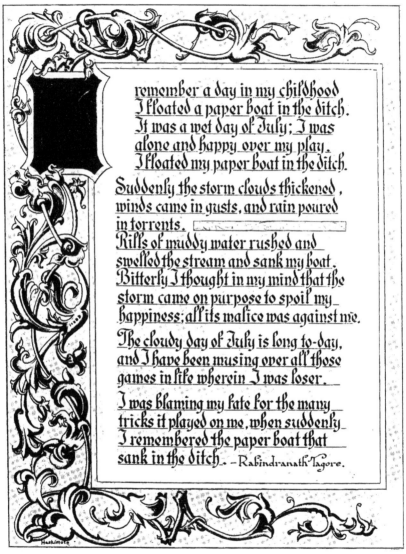

remember a day in my childhood
I floated a paper boat in the ditch.
It was a wet day of July; I was
alone and happy over my play.
I floated my paper boat in the ditch.

Suddenly the storm clouds thickened,
winds came in gusts, and rain poured
in torrents.
Rills of muddy water rushed and
swelled the stream and sank my boat.
Bitterly I thought in my mind that the
storm came on purpose to spoil my
happiness; all its malice was against me.

The cloudy day of July is long to-day,
and I have been musing over all those
games in life wherein I was loser.

I was blaming my fate for the many
tricks it played on me, when suddenly
I remembered the paper boat that
sank in the ditch. — Rabindranath Tagore.

This piece of engrossing is by Tadashi Hashimoto, and was sent to us by Y. Yashiroda, No. 10 Iwai-Kotobukicho, Okayama-city, Japan.

TRUE CHRISTMAS CHEER ...

HELP TO MAKE OTHERS HEALTHY

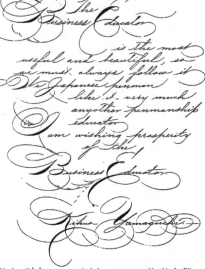

This beautiful letter was received from our penmanship friend, Kikuo Yamaguchi, 537 Daicho, Ashikaga City, Japan, who also sent us some of his pen flourishes. Much interest is being taken in The Educator among the penmen of Japan. We are receiving some very skillful work from them.

The National, State and Local Tuberculosis Associations of the United States

---

Day by day in every way

We learn both form and movement

Every day in every way

We're showing more improvement

Day by day in every way

We're writing better and better

The Zaner way is teaching us

The form of every letter.

A Subscriber

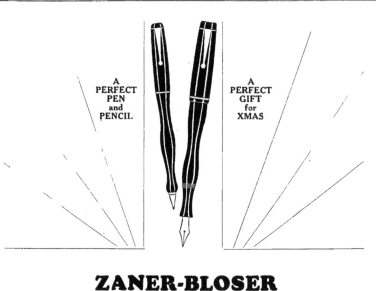

A
PERFECT
PEN
and
PENCIL

A
PERFECT
GIFT
for
XMAS

ZANER-BLOSER

fountain pen
and pencil

Christmas Special Order Blank for
The Zaner-Bloser Finger Fitting Fountain Pen and Pencil

The Zaner-Bloser Co.,
612 N. Park St., Columbus, Ohio

Please send me...Zaner-Bloser "finger fitting" Parker-made
(Quantity)
Fountain Pen and Pencil Sets at the especial low price of $5.50 per set, postpaid.

Check color wanted
☐ Mottled Blue & White
☐ Black
☐ Modernistic Blue & White

Check clip or ring wanted
☐ Clip for Men
☐ Ring for Women

Individual Prices
☐ One Fountain Pen $3.50
☐ One Pencil $2.50

☐ Cash enclosed

☐ Send C. O. D.

Name ....

Address ....

Position ....

Patented in U. S. A. and Canada

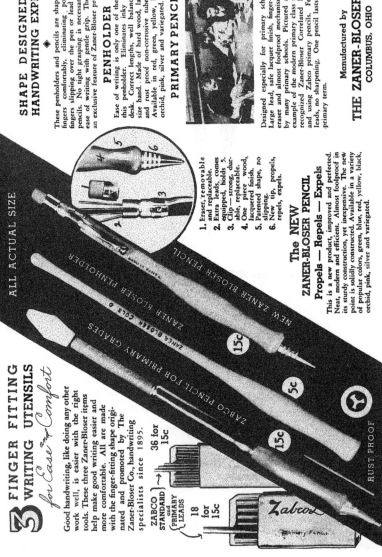

THE €DUCATOR

**DEVOTED TO PENMANSHIP and DRAWING~
DESIGNING, ENGROSSING and BUSINESS EDUCATION**

NEW YEAR

THE ZANER~BLOSER COMPANY
COLUMBUS, OHIO

Zanerian College of Penmanship

Columbus, Ohio

Roundhand or Engrossers' Script Course by Correspondence

Roundhand from a financial point ranks next to business writing. It is beautiful and appropriate for many occasions. A large amount of engrossing is done in this style. Our course covers this work completely. Each lesson is carefully corrected, suggestions for improvement are given, and models are made wherever necessary. This is a most interesting course.

Price of Roundhand or Engrossers' Script Course (including Manual) $12.00

Supplies for Roundhand or Engrossers' Script Course............................ 2.95

Text Lettering and Engrossing Course by Correspondence

Our Text Lettering and Engrossing Course will train you to handle a broad pen successfully, to letter diplomas, and do broad pen lettering for all occasions. It covers in twelve lessons alphabets like the American, Unretouched Old English, German Text, Shading, etc. Teachers can profitably take this course, as well as those who are going into the engrossing business. Lettering as a business or as a sideline is very profitable. You can become quite skillful by faithfully following this course.

Price of Text Lettering and Engrossing Course (including Manual)......$12.00

Supplies for Text Lettering and Engrossing Course 2.85

Advanced Engrossing Course by Correspondence

Our advanced Engrossing Course supplements our Roundhand and Text Lettering and Engrossing courses. It covers standard alphabets, as the Egyptian, Roman, Medial, Old English, etc. It covers the work from fundamentals of lettering to the making of elaborate resolutions, etc. It will train you to make initial letters, borders, scrolls, alphabets, resolutions, memorials, testimonials, diplomas and most of the things done by engrossers. This course lays a good foundation, and if after completing it you desire to go higher, you can attend the Zanerian and complete your training in a short time. The Text Lettering and Engrossing course should be taken before the Advanced Engrossing course.

Price of Advanced Engrossing Course (including text) $12.00

Supplies for Advanced Engrossing Course 2.25

THE ZANERIAN COLLEGE

612 N. Park St.   Columbus, Ohio

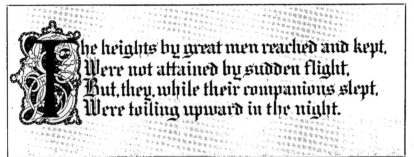

The heights by great men reached and kept,
Were not attained by sudden flight,
But, they, while their companions slept,
Were toiling upward in the night.

Prepared in the Zaner-Bloser Engrossing Studio as a sample of text lettering by John R. Cox. Work of this kind can be used to advantage during the Holiday Season to send Christmas Greetings to friends. It might be well for some of us to begin now preparing handsome cards for next Christmas.

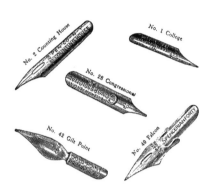

There is ONE
characteristic of all
SPENCERIAN PENS

+ PENMANSHIP + ENGROSSING + EDUCATION +

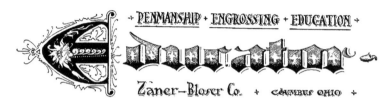

Zaner–Bloser Co. + COLUMBUS OHIO +

—— BY KENSHIRO ——

Volume 42 COLUMBUS, OHIO, JANUARY, 1937 No. 5

Excerpts from a Radio Discussion of Handwriting in Everyday Life

Dr. Harold Davis Emerson

Is it fair to a person who gets a letter to make him or her waste time trying to find out what it is all about? Then aside from the social writing, there is not a letter but that requires a signature and the bane of my life is to decipher signatures. Sometimes they are so hard to read that I hesitate about answering them because I am unable to learn from the signature how to spell the person's name.

Today time means money. Every minute must count and no one is willing to waste precious minutes unraveling poor penmanship or trying to understand what the writer intended. A poor penman is out of tune with the world and certainly finds it difficult to secure employment.

Compliments of Handwriting Dept. of Paterson, N. J., Public Schools

PLAN TO ATTEND THE E. C. T. A.

The Eastern Commercial Teachers Association will meet in Boston, March 24, 25, 26 and 27, 1937. A series of discussions is being prepared on the topic "Foundations of Vocational Testing in Business Education."

Outstanding people in the field of business and commercial education will participate.

It will be a meeting progressive teachers should attend to learn the views of these men and women who are in positions to know the present demands of business.

———

New Officers of the Handwriting Section of the Indiana State Teachers' Association.

Ida S. Koons, Fort Wayne, President

Roy Williams, Bloomington, Vice-President

J. H. Bachtenkircher, Lafayette, Secretary-Treasurer

The eighty-third annual session was held in Indianapolis, October 22 and 23.

We wish one and all a full measure of Health, Happiness and Success for 1937.

THE EDUCATOR

Published monthly (except July and August) By THE ZANER-BLOSER CO.; 612 N. Park St., Columbus, O.
E. A. LUPFER...Editor
PARKER ZANER BLOSER..............Business Mgr.

SUBSCRIPTION PRICE, $1.25 A YEAR (To Canada, 10c more; foreign, 30c more) Single copy, 15c.
Change of address should be requested promptly In advance, if possible, giving the old as well as the new address.
Advertising rates furnished upon request.

THE EDUCATOR is the best medium through which to reach business college proprietors and managers, commercial teachers and students, and lovers of penmanship. Copy must reach our office by the 10th of the month for the issue of the following month.

Modern Handwriting

By E. A. Lupfer, Zanerian College, Columbus, Ohio

No. 5

I saw some of your handwriting.

Does your writing run along freely like the above with a uniform swing? Is each one of your letters unmistakably clear or do your a's look like o's and your o's like a's? Are your r's and i's distinct? Do you get daylight in all of your loops? Write the above sentence and save it for further practice and comparison.

Many people have trouble with the bottom part of the I. Therefore, practice the horizontal oval on the base line. Make the I and retrace the oval about six times. See that you do not scatter the oval. Those who have trouble in making the back straight will find the push pull worked into the back of the I very helpful. Begin the letter at the base line, making the top loop first and making the boat hook at the bottom last. The final stroke should swing across as though you were going to connect on to another letter.

Indian Summer Indian Summer

After practicing the letter individually and with the exercises write the words, **Indian Summer.** Notice the "boat hook" at the bottom is made about the same on both I and S. The loop in the I and S should be the same height and appear to be similar in size. Watch your turns and angles in the small letters.

S S I bi ds wo flu leg qu xth

Here are some interesting letter combinations for practice. Keep reviewing the letters which you have previously studied.

The i is one of the most important small letters. The top part should be sharp and the bottom turns should be rounding. Practice these under turn exercises getting uniformity of size, slant and spacing.

In dotting the i use care. The dot should be twice as high as the i and in line with the i. Most people are careless in dotting the i.

The u is similar to the i. Be sure to study the beginning and ending strokes. They should be the same length and the same curve.

Judge quality of your writing with a scale.

Each schoolroom should have a handwriting scale so that each pupil can judge his own writing and see if his work is satisfactory for his own grade. Some scales are so made that they are easy to handle and the pupils soon are able to accurately judge their own handwriting. Write the above sentence and have each one in the class compare his specimen with the scale and see if the writing is as good as it should be. Then, systematically analyze the writing, show the faults and help to correct them.

The **J** begins with an indirect oval motion. Therefore make a few indirect ovals. Work freely but not too fast.

Remember that the back of the **J** should be comparatively straight. In order to make the back straight retrace it six times, then finish the letter without raising the pen. Before making the **J** study the proportion, spacing and slant. Notice that the top of the **J** is slightly larger than the part below the base line. The top extends three-fourths of the distance from the base line to the line above. The lower loop extends half way between the base line and the next line below.

The backs of **I** and **J** are similar. Practice the letters together. It is good to review the letters which you have previously practiced and to mix them in with the letters you are working upon.

Do not be afraid to make line after line of each letter. Draw a line along the tops and bottoms of your letters to see if your letters vary in size. They do not need to be mechanically the same but aim to make them as near the same height and proportion as possible. Draw slant lines down the back of the **J** and see if the slant of the **J** is the same as in other letters.

J January Jan. June July June July James James James James J

Learn to write the months and various names beginning with **J**. Practice especially the names of the boys and girls beginning with **J**, like James, John, Jane, Joe, Joan, Jesse.

John told his dog to lie down.

In writing this sentence see how well you can make the loops.

The teacher should insist upon the pupils doing careful work in all written work.

(cursive handwriting exercises: D D D O J J fel sc oop ed ton)

These exercises, letters and combinations of letters are given as review work. Each time you study a letter you doubtless will discover something new—something which you previously overlooked.

(cursive handwriting exercises)

(cursive handwriting exercises: j y exercises)

(cursive handwriting: joyous joyous joyous joyous joy)

The **j** and **y** are similar and should be studied together. The loop in the **y** is exactly the same as in the **j**. Keep the loop open, and dot the **j** carefully the same as you dot an **i**. Watch the ending stroke and see that your quality of line is free and smooth.

Get the top turn of the **y** rounding, otherwise your **y** might look like a poor **g**.

The **j** in a word should be no higher than the letters which follow it. Draw headlines to see if your letters are the same height.

(cursive handwriting exercises: G letters)

The **G** begins with an under curve, contains a loop, a sharp point, and finishes like the capital **I**. Stop at the hook before making the final swing, otherwise the letter is made freely throughout. Make about forty or forty-five letters a minute. The loop in the **G** should be larger than the loop in the small **l**.

(cursive handwriting exercises: G G G G G G Good g g good)

Practice the exercises and letter, then write the word **Good**. If you have trouble with the **g** work on the following exercises:

(cursive handwriting exercises: g letters)

Make the slanting oval of the **g** the same as the **a**. Retrace the downward stroke of the loop six times before finishing the loop. Do not raise the pen in making the five connected letters.

g g g g g g g g g g g g g

Study the **g** separately. Compare your letter with the copy. It is a good plan to draw these letters out large on paper with a lead pencil. This you can do at odd moments and you will find it very interesting. Draw head and base lines, also slant lines, erase, and redraw until you get the letter ideal in form.

ng age gu ge og gr go good

Practice these and other combinations of letters containing the **g**. Rewrite the word **Good** to see if you can write it as well as the first time.

good good good good good
o o o o o o o o o o o o o o
some found money order out

If you have trouble with the o's in **good** study and practice them as suggested in this copy. Select words containing the **o** and practice them. The above are good words to work on individually.

The trained runner wins the race.

Write the sentence and preserve it for further study. Your aim in the next few days should be to learn to write this sentence well.

8 8 8 S S S T T T F F F

The capital stem is used today in the **S, L, G, T** and **F**. It is composed of a compound curve. Practice the figure 8 exercise, then practice on the stem itself. Make some **T**'s and **F**'s watching the stem especially.

O O O ~ ~ T T F F Feb. Tues.

The first exercise will help to get the bottom part of the stem graceful and rounding. Retrace the oval six times. Those who have trouble with the cap should make a few of the caps separately. Study the shape and movement. Write the letters and abbreviations many times.

8 8 8 T T T T T T T T T
T T T T Tenn. Thanksgiving

Write the words, Tennessee, Tallahassee, Thanksgiving, Texas, and names of classmates beginning with the capitals **T** or **F**.

Rewrite the sentence "The trained runner wins the race," and see if you have improved it. Pick out the various letters which give you trouble. Watch the **r, s,** and **c**.

Creative Supervision

J. Freeman Guy, 1st Associate Superintendent,
Pittsburgh, Pa.

From the report of the N. A. P. T. S.

The old type of supervisor is passing —the kind that was appointed on age or pull, the kind that makes fortnightly visits, hands out cut and dried specifications for the teacher to follow blindly,

"Hers not to reason why,
Hers but to do or die."

A supervisor is a teacher of teachers. Therefore she must have capacity to invigorate life through learning, she must be able to command respect because of superiority of wisdom, she must be able to inspire, to fire teachers with a burning zeal, to stimulate a passion for professional growth, to originate and try new ideas. She is really creative, she radiates progress, she has the leadership that draws, not drives.

The Creative Supervisor has two characteristics that stand out like mars at perihelion. First, she herself must have constantly accumulating KNOWLEDGE. Knowing and growing are correlative functions. Second, she must have FEELING. She must be sympathetic, considerate, abundantly able to get on with people.

I shall discuss the first qualification, Growth in Knowledge. I shall address my remarks to handwriting under two major thoughts:

GOALS TO BE ATTAINED

TECHNIQUES TO BE EMPLOYED

There are many goals set up for handwriting. Ayres in the Seattle Course of Study in Writing, sets up eleven. Many psychologists shroud these goals in language that Welland Hendricks calls Pedageese. A rolling stone gathers no moss, is clear. To be learned, we should say, "A revolving fragment of the paleozoic age gathers no cryptogamous matter."

Stripped of its verbiage, the goal in handwriting is to train children to write automatically with a degree of speed and legibility that is socially useful.

How well should a child write? What is socially useful? Thorndike, Ayres, Freeman, and others have made extended investigations as to the social demands on writing.

Freeman's investigation shows that commercial schools need a quality of 60 or better on the Ayres Scale. Koos corroborates these findings from 1053 specimens of social correspondence and 1127 specimens from employees of twenty-four occupations. He concludes we cannot justify a quality better than 60 for social correspondence and for most vocations and professions, exclusive of teaching; for teaching and com-

mercial work, a standard of 70 is ample. The standard on the Ayres Scale in the eighth grade is 62 in quality with a rate of 79 letters per minute.

Thus a standard of 70 to 75 words per minute with a legibility or quality of 60 seems to be quite definitely established as a goal to be reached by the end of the sixth year. Analagous goals are established for the other grades in the Fourth Year Book of the Department of Superintendence.

A standard of vocational requirement,—of bookkeeper for instance, is unsound. This standard is needed only by a few.

That Utopia (when handwriting will not be needed for social and business purposes) in my humble judgment, borders on the horizon of the millenium. Even if everybody had a typewriter, handwriting would still be necessary in recording, jotting down items, note taking, signing names, etc. Fancy Milady running to her typewriter when Mrs. Malaprop is quoting a recipe over the telephone. Writing will still be needed inside and outside of school for recording, for social correspondence, keeping account of time, keeping account of sales, notes for speeches of preachers and lecturers, and poetical inspirations, phone numbers, reading papers of other pupils, and memos, signatures for typewritten letters, and countless other functions.

We shall always write first to preserve our own thoughts, and secondly to communicate our thoughts to others. Recording our own thoughts either for permanent keeping or communication demands that a pupil clarify and organize his thinking, a function sometimes

overlooked. A good writing hand frequently is socially useful, such as paving the way for a favorable interview.

Aesthetic appearance formerly was considered a goal. Copper plate writing was aimed at for all. Pupils were drilled on beautiful flourishes, deep shading, fancy letters. Today aesthetic appearance is restricted to form of the letters, regularity of the writing and neatness of appearance. Legibility and speed are the significantly outstanding goals to be attained.

SUMMARY

The goal is to develop sufficient skill to enable pupils to write easily, legibly and rapidly enough to meet present needs and social requirements, to render automatic the recording of thought.

SPEED AND LEGIBILITY

Secondly, let us look at techniques to be utilized. Consider speed and legibility first. It is believed by some that speed and legibility are mutually antagonistic characteristics of writing, that there is a negative correlation between them. As quality increases, speed decreases and vice versa. The evidence does not prove this contention. Without a doubt the law of diminishing returns operates in handwriting as in all other human affairs. My thought is that, when speed is neglected it suffers. Likewise, when quality is neglected, it suffers. The deficiency is due to neglect of training rather than to negative correlation.

Which is more important to emphasize, speed or quality? The Cleveland Survey shows plateaus which indicate desirable standards for each of the grades. For example, in the fifth grade, a rate of 57 letters per minute may be maintained with a quality of from 50 to 70 as measured on the Ayres Scale. In the sixth grade, 64 letters may be written with a quality of 60 or 70. In the seventh grade, 73 letters may be written with a quality of 60 up to 80, and in the eighth grade, a rate of 78 letters may be written with a quality of 60 to 70. These plateaus indicate a desirable balance between speed and quality.

SPEED

Speed of handwriting has too frequently been sacrificed to quality. It is true that greater speed is frequently purchased at an undue sacrifice of quality, but, on the other hand, quality is just as frequently bought at the cost of speed. What the teacher should strive for is a socially desirable quality written at the fastest natural rate of writing for the individual pupil. Practice in speed writing should certainly be given attention in the regular writing program of the upper grades. Most children now write a hand quite legible by the end of the third grade. Following that, speed should be developed.

There should be no speed requirements in the lower grades. In the first grade the first paper writing should be large. In the third grade, writing with a pen may be begun. The size of the letters should be reduced gradually to three-eighth inches high.

MOTOR DEVELOPMENT

The psychological factors in handwriting are **coordination** and **motor development**. Experimental studies show that control of the larger muscles of the arm develop first, and the smaller muscles later. Therefore, Pyle concludes a child of six is not capable of making fine coordinated movements of the hand. On the other hand, it is well known that use hastens and facilitates development. The use of crayons, pens, paint brushes, and scissors hastens the development of motor control of the fingers and hands. The child can profitably begin writing at the age of six using the larger muscles, on the blackboard, or on large sheets of paper with crayon. The period should be short to prevent fatigue.

RHYTHM

Rhythm refers to the relatively equal duration of time used in making unit movements. Nutt found that speed is increased by rhythm of movement. Freeman's experiments show that the development of rhythm has little or no effect on the **quality** of writing. This was corroborated by Nutt, rhythm being a symptom of maturity rather than a quality of writing. The value of counting lies then not in developing rhythm, but in the formation of speed units or unit movements according to the natural divisions of the letter. It is also an important device for controlling the rate of writing. Slight evidence shows that counting by the pupil as he writes, which Freeman recommends, or even writing to the beat of a metronome or to a gramophone record, is probably useful. Writing movements in the first and third quadrants are speedier than those in the second and fourth. Writing with a backward slant, therefore, is to be deprecated. Writing with a forward slant of 45 degrees is quickest, but somewhat illegible. The best authorities, therefore, recommend a slant of not less than 10 degrees from the vertical and not more than 30 degrees. Small writing is speedier than large writing. It is also less legible. Since writing naturally tends to become smaller with age and with the increase of finger movements, it is best to start with fairly large writing and allow it to decrease slowly in size with age. Care should, of course, be taken to prevent it from becoming too small before the

adult stage is reached. Script writing is slower than continuous writing, hence the beautiful legibility of script writing has to be sacrificed to speed. Whenever speed results in a lower quality of work, it is probable that speed should be reduced. In other words, the child should follow his natural rate of handwriting as far as possible.

Good writing is rhythmic writing. The greatest speed is in the middle of a stroke. For example, the down stroke of f is made in about the same time as the other shorter strokes.

Timing is an important factor in writing, as in music, physical education, or in golf.

Timing aids perception of form because the writer must have the form well enough in mind so that the rhythmic strokes may not be interrupted.

The current method of holding the pen, now universally taught, is conducive to a high degree of speed. Paper smooth enough and pens broad enough to prevent sputtering also add to speed.

Plan to attend the next meeting of the N. A. P. T. S. at Toronto, Can.

MOVEMENT

It is widely held that muscular movement is a sine qua non for good writing.

One of the well-known systems of writing advocates three or four weeks on this factor of movement alone, asserting that there is just one correct movement.

Freeman's statistics and photographic studies do not confirm this. His experiments made on both good and poor writers show that there may be more than one favorable position. He points out that the greatest difference in movement between good and poor writers lies in the organization; good writers divide the movement definitely into units, separate them by pauses, and make them conform to the natural units of the letter forms.

Freeman states, "In the first place there is scarcely a writer so far as this investigation indicates, who uses solely the arm movement in the production of the letters. When we confine our examination to elementary pupils, with whom alone we are concerned in public school teaching, we find relatively small per cent in any system or any grade who use the arm movement chiefly. The fingers always cooperate to a greater or less extent, in the formation of the letters. Efforts to de-

velop an exclusive arm movement are not successful."

Freeman found that good writers use the finger movement as frequently as do poor writers. Poor writers use other forms of movement such as hand and wrist with greater frequency than do the good writers. Experiments indicate that the fingers and the arm are the chief factors of writing movement. The contention is that it would be more economical to aim directly at the proper type of speed organization, and not attempt the well-nigh impossible task of developing exclusive arm movement in all children.

Experiments in the University Elementary School of Chicago show that a moderate amount of arm movement is used and that the desirable degree of arm movement comes as a by-product of the adoption of a favorable position and of drill in fluent lateral movement and rhythmic writing.

Furthermore, these experiments have shown that this combination of shoulder, forearm, and finger movements, depends upon the correct holding of the pen and paper. Problems of color, size, beginning and ending strokes, as well as the individual letter forms controlled by these, depend upon the posture of the pen. Problems of slant, letter spacing, and alignment, with the letter forms controlled by these, depend upon the posture of the paper.

These findings are corroborated by a study of the free writing of pupils in allied school subjects in grades six, seven and eight in Pittsburgh. Of 1583 pupils observed during free writing in these three grades, 1443 used the finger movement resting the ball of the hand on the desk, or 91 per cent. The whole arm movement certainly does not carry over into the allied writing activities. I challenge seriously the time and energy expended on muscular movement when experimental evidence strongly indicates it is wasteful for many.

Knapp observes, "It is of little importance how well you **can** write compared with how well you **do** write." Many school children have two styles of writing, one for the writing period, another for the allied writing. Like the girl who carried two handkerchiefs —one for blow and one for show. The trouble was, sometimes she showed the wrong one.

PERCEPTION OF FORM

Perception of form should come, according to Wheat, from the gradual development of the perception of form in the pupil's own mind.

It is good practice to expose the child to the copy, then conceal the copy while he reproduces the letter, then compare with the copy, then try to improve.

Writing constantly, comparison, trial with better success, develops a mental perception of form. Complete perception of form, of course, emerges from much practice. It is in no sense a substitute for practice.

Perception in writing is not wholly visual, but partly kinaesthetic or muscular. A good writer gets the feel of the letter. This is a kinaesthetic image as real as the visual image. The skilful writer uses vision only for the general placement of his writing on the page and the direction of the line of writing. The kinaesthetic image does the rest. A good writer is practically unconscious of kinaesthetic perception.

LEGIBILITY

The most important factor in writing is legibility. We write in order that we may later read! If writing is illegible it defeats its own end.

Contrary to general opinion, the spacing of words has more to do with legibility than any other single element. Words insufficiently spaced seem to make one continuous word and the writing is very difficult to decipher.

Flourishes at the beginning and the end of a word are to be deprecated chiefly because they interfere with proper spacing. Words in a sentence should be spaced about a quarter of an inch, roughly the width of the letter m.

Next in importance is the spacing of lines. These should be wide enough to prevent the serious overlapping of loops and tails.

Slant is important. It is a well-known fact that writing composed of imperfectly formed letters, if regular in form and slant, can usually be read with ease. Vertical writing is more legible than slant writing but a compromise has to be made, since slant writing is more speedy than vertical. The form of letters used in the "script" writing of England and the "library" hand of North America leads to legibility. The compromise of a fairly well-rounded letter found in a good "running" hand is generally regarded as satisfactory.

The form and size of letters in writing is important. Crowding letters fosters illegibility. Finger movements lead to small writing and consequently loss of legibility. Large writing, however, is slower than small writing, owing to the greater distance the pen has to cover.

Lastly, legibility is dependent on the regularity of letters and regularity of slant of the writing.

The arrangement of the writing on a page enhances legibility such as: neatness of appearance, non-crowded lines. Pupils should be trained to plan not to run out of space. The addressing of

envelopes gives splendid practice in this line and should be utilized in the upper grades.

Experiments have shown that legibility, or excellence in handwriting, does not depend upon a special type of movement, but upon the proper combination of shoulder, forearm, and finger movements. This combination of movements differs in individuals as their length of fingers and arms differs, and as their ages and degrees of physical control differ.

Rate of improvement in quality of writing is steady from second to eighth grade, slightly greater from the fifth to the eighth grade.

Pupils should be taught legibility with versatility of position. They should be taught to use different materials under different physical situa-

> Training children to write well is also training them in many of the elements that go to make up character.

tions. For example, use of pads and notebooks; writing on knees, on books; writing while standing or bending over; writing with pens, fountain pens, pencils, crayons, or stylus. A signature should be legibly written under any and all conditions.

Legibility is a mark of literacy highly prized.

Many men in World War remained in ranks of privates on account of inability to write legibly while others less capable were promoted.

Summarizing, factors in securing speed are:

1. Ease of movement
2. Rhythm of movement
3. Slant of writing
4. Size of letters
5. Continuity of letters
6. Method of holding pen and placing paper
7. Kind of pen and paper

Summarizing, legibility is secured by:

1. Spacing of words
2. Spacing of lines
3. Slant of writing
4. Form and size of letters
5. Regularity of letters and slant
6. Absence of flourishes

INDIVIDUAL DIFFERENCES

Handwriting is frequently taught as though all children had the same abilities and the same difficulties. Writing is dependent upon the organization of a complex set of habits growing out of innumerable inherent movements. Writing, therefore, tends to become individual in character, because the basic elements of arm and finger movements, which go into its make-up, are individual. The pressure of a writing system may disguise this individuality for a time, but as soon as control by the teacher is relinquished, individuality begins to assert itself. Not only is this true of individuality, but the two sexes also tend to write differently. Apart from the immature form of childhood, writing may be said to be either masculine or feminine in character. Competent judges can distinguish sex in handwriting correctly between 60 and 70 per cent of the times, some 10 to 20 per cent more frequently than chance. Some males write a feminine and some females a masculine hand, but in general, each sex tends to keep to its own type.

Such wide individual differences appear in school pupils that if, in rate of writing, some educational Pied Piper should exchange the better half of the fifth grade pupils with the poorer half of the eighth grade pupils, neither the teachers nor the supervisors could tell the change.

PROVISION FOR INDIVIDUAL DIFFERENCES

First, rate the applied writing at least once a month in grades 3-8, perhaps oftener. Second, since the law of diminishing returns operates in all skills, excuse those pupils from special drill who have exceeded by 10 per cent the standard speed and quality for the grade, providing this standard is maintained in the applied writing. Third, adjustment should be made for the age of the child. Coordination of muscles is not well developed in small children. Pyle maintains that there should be no writing except blackboard or crayon writing on large paper in the first year. Freeman recommends blackboard and large pencil in the first and second years. The pen may be introduced in the third year. Fourth, expect and welcome individuality in style and form of writing. Allow for differences in position and movement. Investigators find that there is less variation in position than in other factors. Marked changes in adjustment of position is necessary for strongly left-handed pupils. Yet the variation must not becloud legibility. Printing press uniformity is impossible and unwise, contrary to human nature. Hand-made goods are marked by their individuality, so is handwriting.

Holley says, "The movements utilized in handwriting probably should be secured indirectly by focusing the child's attention upon a good product instead of upon the way of attaining it. There seems to be little relation between the form of movement that one uses and the quality of his handwriting. Individuals differ so much in their physical makeup that it probably is natural for them to vary widely in the ways in which they get results. A little freedom in the field of handwriting, probably, will do no harm."

From our discussion of individual differences, it follows that, DIAGNOSIS of individual difficulties is imperative. Diagnosis of difficulty and remedial instruction therefore involves **individual instruction** rather than class instruction. This is harder to do, but pays big dividends. We need less mass instruction and more, much more individual instruction in handwriting. An adaptation of the Morrison technique to handwriting is wholly feasible. Start the unit with the whole class. Then follow with individual help according to needs.

DIAGNOSIS

Teacher diagnosis of pupil errors does not solve our problem. That goes only part way.

Pupils should be taught to diagnose their own deficiencies in writing, using scales like the Ayres and the Freeman, as well as personal judgment of quality.

Pupils should know that these factors contribute to legibility: **Uniformity of slant, uniformity of alignment, quality of line** of the letters (smooth, regular, or broken); **adequate spacing** between letters, words, and lines, (uniformity, too close, too far apart); **letter formation** (large, too small, uniform, irregular, open, angles for curves as in m); **position**, develop an appreciation of the relationship between correct body adjustment and an efficient writing production. Gray adds to the above factors of **heaviness, of neatness, free from blotches, carelessness.** Miss Nystrom adds **irregularity of color** as another defect. But this has lower weighting than size, slant, letter and word spacing, beginning and ending strokes, and alignment.

We should equip the child with **methods of work** so that he will attack his writing problems intelligently.

"Think, children, think" is fragrance wasted on the desert air. Furnish an apperceptive mass for thinking. Give the criteria for thinking. Furthermore, when he is writing, the less thinking about mechanics of writing, the better. Good writing is automatic.

LEFT-HANDEDNESS

Another problem in individual differences is the left-handed pupil: About four per cent of pupils are naturally

(Continued on page 26)

The above scroll was made by Burton O'Mealy, 2026 S. E. 56th Ave., Portland, Oregon, for the Portland Community Chest. The scroll was presented by the mayor honoring the 1100 leaders of the Boy Scouts, Girl Scouts, 4 H Clubs, and other youth character building organizations.

"Mr. Meadows Says"
BY GEORGE A. MEADOWS
Pres. Meadows-Draughon
Business College, Shreveport La.

DO YOU KNOW BUSINESS ENGLISH?

The following test represents a lesson given at Meadows-Draughon College. The stenographer, secretary or accountant who expects to get very far in his or her profession must have a good command of Business English.

Read the sentences below and underline the words which you think should be used.

1. A fat man with a little boy WAS-WERE standing on a box.

2. A set of volumes WAS-WERE sent to brother John.

3. Each of the trains HAS-HAVE a sleeper.

4. Which of these coats LOOK-LOOKS best?

5. Have you WROTE-WRITTEN your lesson?

6. It was not ME-I.

7. THEM-THEY that study grammar talk no better than I.

8. What monument IS-WAS that which we passed?

9. Pleasure, and not books, OCCUPY-OCCUPIES her mind.

10. Sarah, will you please SIT-SET the pitcher on the shelf?

11. Ruth, will you LIE-LAY this picture in the box?

12. Politics IS-ARE the general talk at this season.

13. The wages of sin IS-ARE death.

14. WHO-WHOM did they say committed the crime?

15. They invited Sally and I-ME to the supper.

16. She never went to NO-ANY school.

17. I heard of HIM-HIS coming home.

18. Tom differs WITH-FROM Sam in opinion.

19. He sees WELL-GOOD for one so old.

20. The velvet feels SMOOTH-SMOOTHLY.

21. They waited for the committee to make THEIR-ITS report.

22. Bookkeeping is not AS-SO difficult as shorthand.

23. There are differences between you and I-ME.

24. It DON'T-DOESN'T seem possible that it is you.

25. WHO-WHOM am I supposed to be?

Check the words which you have underscored with the following list which shows the correct words you should have used in each sentence:

1. WAS	14. WHO
2. WAS	15. ME
3. HAS	16. ANY
4. LOOKS	17. HIS
5. WRITTEN	18. WITH
6. I	19. WELL
7. THEY	20. SMOOTH
8. IS	21. ITS
9. OCCUPIES	22. SO
10. SET	23. ME
11. LAY	24. DOESN'T
12. IS	25. WHO
13. IS	

A. W. KIMPSON

A letter has been received from our old friend and former contributor, A. W. Kimpson, who in renewing his subscription states that he has for the past 19 years been conducting a show card shop at 231 Pine Avenue, Long Beach, Calif. His son has been with him for the past eight years.

Mr. Kimpson has turned out some very fine pen work and engrossing and we hope that we may have the pleasure of seeing some of his recent work.

The Educator is always glad to hear from its old friends, telling us what they are doing and how they are getting along.

Roger L. Barnett is now employed as an engrosser in the M. L. Harris Studio in Chicago. Mr. Barnett is a young man of unusual talent. He is a nephew of the well-known penman and engrosser, C. A. Barnett of Cleveland.

The Zaner-Bloser Co.,
Columbus, Ohio,
Gentlemen;—This is a specimen of my writing after completing the work in Z. & B. Manual 96, and which is submitted with the hope of obtaining a High or Business School Certificate.
Sincerely yours,
Beatrice Edwards

A specimen by one of J. M. Tice's students in the State Teachers College, Whitewater, Wis. Mr. Tice is to be complimented on the dashy, excellent business writing secured from his students. It would be fortunate, indeed, if more normal schools trained their students to write like they do in Whitewater.

These letters were made by that renowned penman, L. Madarasz. The cut was loaned to us by our good friend, C. W. Jones, of Brockton, Mass.

Variety Capitals

Ornamental Penmanship

No. 15   **Script by the late A. M. Wonnell**

Signature writing is very interesting. To combine a number of letters systematically and skillfully requires thought. All crossings should be at right angles. The shades should be distributed fairly evenly and the spaces should be divided up into equal parts. The ovals should be of about equal size wherever possible to make them so. The joinings should be natural and not strained.

Study the above combinations and let us see your efforts in imitating them. If you can improve on any of the combinations do so. There are many ways of writing a signature. The more you study combinations the more skillful you become. Practicing on these combinations should help you to acquire more skill for writing plain business writing.

Study the location and shape of the shades. Watch the slant and above all get a light delicate touch.

If you do not have a well balanced oblique penholder send us your penholder and we shall be glad to check it over. It requires good tools to produce good work. Change your pen often.

                                        Editor

Tinted Cardboard Work

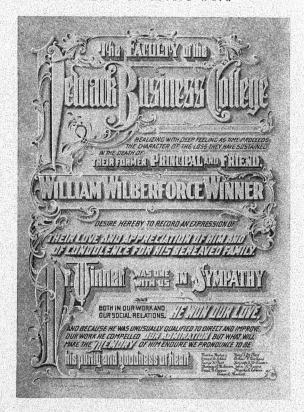

Very beautiful effects can be secured by using gray or colored cardboard, tinted washes, white and black ink.

Pencil out the entire design, being careful with the location, size, and form of each word and letter. Give the initial letters and ornaments extreme care.

Where a colored board is used it gives a pleasing effect to use washes of the same color.

This beautiful flourish was made by one of America's finest penmen, one whose work has not often appeared in penmanship magazines. This penman was O. A. Hoffman, who for many years was located in Valparaiso, Indiana.

This flourish shows a command of the pen equalled by but few. Place this specimen in your scrapbook along with your other masterpieces. The original of this beautiful piece was loaned to us by F. A. Hatchett, Benton, Ill.

A DISTINGUISHED INDIAN WAR VETERAN AND PENMAN

Colonel Albert Fensch maintains an unusual high interest in good handwriting. Each year in December he stocks up with a large supply of penmanship Christmas Cards which he sends to his many friends. Colonel Fensch is 80 years of age and is National Adjutant General of the United Indian War Veterans. He gives much of his time and experience to this work and is a real friend to the Indian War Veterans.

In 1878 he was engaged in a campaign against the Northern Cheyennes and in 1879 he was campaigning against the Southern Utes. He also participated in the campaign against the renegade Navajos and Apaches. In 1882 to '84 he was engaged against the Apaches and participated in the Sioux campaign in South Dakota in 1890 to 91. His services included the Spanish-American War, the Philippines and World War. He was awarded the Certificate of Merit for bravery in action against the Indians in Kansas in 1879. In the Philippines he was a dispatch messenger in hostile territory.

After the Spanish-American war he retired. Mr. Fensch has rendered very valuable service during three of the American Wars, and is at the present time working in the interest of the Indian War Veterans.

Mr. Fensch has also prided himself on his line penmanship and has never lost interest in the Queen of Arts. Whether Mr. Fensch would agree that the pen is mightier than the sword we do not know, but we do know that penmanship has occupied a very important place in his life.

Col. Fensch resides at 740 S. Hauser Blvd., Los Angeles, Calif.

THE COVER PAGE

The cover page this month was prepared by Claude D. Scribner, handwriting expert, engrosser, photographer, artist, and engraver of Springfield, Mass.

The story of C. D. Scribner would furnish excellent material for a real inspirational book, as he has had an extremely extended and valuable experience. The story of his life is an inspiration to any young man or woman interested in any phase of penmanship, engrossing or art. It is gratifying to have Mr. Scribner state that all through his experience his ability in penmanship and engrossing has stood by him. Mr. Scribner first came to Columbus to specialize in penmanship, engrossing and art in 1902. After qualifying himself he returned to Boston, his home town, and conducted an art school by mail for two years. He then went to Belton, Texas and worked for A. J. Embree, a man interested in pen work and who owned a fine printing plant and who also had taken a course of lessons in pen art from Mr. Scribner. Together they established a magazine known as "Pen and Ink Art" which was published by them for a year. The latter part of 1905 he went as artist with the great Texas Newspaper, The Dallas News, where he remained a year. He then went with the A. Zeese Engraving Company accepting a position as artist where he remained four years. Oklahoma City then called him where he worked with the Standard Engraving Company. He had charge of their art department for seven years.

In 1917 he went back to Dallas where he helped to illustrate the new Southwestern Buttler Bros. Big Catalog which required about two years. He then entered business with Mr. E. Suhler and established a commercial art studio. In 1922 he sold out his interest in the studio and went back to the art department of the Standard Engraving Company in Oklahoma City where he remained until 1924. He then received an appointment as Captain from the Governor's Staff and was given the Chair of Penmanship and Drawing at the State Military Academy at Claremore, Okla. In 1926 he returned to the A. Zeese Engraving Company of Dallas as a finisher and proofer in the Engraving Department. He remained there until 1929 when he went to the Service Engraving Company, San Antonio, Texas. We next find him in the Southwestern Engraving Shop at Atlanta, Ga.

The next year he went to San Francisco with the New Method Engraving Company, then back to Canton, Ohio. Later he went to Dallas with the Harper Standard Engraving Co.

In 1932 he established the Graphic Arts Engraving Company in San Antonio, Texas, and operated it for two years. The first part of 1934 he went with Norfolk Engraving Company, Norfolk, Va., as artist and engraver, where he had charge of the production for two years. For the past year he has been with the Phoenix Engraving Company, Springfield, Mass.

Mr. Scribner is a talented musician, receiving early training in music in Boston, and has played in most of the noted bands and orchestras in the Southwest. He played at the Greenwall Opera House at Dallas, Texas, matinees and nights for seven consecutive seasons, also in the Majestic Theatre, Dallas, and the Liberty Theatre, Oklahoma City. He also played with travelling bands such as Niller Bros., 101 Ranch Show Band, and many other notable bands.

He has studied penmanship personally and by mail with most of the notable penmen beginning with D. T. Ames, Chas. T. Rollinson, Zaner and Bloser, Dennis, Madarasz, Tamblyn, etc.

During all of these years he has given special attention to handwriting and questioned documents and has been in close touch with the men in the questioned handwriting work. He has had many cases in questioned handwriting in Oklahoma City where he has commanded the respect of those connected with the courts. He still follows questioned handwriting on the side, making examinations and reports on handwriting and questioned documents. He has made a special study of photography, chemistry, paper, ink, etc.

While in Oklahoma he established the Bureau of Engraving and Electrotyping Company and was a charter member of the first photo-engravers union in Oklahoma. He played professional music and carried a union card for twenty-two years.

Mr. Scribner is happily married and has one grown daughter.

The work on the cover page which Mr. Scribner has been so kind to prepare for us will give you some idea of his ability and some idea of what you may hope to see from Mr. Scribner in future issues of The Educator.

We feel proud that the founders of The Educator had a hand in training so capable and experienced an artist.

ORNAMENTAL CARDS

Some very fine cards written in ornamental have been received from L. A. Ware, 309 W. Harrison St., Bozeman, Mont. We wish to compliment Mr. Ware on the work he is doing.

PENMANSHIP TEACHER

Janith M. George

Miss Janith George is the penmanship teacher in Goldey College, Wilmington, Del. Miss George is securing excellent results from the students. We examine specimens from her students quite regularly and find the work up to our various certificate standards. Miss George is a very capable and well grounded teacher and is a very valuable addition to the Goldey Staff.

Goldey College has been noted for years for its exceptionally fine work in handwriting.

DOING FINE WORK

Along with a club of subscriptions to The Educator, we received a package of specimens from Mr. R. R. Reed of the Platt-Gard Business University, St. Joseph, Mo. Mr. Reed is still turning out his usual high-class work.

Canada's distinguished educator and penman.

This specimen was engraved from a print. The original was made many years ago by that prince of a penman, E. J. O'Sullivan, Montreal, Que., Canada. Mr. O'Sullivan has enjoyed the reputation of being one of the most skillful penmen on the continent.

GOLDEN WEDDING ANNIVERSARY BOOK

Probably the finest thing we have had the pleasure of examining in the way of a Golden Wedding Anniversary Book has been received from E. H. McGhee, the engrosser of Trenton, N. J. The book is bound in a fine blue seal skin cover trimmed in gold. It contains about forty pages, many of which are highly illuminated. Other pages contain photographs of the family with pen drawings. The book was presented to Mr. McGhee's father and mother. A book of this kind would be cherished by anyone, especially when prepared by their son.

COME AGAIN

A unique Christmas Card was received from **S. J. Shaw, 45 Santa Barbara Avenue, Long Beach, Calif.,** which consisted of a skillfully drawn portrait of himself by the use of a mirror. Mr. Shaw is one of the old guard in the penmanship work and finds the pen a very excellent way of spending his time.

In Memoriam

Sarah Katzenberg

Born March 8, 1864   Died October 8, 1935

Whereas, on the eighth day of October, 1935, the Almighty, in His wisdom, deemed it expedient to take from us our affectionate, tender, and sympathetic wife, mother, grandmother and aunt **Sarah Katzenberg**; and

Whereas, the earth that nourished her, the said Sarah Katzenberg, has claimed her mortal remains to be resolved to earth again; and

Whereas, she, the said Sarah Katzenberg has left behind her a bitterly distressed and grief-stricken husband, children and grandchildren; and

Whereas, she, the said Sarah Katzenberg was always an impartial, constant and faithful friend and member of the

Katzenberg Family Circle, Chicago Branch

Now therefore, be it respectfully and reverently resolved, that the date of our bereavement be and the same is hereby spread upon the records and minutes of the Katzenberg Family Circle, Chicago Branch, it being the date herein above set forth; and that date be commemorated with fitting ceremonies by the Katzenberg Family Circle, Chicago Branch in the next ensuing year, and for every succeeding year thereafter.

Dated at Chicago, Illinois, this second day of February, 1936.

Katzenberg Family Circle, Chicago Branch

Henrietta Katzenberg Friedman
Secretary

Pauline Katzenberg Rivkin
President

Music, when soft voices die,	Rose leaves, when the rose is dead,
Vibrates in the memory;	Are heaped for the beloved's bed,
Odors, when sweet violets sicken,	And so thy thoughts when thou art gone,
Live within the sense they quicken.	Love itself shall slumber on.

Percy B. Shelley

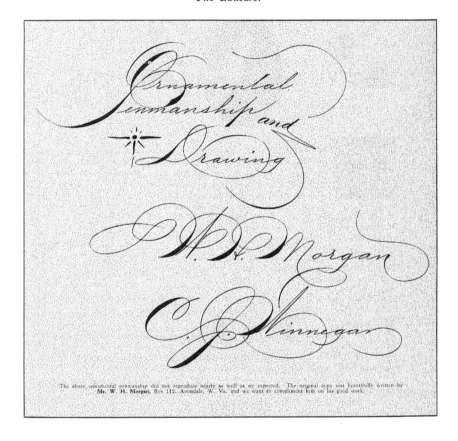

The above ornamental penmanship did not reproduce nearly as well as we expected. The original copy was beautifully written by Mr. W. H. Morgan, Box 112, Avondale, W. Va., and we want to compliment him on his good work.

Written by E. Iwasa, Misono 281, Kamata-ku, Tokyo, Japan.

BOOK REVIEWS

Our readers are interested in books of merit, but especially in books of interest and value to commercial teachers including books of special educational value and books on business subjects. All such books will be briefly reviewed in these columns, the object being to give sufficient description of each to enable our readers to determine its value.

Public Speaking for Executives, by Charles W. Mears, Dean, Cleveland Advertising School; Promotion Manager, Cleveland News; Author of "Salesmanship for the New Era." Published by B. C. Forbes Publishing Company, 120 Fifth Avenue, New York City, N. Y. Cloth cover, 194 pages.

A PRACTICAL BOOK WHICH WILL HELP YOU PRESENT YOUR MESSAGE CLEARLY AND FORCEFULLY.

This book aims to give practical help to the business man who is called on to speak before groups small and large, both within his organization and without.

In order to be practical it does not set up as its goal the perfection of genius. The possibility exists that a business man may lose some of his business prestige by becoming known as an orator. But there can be no question that the ability to stand before an audience and say one's say creditably is an asset both to the man and to his business.

The author writes as a business man. His lifelong interest in persuasive business communication has necessarily entailed public speaking. Through many profitable contacts with able speakers, chiefly in the field of business, through research into successful methods and by many appearances on the platform, using his own experiences as laboratory tests, he has learned what this book presents. Much of its material deals with what not to do. Rocks and shoals menace the public speaker as they do the mariner and, after all, it is by avoiding them that both speaker and mariner bring the ship safely into port.

FREE WITH YOUR SUBSCRIPTION TO FORBES MAGAZINE.

Whether you are a poor speaker or a good one, you will want to possess this fascinating and human study which covers all phases of the subject. Many books on public speaking are as dry as dust. Mr. Mears has made his message on how to succeed an entertaining story which makes public speaking an exciting adventure.

Remember, you get it FREE with a year's subscription to FORBES, New York City, the magazine that has clarified thoughts of business executives throughout America on all phases of business life.

This ornamental alphabet has been received from Mr. C. A. McCluggage, 2309 State St., Quincy, Ill.

Lessons in Modern Engrosser's Script

Prepared in the office of The Educator

No. 5

Practice the straight line exercise with a view of developing a uniform pressure. See if your shades are the same thickness at the top as at the bottom. Also try not to get your shades too heavy. It is better to have work neat and delicate than to get it too heavy and clumsy.

Work on the t exercise. Be sure that you get the turn at the base line graceful and that the tops are squared off. Ordinarily the squaring of the tops of the t should be done with one stroke of the pen and not necessarily retouched. We retouch only when a mistake is made.

Study the similarity between the a, t and d. The d is the same as the a and t combined. The t is an extended i and the body of the d is the same as the body of the a. Study the individual letters, then work upon the words. Practice each word separately and where necessary break the words up into individual letters and practice upon them. Be sure that your shades are uniform in thickness and not wedge shaped. Send your work to The Educator for a few free criticisms. Be sure to enclose return postage.

Be a real student of script. It is one of the most profitable lines of pen work.

CREATIVE SUPERVISION

(Continued from page 15)

left-handed. Experiments have shown that changing a strongly left-handed pupil to right-handed is liable to be injurious to the nervous system, manifesting itself in speech defects. Wallin disagrees. In St. Louis he found little evidence to support the notion that there was danger of bringing on speech defects from change. Parsons, in Elizabeth, New Jersey, also disagrees. He reports, "Not a single case of defective speech could be traced to reversal of manual habit." Although these two investigators seem to disagree with the results of other workers, yet the preponderance of evidence indicates

that changing a confirmed left-handed child is doubtful practice. If a child changes easily, showing that left-handedness is not persistent, or intrenched in his physical mechanism, no harm is likely to follow. These are probably not genuine cases of inherent left-handedness.

A teacher replied to an observer, "John always writes with his right hand in the writing class, and does very well too, but I let him use his left hand the rest of the time, because it is so much easier." This is sheer disregard of the laws of habit formation, to say nothing of the waste of time. If a left-handed child has progressed into the intermediate, or upper grades and writes well left-handed, by no means should his nervous mechanism be tampered with.

Two other reasons are advanced why children should write right-handed:

1. Left-handers are handicapped. School equipment is built for right handed individuals; for example, tablet arm-chairs.

2. Our custom of writing with the line moving to the right is adapted to right-handed people.

Summarizing: If change from left to right in early grades takes place without conflict, probably a wise procedure. If left-handedness is dominant, persistent, it is dangerous to attempt to change him, especially in upper grades. The weight of evidence seems to be that changing innate left-handers may result in nervous disorder, even speech defect.

A New Years Greeting

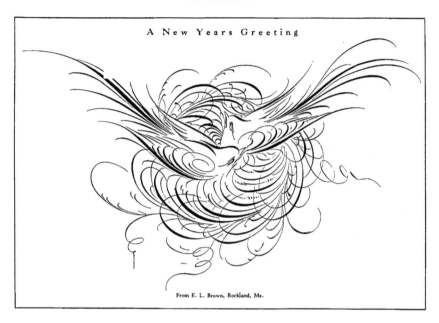

From E. L. Brown, Rockland, Me.

Signatures by M. A. Albin, 3823 SE 65th Ave., Portland, Oregon.

AS APPLIED TO ASPIRING PENMEN

Have confidence in yourself. Believe in your ability to master any style of pen work. Only by having faith in yourself, can you equal or excel the work of the masters. Have high ideals and back them up with midnight oil. You can if you will, regardless of what others think of you.

HOW TO RULE CARDS

Few penmen can write straight. On careful work where a straight line of writing is desired rule your cards with charcoal. An ordinary soft burnt stick will answer the purpose. Fold a card in the middle and rub one edge of the folded card over the charcoal; insert a card in the folded card and rub the fingernail along the edge containing the charcoal. A straight, clear line will be the result. The position of the line can be regulated by folding the card above or below the center. The charcoal line can be quickly rubbed off with a handkerchief. When ruling dark cards use soft chalk. It takes very little time to rule cards and it pays.

By the late S. M. Blue

Mr. Warner Dante Tomlinson.
Minneapolis, Minnesota.

Signatures written by O. E. Hovis, 88 Biltmore St., Springfield, Mass.

Portrait by J. B. Hague, The Haring Studio, 15 Park Row, New York City.

LESSONS IN CARD CARVING
By J. D. Carter, Deerfield, Ill.
Lesson No. 4

This lesson shows how Holiday cards, etc., can be made by combining knifemanship, pen work, and photography. First of all work out a good design and cut it as suggested by the copy. Practice on the flower. First draw several circles in order to get the proper shape. Let me see your efforts.

C. E. CHAMBERLIN WILL BE LISTED IN PROF'S WHO'S WHO

Lauded As One of America's Most Outstanding Educators By National Publication

Among the college professors recently receiving national recognition in publications which carry the names of noted men of America is Prof. C. E. Chamberlin, head of the department of business administration. The biography of Mr. Chamberlin appears in the "Who's Who in American Education" for 1935-36.

The sketch, with the abbreviations omitted, appears below:

"Chamberlin, Charles Edward, Professor Business Administration, San Marcos, Texas. Born May 21, 1879, Shelby County, Ill.; son of D. W. and Ruth Ann Chamberlin; married Eva S. Mayhew, Coles County, Ill. (Etna), March, 1905; children: Geraldine, Mildred, Jessie Lee.

"Education: M.S.C., Ellsworth College, Iowa Falls, Ia., 1910; B.S., Southwest Texas State Teachers College, 1927; M.A., State University of Iowa, 1930.

"Experience: Head Department of Commerce, Ellsworth College, 1908-12; head Department of Commerce, Jamestown College, Jamestown, N. Dak., 1913-15; Supervisor of Writing and Assistant in Department of Commerce, Chattanooga Public Schools, 1915-18; head Department of Business Administration and Auditor, Southwest Texas State Teachers College, 1918-20; head Department Business Administration and Treasurer, Southwest Texas State Teachers College, 1920-28; Professor of Business Administration, 1928-36.

"Member: Southwest Texas Golf Association; the local school Men's Faculty Club; local chamber of commerce. Research of general interest: Tests in Commercial Education and Public School Accounting. Fields of Special Interest: Commercial Education; accounting."

Mr. Chamberlin received his training in penmanship in the Zanerian College.

LESSONS FOR EDUCATOR
Just received a package of lessons from **E. L. Brown.**
You'll enjoy them.

Fairfield County Penmanship Contest

A Class Creed

I believe in Class Spirit – the foundation of all motives in school life.

I believe that success and achievement are only obtained by class and school unity, cooperation and team work.

I acknowledge that to be a member of a progressive and worthwhile class I must attend to myself only – not to others.

Ruth Thompson

Great interest is created each year in handwriting in Fairfield County by the contest which is annually held at the County Fair in Lancaster, Ohio. R. M. Eyman, the superintendent, is greatly interested in handwriting and he and his teachers are doing a great job of training the children to write well. The specimen herewith was written by Ruth Thompson, one of the eighth grade contestants. Her teacher is Hazel Wheeler, Pleasantville, Ohio.

By the late H. B. Lehman

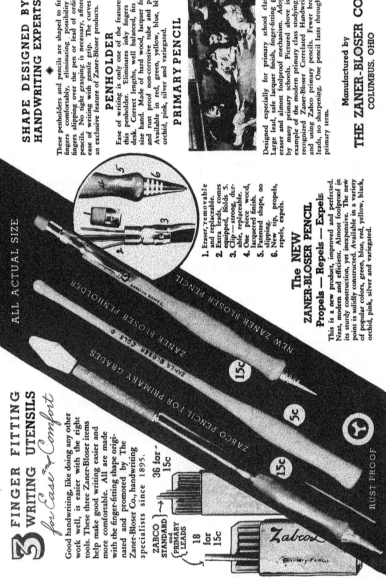

Vol. 42   FEBRUARY, 1937   No. 6

THE
EDUCATOR

ZANER-BLOSER CO.
COLUMBUS, O.

Summer School

You can attend the Zanerian any time dur-
ing the summer and take special work in

Methods of Teaching

Supervision

Blackboard Writing

Business Penmanship

Professional Penmanship

Ornamental Penmanship

Engrossers' Script

Text or Diploma Lettering

Engrossing

Illuminating

Commercial Lettering

Come and spend a profitable summer and prepare for something better.

Whether you are a student, teacher or professional you are urged to come to The Zanerian where you can improve your penmanship, your teaching, and your earning ability.

The Zanerian has trained thousands and has helped them to secure good positions.

Prepare for the future.

The Zanerian College of Penmanship

612 N. Park St.   Columbus, Ohio

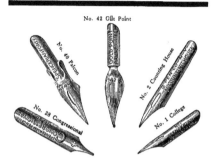

* PENMANSHIP * ENGROSSING * EDUCATION *

Educator

Zaner–Bloser Co. + COLUMBUS OHIO +

———— BY KEASHIRO ————

| Volume 42 | COLUMBUS, OHIO, FEBRUARY, 1937 | No. 6 |

PLACE OF HANDWRITING IN THE SCHOOL PROGRAM

The energy with which the child seeks to improve his writing will depend in part on his recognition of the importance of handwriting in modern life. The teacher should be aware of the many and abundant uses to which handwriting is put and of the value to the individual and to society of efficiency in handwriting, and should take advantage of favorable opportunities to pass on to the child information concerning these points.

Convincing evidence of the continued and ever-increasing importance of handwriting in the United States is found in the increase in the amount of handwriting materials used in recent years. For example, comparable figures for the years 1914 and 1927, taken from the Statistical Abstract of the United States, enable us to calculate the increase in the value of certain materials used in writing which were manufactured during these years. During the period between these years, the value of writing ink manufactured increased from $2,784,-000 to $5,342,000; the value of lead pencils increased from $8,328,000 to $24,500,000; and the value of fountain pens increased from $6,865,000 to $23,255,000. The opinion is sometimes expressed that the use of typewriters is rapidly displacing handwriting. That this is not the case is shown by the value of pens. The figures for typewriters are $24,500,000 and $69,-112,000.

These figures show clearly that the American people are doing much more writing than formerly, with pen and pencil as well as with the typewriter. Handwriting as a subject of instruction is, therefore, of increasing importance because of the sheer amount of handwriting which the American people do.

This argument from the amount of handwriting which is done may be supplemented by the argument that the quality of handwriting is important. Some time ago the supervisor of training of a large department store consulted a specialist in handwriting to get advice on the methods of improving the handwriting of sales clerks. Many of the tickets made out by clerks were so illegible that they caused serious errors in the delivery of goods or in the entering of records. Much of the carelessness in handwriting which characterizes the pupils of the present-day school is probably due to the low value they set on handwriting.

A TRIBUTE TO UNKNOWN TEACHERS

By J. W. Studebaker

Commissioner of Education.
(Reprinted from School Life)

This month carries our thoughts toward two great men in history—Washington and Lincoln. Each, as the world well knows, made an in-

J. W. Studebaker

delible contribution to human progress.

Today, as I write this message to schools of the Nation these men helped build, my thoughts keep turning to the teachers who are guiding the childhood of the Nation's future leaders.

Unknown, save to the few in his own community, the teacher stands with staid concern for the ultimate good of the boys and girls. He seeks to bring better order out of confusion. He keeps the faith in human endeavor that made Washington and Lincoln live on in the hearts of men and women.

We well know that cheers for great deeds may be muffled over night or silenced forever by tomorrow. Mere popularity may sink into oblivion when a new hero mounts the rostrum calling some different ware. Even the most loudly applauded effort becomes only a small part of the record of mankind.

But the teacher's daily work with his pupils, his quiet kindliness, his unassuming leadership, his thoughtful and gracious deeds, his silent inspiration—these live on in the hearts of men and women. These go into life's eternal pattern.

Great, even as Washington and Lincoln were great, is the teacher who leads the youth to an admirable way of life.

SWING OUT OF IT

Another milestone is past. No doubt at times the world seems cock-eyed and the people act daffy, and mayhaps you are a little that way yourself at times, but throw back your shoulders and don't let the blues get you down. Other successful men at one time or another felt just as you do.

THE EDUCATOR

Published monthly (except July and August) By THE ZANER-BLOSER CO., 612 N. Park St., Columbus, O.
E. A. LUPFER................................Editor
PARKER ZANER BLOSER..............Business Mgr.

SUBSCRIPTION PRICE, $1.25 A YEAR (To Canada, 10c more; foreign, 30c more) Single copy, 15c.
Change of address should be requested promptly in advance, if possible, giving the old as well as the new address.
Advertising rates furnished upon request.

THE EDUCATOR is the best medium through which to reach business college proprietors and managers, commercial teachers and students, and lovers of penmanship. Copy must reach our office by the 10th of the month for the issue of the following month.

Modern Handwriting

By E. A. Lupfer, Zanerian College, Columbus, Ohio

No. 6

BLACKBOARD WRITING

Lower grade students should be started at the blackboard. Blackboard work may be continued throughout the grades, and is especially recommended where students have special trouble in mastering certain letters. At the board the movement is large, the forms are large, and the tools are coarse which makes it easier to master writing first on the blackboard before using paper.

We have here a young man demonstrating how to write on the blackboard. Stand well back from the board, hold the chalk as indicated in the illustration between the first and second fingers and the thumb letting it point towards the palm of the hand.

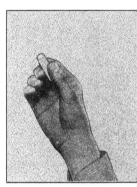

How to Hold Chalk

The teacher should use the blackboard frequently to show how good writing should be done.

How to Stand at Blackboard

Blackboard writing makes the handwriting lesson interesting. Try it occasionally.

Position of Paper

This illustration shows how the left-handed writer should hold his paper. Many times the left-handed writer is neglected until incorrect habits are established. It is important that correct position be secured from the beginning.

Correct position of the body, arm and pen.

Position of Hand

Top view showing the correct position of the hand and paper. Notice that the pen point is directly in front of the body.

Study the curvature of the fingers. Check your position. Do not grip the penholder.

The paper is tilted to the left.

Before writing this sentence see if your paper is in the right position. Do you move your paper in writing across the page? It is best to write directly in front of you and not too far to the right.

T Tuesday Tues. Thursday Thurs.

F February Feb. Friday Fri. F F

The above copy is given for added practice in making **T** and **F**.

t t t t t t t d d d d d d
l l l t t t t t t t t t t
d d d d d d d d d d d d d

The small letter **t** is an **i** with the extended part and the crossing. Be sure that the crossing is placed in the proper position and neatly made. Practice the retraced exercise without raising the pen.

The **d** is a combination of the **a** and **t**. Cover the top of your **d** and see if it makes a good **a**.

Keep comparing your writing with the copy. Know your mistakes and correct them.

Here is a fine lesson on the **K**. Write the sentence to find out what parts need more attention, then practice on those parts in a systematic way.

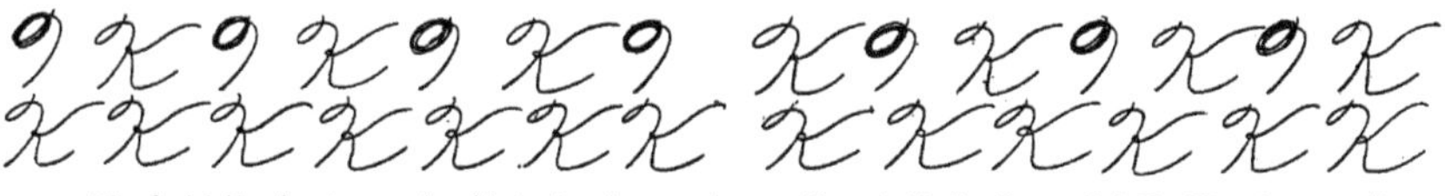

9 K 9 K 9 K 9 K 9 K 9 K 9 K
K K K K K K K K K K K K

The first letter to give you trouble in the above sentence will probably be the capital **K**. Therefore practice retracing the beginning part. This will help you to curve the first down stroke. Notice that the oval exercise should not be much more than one-third of the length of the entire stem. Make the exercise, then make the letter **K** and repeat. After practicing a page or two of the exercise try the **K** alone.

In this exercise attention is given to the final part of the **k**. Curve the top of the second part and have the loop swing around the first section, thus tying the letter together. See that the final stroke is the same as in the **i**.

Here are additional copies for practice. If you have mastered them go on to the next copy. If not, give them considerable of your time.

Again we spend a little time on the capital and small letter G. You will find the large tracer good form study. The third exercise is a new one. It is important in making the straight stroke just before swinging into the "boat hook" on the base line.

Additional practice is given for the capital and small letter **f**. The back of the small **f** should be rather straight. Therefore, the push-pull and retrace exercise should be mastered. Does each one of your f's contain an **i**? Get the top and bottom loops the same in size.

Give the muscles of the arm a good work out on the above exercises. These exercises are intended to help in making the capital letters, P, **B** and R. They will help to make the retraced stem and to get full graceful ovals.

Be sure that your pen pressure is no heavier on the downward strokes than on the upward strokes, and that you roll the exercises out freely. No finger movement should be used in making these exercises. To check the rate of speed time yourself with a watch. You should make about 200 down strokes per minute.

It takes a little more control to make a single retraced oval exercise than it does to make the running general exercise. See if you can make the first oval well shaped and keep on the track. Notice the direction as indicated by the arrows.

Changing direction of movements is always difficult and, therefore, the push-pull and indirect ovals are made together. You will see quite a resemblance between these exercises and the capital letter P. The main difficulty is in the size of the ovals.

Make the retraced stem, then swing gracfully and freely into the oval. Make the oval with a rather quick motion. Try to keep the oval about half as large as the retraced exercise.

P P P P P P P P P P P P P

Penman Penman Penman Pen

Penmen are in demand. P P

This copy contains some very good points for you to work out. Study the dotted lines and check marks.

You will notice in the second illustration that the oval should be as wide at the top as at the bottom. Avoid getting a point at the top of the P.

In the word **penman** notice the rounding turns. Are your turns all equal? Close the **a** for someone said that an open a indicates a talkative nature and you wouldn't want to be misjudged.

Preposition, Pronoun, Phrase . Paragraph.

Punctuation, Pronunciation, Parenthesis

Period. Proper name, Predicate, Participle

Additional interesting words for practice. Remember that after you have acquired a fair degree of skill in making an individual letter you should apply it in words and sentences. The more you use your writing the better it should become if you always do your best.

p p p p p p p p p p p

pen pin pure prepare prefix

The small p makes a very interesting lesson. Curve the beginning stroke and notice the height of the top retrace. It should go about twice as high as the oval. Retrace the oval about six times, then finish the same as the i. Notice that the letters when slant lines are drawn should be divided into about three even spaces. The oval or body part of the p is exactly the same as an inverted **a**. Since you close your a at the top you should close the p at the bottom.

Never get a loop at the top of the p.

Practice these easy words as well as other additional words. Have someone hold a watch while the class writes. See how many letters each one makes in a minute or two. Count only those letters which are legible and well made. This will prevent carelessness.

Freedom and Grace in Writing Depend upon a Free and Graceful Movement

Historical Background of Handwriting Instruction

From San Francisco Public Schools Monthly Bulletin

Consideration of the present status of handwriting and modern trends in instruction stimulates conjecture as to what is to be the future position in the curriculum of this controversial subject. Whether our alphabet in its present cursive form has completed the cycle of its development and whether there exists possibility of evolving newer and simpler forms are a few phases of this arresting problem.

Throughout the ages some means of expressing human experience has been indispensable to mankind. As the child of today crudely expresses his ideas with paint or crayon so in past ages primitive man set down in bold and lasting outline what his life experiences must have been. Between that sign-maker of yesterday and the child of today lies the story of the greatest contribution to the civilization of man, the development of the art of writing. It has required eight thousand years of transition for the alphabet to reach its present form. How the transition took place and through what steps writing became an integral part of the school curriculum is subject matter worthy of investigation.

Writing as a Tool of Expression in Ancient Times

The real source of all alphabets may be traced back to the pictographic expressions of tribal history, tribal legends, and tribal pastimes of earliest man. From the pictorial representation the next step was the symbolic exemplification of an idea which was later supplanted by the phonetic or sound sign. That briefly was the history of the alphabet. Probably the beginning of writing occurred in the early civilizations of Babylon and Egypt. Egyptian hieroglyphics were developed from elaborate pictures to a system of quick strokes, the essential elements of which were later simplified into the Phoenician alphabet.

The Egyptians were primarily concerned with writing as typified by their hieroglyphics, use of which was confined to the inscriptions carved on the walls of temples and palaces. For this reason the position of the hieroglyphs in the sentence was secondary in importance to the decorative effect. Hieratic writing was a simplified cursive form of hieroglyphic writing resembling modern shorthand and used chiefly in copying important literary productions. A third type of

writing called the demotic, was used for the ordinary purposes of daily life such as personal letters and business records. Reeds, bruised to give a brush-like appearance ·or sharply cut to resemble pens; stone, wooden, or ivory ink-wells resembling palettes; black or varying colors of ink imitative of the subject dealt with, constituted the writing tools of the professional Egyptian scribe.

The idea-signs, picture-signs, and sound-signs also prevalent in Babylonia finally evolved into a writing in which sound-signs for words and syllables were used. Like the Egyptians,

> We have faith in education as the foundation of democratic government . . . Our schools need the appreciation and cooperation of all those who depend upon them for the education of our youth—the state's most valuable asset. Our schools are today enabling America to achieve great results.— President Franklin D. Roosevelt.

the Babylonians failed, however, to develop a real alphabet of single letters.

Interesting methods of instruction in handwriting were followed in both Egypt and Babylonia. In Babylonia "primary" schools often numbered as many as 60 six-year-old children to the classroom. They practiced their writing lessons seated on low stools holding their damp clay tablets and grasping their pointed reeds tightly as they made little wedge-shaped marks on the wet surface. Perhaps our idea of blackboards is not so modern after all, for these children too, modelled their writing after the enlarged copy inscribed on a large clay tablet which was placed on a raised platform in front of the room. Wise old sayings comprised the subject matter of these earliest of "copy books." The schoolmaster pursued a definite technique of instruction which consisted of oral reading of the maxim, repetition by the pupils, and a careful explanation by the teacher of the distinguishing characteristics of the various signs. This was followed by close application of the pupils to their assignment, a difficult task because the script was small and compact and had to be fitted into a small area. Historians tell us that on many

of the unearthed tablets spelling and handwriting were perfect, a testimonial to the efficacy of their teaching method.

To the Egyptian schoolboy, learning to write was also a difficult task. He was confronted with the necessity of learning to draw the numerous hieroglyphs, memorizing them, and knowing how to assemble them in various ways to express meaning. The average school boy was required to learn only the chief hieroglyphs and those chiefly for religious purposes. Boys destined to become priests were expected to acquire fluency in the sacred script. Ordinary school boys were required to attain skill in the use of simplified hieratic script in common use. Writing exercises composed of sacred passages, words of wisdom, and magic formulas were first practiced in vertical lines on whitewashed boards or limestone slabs before the boys were permitted the use of the expensive papyrus paper. The career of professional scribe was the goal of most ambitious boys, so that special training schools existed for that purpose. Often boys were apprenticed to professional scribes already established in practice.

The Egyptians and Babylonians progressed no farther, however, than the selection of a certain number of signs to signify particular sounds or syllables. A single letter alphabet was the achievement of the Phoenicians, the so-called "Yankees of the Mediterranean." They were a practical people, and their commerce with other nations entailed a simplified method of keeping accounts and labelling their cargoes, so it was they who formed an alphabet with the unnecessary details omitted and arranged in the ordinary fashion that we have it today. With these early business men, speed and legibility were primary requisites in writing. Consequently they developed a method of quick writing which was easily read and composed entirely of consonants. They used only the capital form of the letter, not the capital and small letters as we do, and adopted the method of writing in long straight lines in either the left-right or right-left sequence as was suited to their convenience.

It was fortunate that in the westward progress of the Phoenician alphabet that the Greeks should be the first to receive it, for it was they who brought it to an almost final perfection. By adding the necessary vowel sounds and omitting non-essential consonants, they fitted it to the peculiar needs of their language. In its final form the Greek alphabet numbered twenty-four letters, and the left to right sequence of writing was eventually adopted by them.

In early Greece primary day schools flourished and schoolmasters were numerous. Writing occupied a place of prominence in the curriculum. Little boys practiced their writing exercises seated on stools. The copy was placed on a "white blackboard" with dark colored chalk. Writing tools for beginners consisted of the sharp-pointed metal stylus and wax "slates." Motivation played its part in instruction because it was only the good writers who were permitted to write with ink and reed on the prized papyrus rolls.

From the Greek sprang the Latin alphabet which was by far the most important of all alphabets. The dominance of the Latin people led to the use of their alphabet exclusively in the Roman Empire and, later, in all Christendom. It was the Latins who were the first of all the Italic people permanently to adopt the left to right sequence in writing. By 200 B. C., six hundred years after they had received it from the Greeks, the Romans had their alphabet completely formed in the capital shapes and phonetic values which were thenceforward retained. During the early period of the Empire two types of characters were used, the capital and cursive. The capitals were square-shaped and slightly ornamental and used entirely for inscriptions and writing of importance much as we employ the use of capitals today. The cursives comprised the running characters which were the originals of our small letters, their chief purpose being for correspondence or any written matter requiring speed. From this cursive hand developed a variety of handwritings, chief among which was the "semi-uncial" or sloped and slightly curved letter form which was later to evolve into the finest type of medieval script. It flourished in the monasteries and because of its clearness and compactness increased in favor until the temporary period of decline resulting from the invention of printing.

Methods of teaching handwriting in Rome were patterned after those of Greece except that girls shared in the severe and harsh instruction in the primary schools as well as the boys. Wooden tablets coated with wax were used as an economy measure so that the writing could be smoothed out and the tablet repeatedly used. Writing as a common school subject did not occupy the prominent place in the schools of Rome that reading and arithmetic held.

Writing as a Tool of Expression in the Middle Ages

Handwriting in the Middle Ages was a specialistic art for the purpose of copying and illuminating manuscripts. To the monasteries of that time we are indebted for the perfection of writing as a fine art. Both capitals and small letters were used. The Roman capital letters used by the monasteries resembled strongly our capitals, but were vertical in character. For writing on parchment or vellum they chose the "uncial" letters. These "uncials" were the forerunners of the simplified "semi-uncial" or "miniscule" letters used for many centuries in Europe. They had the requisite speed essential to the vast amount of copying necessitated by the revival of Greek learning. Thenceforward capital letters were used for chapter headings and the beginnings of sentences or paragraphs.

THE CHILD FIRST
America today faces a choice between the child and the dollar. It cannot afford not to put the child first. Any other policy destroys progress. Only as the schools move forward today can government, industry, and the standard of living move forward tomorrow.—The N. E. A. Journal.

The events which led to the compilation of the gospels were of great moment in the writing movement. They were directly influential in spreading the use of letters and in creating schools for the study of "reading and writing." The Gothic Bible, one of the most beautiful existing manuscripts, was a product of that period. The "black letter" form of letters variously known as Gothic or old English and first used by medieval scribes near the end of the twelfth century, has been attributed to the ingenuity of the Irish people. Because it was not easily legible it gradually fell into disuse.

Education in the Middle Ages was far from universal. Usually only children who lived near the monasteries attended school. The school life of the Anglo-Saxon child was typical of that of later medieval times. Writing methods were primitive. Books, hand-written upon parchment, were rare and costly articles which children were not permitted to touch. Words or sentences were therefore written on the blackboard by the "master." The children first recited them aloud and later traced them on wax tablets after the Roman manner.

The copy, set for boys to imitate in learning to write in the monastic scriptorium, was usually the doggerel line introducing every letter in the alphabet. It is not likely that there was

any considerable amount of written work in the Middle Ages in the nature of drill exercises. The "Vulgaria" which was the first book of exercises to be translated into Latin was printed in England in 1483, but it was probably for training in speaking rather than in writing Latin.

There were two main branches of good writing in everyday use, the "professional expert scripts" and the fluent "cursives" or running hand. Before the invention of printing, the scribes' scripts were brought to the highest possible perfection. The first printers strove to reproduce as nearly as possible the fine handiwork of the scribes. In Italy they adopted the style newly introduced by the Humanists. Consequently some of the earliest books are still artistically the most beautiful specimens of the printer's art. Previous to the development of printing, speed was the predominating factor in writing due to the need for copying so many documents.

Later Developments

After the Renaissance, letter writing, theme writing, and compositions of orations became a regular part of the school work, and involved the use of writing, although Latin speaking tended to minimize the relative importance of writing. When Latin speaking was given up in the schools in the seventeenth century, writing became far more important as the basis for school work. After the Reformation, primary schools increased and as a result most girls learned to read and write. Mulcaster, an early schoolmaster, advocated coeducation, saying that one ideal of training for girls was to "write fair and swiftly."

The advancement of writing in the Renaissance schools was seriously handicapped because the schoolmasters were often "very indifferent writers." Up to the end of the first half of the seventeenth century, grammar school boys learned to write either by attending in addition to their regular school a special writing school kept by a "scrivener" or arithmetic teacher or by receiving instruction from a "peripatetic scrivener" who visited the school at various intervals during the year. In the intervening time the schoolmaster was expected to provide practice in the mastery of the art. This was probably an example of school supervision as it existed in that period. The latter method prevailed chiefly in the country. Girls of well-to-do families frequently learned writing from tutors specially qualified in that subject.

The sixteenth and seventeenth centuries marked the period of great advance in the art of writing, particularly in England. School statutes in many instances made it a required subject of instruction in the schools. Schools definitely termed "Writing Schools" sprang up. Statutes enjoined the trustees to "teach the scholars to write which is observed according-ly." Probably such writing schools were the outgrowth of the monastic schools of the Middle Ages.

Famous schoolmasters, among whom were Ascham, Mulcaster, and Coote treated of the subject of handwriting instruction in their writings. Ascham in his "Scholemaster" advocated much more written work in the schools than he found. His championing of writing instruction was coupled with an intense pride in his own calligraphy. At that time, too, appeared the first copy books containing directions in posture and materials for practice. Brinsley spoke of the difficulties in teaching writing due to the "often changing of hands" by schoolmasters employing different kinds of writing. He wrote, as well, that children entering the grammar schools had had no adequate preliminary training in writing and reading. Coote contributed a methods book, "The English Schoolmaster," in which was provided a copy of handwriting. Richard Lloyd in his book dealt directly with the rules of the art of writing and the pedagogy of writing including detailed directions for posture, the use of copies, and the making of the pen. Peter Bales, one of the earliest and best known writing specialists of the sixteenth century, stressed the necessity for speed when he said "Man should write as fast as man can speak." Edward Cocker wrote over twenty books of calligraphy and he was the first to publish engraved copylines. The most comprehensive collection of all types of writing was contributed by George Beckham in the eighteenth century in his "Universal Penman." The invention of lithographic printing introduced a more reliable method of reproducing good copies of penmanship.

A survey of the school statutes of this period disclosed many interesting practices with regard to handwriting instruction. As early as 1541 in England pupil monitors assisted in the correcting of the writing papers of their fellows. Writing was often taught on Saturdays and half-holidays, or at any time outside of the regular day. Prizes in money were given and exhibits preserved for "posterity." Qualifications of writing masters consisted of the ability to write a "fair secretary or Roman hand" and the ability to impart this knowledge to children. During the seventeenth century the grammar schools charged extra fees for the teaching of writing. Class distinction prevailed in the better schools where only the children of the more prominent families were taught to write.

Developments in America

Simultaneously with the forward movement of education in England, schools were urged and instituted in America. The famous Massachusetts Law decreed the teaching of reading and writing. Parochial and charity schools taught writing to both boys and girls. In many districts the writing school became a regular institution. The School of the Three R's was a later outgrowth of the writing school. In preparation for college the child of seven or eight entered the Latin grammar school to learn reading, writing, and Latin. In the grammar school writing was often taught in a separate building by a resident scrivener or by a peripatetic scrivener. The art of the scrivener was very elaborate and was characterized by many flourishes. Teaching was chiefly by dictation and involved intensive drill. Due to its difficulty, lack of practical value, and the expense entailed for materials and special lessons, writing was not as important in the curriculum as reading.

The beginning of the district school in the nineteenth century marked a further step in the advance of handwriting as a school subject. Materials were cheaper and easier to obtain. Sometimes the master "set the copy" at the top of the paper for the pupils to practice. Often engraved slips were used. Caleb Bingham published a set of engraved lines. Exhibits at the close of the school term featured copy pages with "edges beautifully bordered with birds, flowers, and ships."

This period marked the appearance of the first copy book consisting of over twenty pages and containing ten or twelve practice lines below the copy which extended across the top:

PPPP Prac PP Practice
Practice makes Perfect

From the administrative viewpoint the Boston school system presented interesting practices. Children were required to purchase their pens, paper, and either printed or engraved copy slips. A period varying from thirty minutes to one hour was devoted to daily drill. Even in that period a "system of writing" was used and considered satisfactory.

The years between 1869 and 1930 marked the rise of the various systems of handwriting, some of which are still in vogue.

Modern Trends

The history of handwriting from its inception in primitive times until today indicates that it has served four chief purposes:

1. To indicate ownership

2. To commemorate deeds and persons

3. To keep records

4. To communicate thoughts to other persons.

The need today is for a rapid, legible, and an easily taught cursive system. The writing must be such that the thought expressed may be read easily and rapidly. The values which are important in developing a program of handwriting which will meet such needs are:

1. Individual and group instruction

2. A definite technique of study

3. A means for the individual pupil to progress at his own rate

4. A procedure which provides growth in the development of social habits as well as the skill to write

5. A use of tests as an aid in instruction

6. Group progress.

Recapitulation

The important steps in the development of handwriting and handwriting instruction may be summarized as follows:

1. The beginnings in handwriting were made in Babylon and Egypt where the earliest civilizations were produced.

Ornamental penmanship from the pen of Mr. C. A. McCluggage, 2309 State St., Quincy, Ill.

2. The Phoenicians simplified the Egyptian alphabet to meet the needs of commerce.

3. The Greeks added vowels to the alphabet of the Phoenicians and brought it to an almost final perfection.

4. The Latins seem to have been the first to adopt the Greek modification by which the letters took their permanent shape from left to right sequence.

5. The events which led to the compilation of the Gospels were of the greatest moment in the history of writing.

6. Out of the smooth and legible cursive script of the Romans developed the style of writing we have today.

7. The qualities of fluent cursive writing are three:

   (a) Legibility
   (b) Speed
   (c) Beauty

8. Writing in the Middle Ages was a specialistic art for the purpose of copying and illuminating manuscripts.

9. The first book of exercises, called "The Vulgaria" consisting of sentences for translation into Latin and vice versa, was printed in England in 1483.

10. After the Renaissance letter writing, theme writing, compositions of orations became a regular part of the school work and involved the use of writing.

11. The first English teacher to treat educationally of writing was Mulcaster.

12. One hindrance to the advance of writing in the Renaissance Schools was the fact that the schoolmasters themselves were often very indifferent writers.

13. Brinsley (1612) gave a full account of the practice of "writing teaching" in the schools.

14. The establishment of Charity Schools at the beginning of the eighteenth century led to the establishment of handwriting as a permanent subject in the curriculum.

15. The invention of lithographic printing introduced a more certain and exact method for reproducing good copies of penmanship.

16. The copy book made its first appearance during the great educational awakening in America, 1838-1861.

17. Horace Mann said, "Handwriting is one of the most important aids in the acquisition of all parts of written language work."

18. The need today is for a rapid, legible, and an easily taught cursive system. We need to write so that our thoughts may be read easily and readily.

Man has always experienced the urge to express himself in writing. The adaptability of this tool of expression to his need and purpose is the theme which is interwoven in the history and development of writing. Perhaps this need is the vital factor which will determine the future course of handwriting as a school subject.

Rosamond DuBois is a student of J. M. Tice, in the State Teachers College, Whitewater, Wis., where she is preparing as a teacher. We receive hundreds of specimens from Mr. Tice's students which show dash and grace, such as the work above.

"Mr. Meadows Says"

BY GEORGE A. MEADOWS

Pres. Meadows-Draughon
Business College, Shreveport, La.

Some noted authority has said that TECHNICAL TRAINING counts for 10 per cent and PERSONAL QUALITIES for 90 per cent, when it comes to making a success in life.

Assuming this to be correct, and that you are giving the necessary time to your course of training, is it not well for us to give more thought and study to the development of the necessary PERSONAL QUALITIES?

First, let us take PERSONAL APPEARANCE: That's the first thing that an employer or the public sees and is influenced—FAVORABLY or UNFAVORABLY—by. If our appearance is one of neatness, from a clothes standpoint; if we radiate cheerfulness and happiness; if our appearance and manners are such as to win confidence and make people like us and want to do business with us, that, of course, is going to have a great deal to do—more than anything else, in fact—with our making a success.

Then, we must not overlook energy or industry and initiative. People like to have people around them who are quick to think and move and who do not tire out easily; people who seemingly enjoy their work and who do not mind how much they do or how long the hours; they also like to have people around them who can see and find things to do, without having to be told; people who can manage to keep themselves busy when the employer, or his immediate superior, has other things that require his attention.

Then there is CHARACTER, which, perhaps, should be listed as the FIRST requirement of success, for, without character, there can be no genuine, lasting success. Character inspires confidence, which causes people to trust us and come to depend on us. To say that one is of good character, means that he is honest, trustworthy,

and dependable—something absolutely required, if one is to advance very far in the business world.

Loyalty, like some of the other personal qualities required, should, perhaps, come under the heading of character; still it is one of the personal qualities that should be emphasized. Every business establishment and institution is looking for employees who can be depended upon to be 100 per cent loyal—young men and women who would never hesitate to boost or defend the establishment or institution when the occasion presented itself.

One's attitude and the ability to adjust himself have a great deal to do with his success in life. A person must be agreeable and must have a cheerful, optimistic outlook. He must also have the ability to get along with other people—must use tact and diplomacy and avoid friction.

AMBITION is another very important personal quality when it comes to achieving success. As I have often said, it is the DRIVING force in one's life. It is the thing that makes us feel that we must keep on keeping on; that there are no such words as "can't," "cannot," or "impossible." Really, if we have ENOUGH AMBITION, we can do almost ANYTHING we set our hearts on doing!

IMAGINATION is another quality that is very essential, if we are to succeed in life, for unless we are able to visualize things, to see ourselves succeeding in a big way during the years to come, we can hardly hope for more than mediocre success. Someone said years ago, during the days of the Model "T" Ford and the expensive, luxurious Cadillac, "If you want to ride in a FORD car, THINK Ford; if you want to ride in a CADILLAC, THINK Cadillac!"

To develop the afore-mentioned

qualities, one only has to do a little ORDINARY thinking as he goes along —just keep these fundamentals, or principles, IN MIND. If one will DO that, and he is PERSISTENT enough, and has ENOUGH AMBITION, he can create a demand for his services— make people WANT to hire him—go far in the world!

$1580.00

Minneapolis, Minn., Apr 2-07

National Bank of Commerce

Pay to James M. Irwin & Co or order

Fifteen Hundred Eighty Dollars

D. B. Moon & Co.

By F. B. Courtney, Detroit, Mich.

R. L. Turner.

S. B. Brown

Harrison

H. Harmon

P. R. Spencer

G. W. Eastman

W. P. Cooke

W. H. Doughty

G. A. Grimes

Ornamental Penmanship

No. 16   **Script by the late A. M. Wonnell**

Ornamental penmanship helps one in acquiring skill in business writing. It lightens the touch, gives one more freedom and force, and refines the shape of the letters. Every teacher can profitably devote some of his spare time to the practice of ornamental penmanship.

Ornamental penmanship is appreciated by the average person. Students delight in seeing fine ornamental penmanship. It, therefore, creates confidence in the minds of pupils when the teacher is able to write a skillful ornamental hand. It is a fine art and should not be confused with a plain style of business writing for business purposes. It is a help in mastering business writing rather than a final style for business purposes. Ornamental penmanship can be used to advantage in social correspondence. Those of you who like individuality certainly can get plenty of individuality into your writing by studying ornamental penmanship. If you desire to get a little satisfaction and pleasure out of life other than dollars and cents alone, get out your oblique and work on these lessons.

Practice each letter separately, especially those letters with which you have trouble. Study the location of the shades. Swing into the shades with a free movement in order to get clear cut lines.

A nice shade is one which bulges with considerable snap. The shade is made by increasing the thickness quickly and diminishing quickly. Begin and end every shade with a hair line. Have the shades at the bottom of capitals **N**, **H**, etc., swing into a hair line. It is beauty and grace we are after in ornamental penmanship; therefore, look well to your pens and ink. Change your pen often or whenever needed. If your ink becomes too thick, thin it with water.

In ornamental penmanship one is allowed to write slower than in business writing and the pen may be raised more frequently. The shades, too, afford one some rest. At least it seems that the shading on the small letters makes writing easier rather than more difficult.

Let us see your best efforts on the above copy. If you will send postage, a few free criticisms will be given you. Let us see what you can do.

A Penmanship Quiz

By W. A. Larimer, Instr., North Texas State Teachers College, Denton, Tex.

1. Bending the first joint of the first finger...indicates excessive pressure on the penholder.

2. Figures............. and .... extend below the line of writing.

3. The upper-loop letters ...., ..., ..., ..., and .... extend 3 spaces above the base line.

4. Figures 3 and .... compare closely in the size and form of their lower parts.

5. Capital Q is an enlarged form of figure ....

6. The capitals ...., ..., ..., ..., ..., and .... should not be connected to following small letters.

7. Small u has .... stops in it.

8. Small ...., ..., ..., and .... end alike with a "sore thumb".

9. Commendation of good work ....the best students.

10. .... and ....are two essentials in good writing practice.

11. The spacing of the letters in a word should be...

12. The main slant of writing is determined by the direction of..................
....lines.

13. The pen should be so held that it points to the ....of the elbow.

14. A teacher of handwriting needs to be a good writer on the....................
....

15. Correct writing posture is ....to the health.

16. The .... is used frequently by the good teacher of writing for illustration purposes.

17. The value of good writing is much ....-rated in our schools.

18. Small............contains the longest straight line in the small letter group.

19. Capitals ...., ..., and .... have the same type of base formation.

20. Small .... and t are the same height above the line of writing.

21. The last part of capital W is the same general form as final ....

22. The members of the "a" family are ...., ..., ..., ..., and ....

23. Numerical count refers to the number of distinct.................................... used in making the letter.

24. Instruction to the class should be .... by individual instruction and personal criticism.

25. The removal of the upper stem of small d leaves small ....

INSTRUCTION: Do, in each case, exactly what the question or statement calls for.

1. **Write** the word "Blackstone" and show how you would test it for slant

....

2. **Make** oval drill to use in developing capitals E and C. **Show** direction by using arrow and name the oval.

....

3. The letters made one space high (one-fourth the height between lines) are:

....

4. **Make** "figure 8" drill and five letters that make use of this movement.

....

....

5. The numerical count for the following form is: (Place figure on blank.)

E............, B............, M............, f............,
4............, G............, a............, Y............,
L............, q............

6. **Write** the word "Pittsfield" and show how you would measure it for correctness of heights of letters.

....

7. **Make and name** the oval drill to be used in developing capitals N, Q, Z.

....

8. **Write** the letters, capital and small, that are made three spaces above and two spaces below the base line. (Total length.)

....

9. **Write** five words that may be used in developing form and use of small "g".

....
....

10. **Write** five letters that may be found in part, at least, in small "J".

....

(See how many of these questions your class can answer.)

A beautiful flourish by M. A. Albin, principal in the Pacific Business College, Portland, Oregon. The title of this drawing is "The Early Bird Catches the Worm".

A FRIEND OF THE BUS

Johnnie Brown was kept after school to write his misspelled words fifty times. The artist, David J. Person, Carthage, N. D., made the above sketch of him after Johnnie discovered that the schoolbus had gone and his teacher had to haul him seven miles in her machine to his home. Let there be more buses.

MEADOWS ELECTED DEPARTMENT HEAD OF NATIONAL BODY

George A. Meadows, president of Meadows-Draughon College, and regular contributor to the Educator, has returned from Cleveland, Ohio, where he attended the National Association of Accredited Commercial Schools and the National Commercial Teachers' Federation. Approximately 1,000 persons, from all sections of the country, attended the two conventions.

Mr. Meadows had the honor of being elected president of the private schools department of the National Commercial Teachers' Federation.

At a recent meeting in Dallas, Mr. Meadows was elected regional secretary of the National Association of Accredited Commercial schools. This association carries approximately 250 of the leading private commercial schools of the United States on its membership rolls.

Mr. Meadows was accompanied to Cleveland by Mrs. Meadows. They visited leading commercial schools in Chicago as well as in Cleveland and other cities.—Shreveport Journal,

Charlton V. Howe

Earl A. Lupfer

E. C. Enriquez

These exquisite cards were written by E. C. Enriquez, Pineda, Pasig, Rizal, P. I.

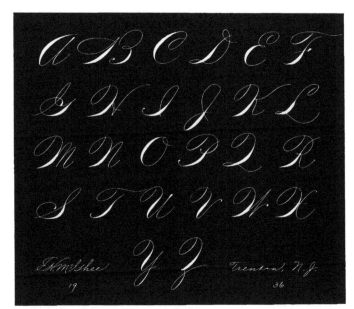

This beautiful alphabet was made by E. H. McGhee, the engrosser of Trenton, N. J., whose lessons and specimens have appeared in our columns.

These signatures were written by M. Otero Colmenero, the skillful penman of San Juan, P. R.

Lessons in Card Carving

By J. D. Carter, Deerfield, Ill.

Lesson No. 5

In Lesson No. 5 I have attempted to show one of many ways to use card carving on any occasion in decorating cards that have been printed on press by using decorative type.

I am hoping a number of you have followed the work in card carving so you can use the above method in making interesting things that will appeal to your friends and all that may see your work.

If you should want a printing cut made special for printing I am sure the Zaner-Bloser Company can do it to your complete satisfaction.

The carving in this lesson can be done with knife, pen, or a safety razor blade in a special holder. The cutting of the rose can be more easily made with the back end of a pen ground special for that kind of work.

I am interested to know that each of you have made progress in your work and shall be glad to exchange a specimen of card carving with the readers of The Educator that enjoy doing any kind of card carving.

You send me some of your best work for exchange on card and I will attempt to send in return something as good from work of my own choosing.

What have you? May I be favored with a pleasant exchange?

Criticism on your lesson and return of same if return postage is enclosed.

42,000 BOYS IN THE CCC CAMPS ARE TAUGHT TO READ AND WRITE

It is reported that the above number of young men have been taught the art of reading and writing. It is difficult for one to realize there are so many illiterate young men in the United States. However, when you stop to consider the number of letters which the average office receives from business men whose signatures are illegible we are not surprised at the large number of young men not being able to write. When we receive an illegible signature to an order it is naturally provoking, for ordinarily poor signatures are an indication of lack of care rather than a lack of ability.

Louis Teller, 948 N. Plankinton Ave., Milwaukee, Wis., writes very beautiful engrossers' script. The Educator is always anxious to see skillful work from anyone.

INTRODUCING PRINTING

In the first and second grades of the Chicago Public Schools printing is to be taught in place of cursive writing. Many school officials will watch the results of this change with much interest.

A. J. Williard, the penman, is now employed in the Pennsylvania State Department at Harrisburg, Pa. Mr. Williard is doing unusual skillful pen work. His pen flourishes are especially attractive.

THANKS

An attractive ornamental letter containing a much appreciated list of subscriptions is hereby acknowledged from J. W. Hepburn of the Hepburn Business College, Calgary, Alta., Canada.

IDENTIFIED

He: "That driver ahead must be Harold, the boy who failed to pass the finals."

She: "Why?"

He: "He seems to be as careless with his driving as he is with his handwriting."

Chicago   Illinois

To all to whom these Presents may come

GREETING

s an expression of the high personal esteem and fraternal regard in which

Elmore J. Green

is held by our members, and in recognition of the valuable contribution he has rendered to the Catering profession by creating such high ideals in cuisine, we have on this twenty-third day of August, A.D. 1933, unanimously elected him an

Honorary Member

In Witness Whereof, We have hereunto set our hands and caused the seal of The International Stewards' and Caterers' Association to be affixed.

Raymond J. Kief
President

Wm. H. McMahon
Secretary

A very fine piece of engrossing by C. L. Cook, of the Harris Studio, Chicago, Illinois. Each piece of work we receive from Mr. Cook seems to be a little better than the preceding ones. The lettering and the dainty ornament in this piece are particularly fine. Also notice the strong script. We congratulate Mr. Cook upon his fine work.

A pen drawing by the late P. W. Costello. While his business was engrossing, he delighted in making pen drawings and acquired a high degree of skill in portrait work.

There is no accomplishment a young man or woman can possess equal to a good handwriting. Beautiful penmanship is the key to the favor of business men and those who acquire it are sure to be wanted in business.

Written by: H. Moriyoshi, No. 24, Showamachi, Sumiyoshiku, Osaka, Japan.

NEW PENMANSHIP TEACHER

The West Virginia Business College recently employed Kathryn Payne to take charge of their penmanship work. Miss Payne is a former student of Miss Alma Shackleford and Kelvin McCray, both Zanerians. Miss Payne is a college graduate and is trained in business college work.

Mr. **Fong Dong Chu**, Box 25, Kapaa, Kauai, T. H., states that he did quite a good business around Christmas, doing pen work. He sold over 120 handmade Christmas Cards, a sample of which he sent us. It is composed of ornamental penmanship, lettering, knifemanship, pen drawing and color work. All in all it is very pleasing, delicate workmanship.

Mr. **J. G. Wootton** is teaching in the Draughon's Business College, Winston-Salem, N. C. Mr. Wootton is an expert penman.

Lessons in Modern Engrosser's Script

Prepared in the office of The Educator

No. 6

[handwriting practice specimens in engrosser's script: letter drills and words including "bills bulbs", "husk black", "effort offhand bluffed", "comfort flaked friendship luck"]

The loops should be three spaces high and of uniform size. The tops are rounding and full. Study the straightness of the backs. There are many details to master in this lesson. You can not make good letter forms unless you have a good mental picture of them. Study first, then practice much.

THE EASTERN COMMERCIAL TEACHERS ASSOCIATION AND THE BUSINESS EDUCATION COUNCIL

Coincident with the significant changes of the past twenty years in our political, social, and economic life, commercial education made phenomenal strides in our public and private schools. With the changing conditions of this period, new problems presented themselves to commercial educators. None proved more challenging than the preparation of commercial students for gainful occupations, properly trained to meet the demands made by employers.

Two years ago a movement was initiated to seek a satisfactory solution of this problem. As the first step, the Business Education Council was organized under the sponsorship of the Eastern Commercial Teachers Association and the National Office Managers Association. Two of the outstanding aims of this Council are the standardization of vocational objectives in commercial education and the construction of standard tests for business employment.

Frequent conferences have been held by the Council and sub-committees have been diligently making a thorough study of every phase of the problem. Their investigations and efforts have resulted in the formulation and administration of tests in the following subjects: Stenography, Typewriting, Bookkeeping, Machine Calculation, Filing, General Information, and Fundamental Operations. In form, scope, content, and administration, these tests differ considerably from the traditional academic type of testing in these subjects. In addition, a personality rating chart has been devised.

A detailed report of the accomplishments of the Business Education Council will be made and plans for the future outlined at the annual convention of the Eastern Commercial Teachers Association which will be held on March 24, 25, 26 and 27 at the Hotel Statler, Boston, Massachusetts.

DESIGNING AND ENGROSSING

By E. L. BROWN

Rockland, Maine

Pen Drawing Cover

Simple designs are often more effective than elaborate ones, likewise short speeches often make more lasting impressions than great orations. Therefore, your constant aim should be in the direction of simplicity. However, good judgment must ever be a leading factor whether your work is elaborate or simple in design.

Lay off your drawing about one-third larger than the copy, or make a rough sketch same size of design on cover. It is always better to make small sketches giving special attention to form, arrangement and balance in the design, then enlarge them to the desired dimensions. Pen drawings are usually made larger than the required cut (one-third to one-half larger) but this is not always necessary. This design represents a Northern winter effect, and would make a nice Christmas or New Year's card if reduced in size.

The old home nestled in the mountains surrounded by snow-covered spruces, and the smoke curling upward from the chimney give impressions of a calm, Northern winter evening. One can easily surmise that a delicious supper is awaiting the man of the house who is wending his way through deep snow, soon to enjoy the comfort and happiness of the family fireside. Modern inventions have changed much of the charm and character of the olden times, when women wove their cloth; ox-teams plowed the fields, and men hunted the woods for fresh meat.

Pen technique is a fascinating study. The pen work of Franklin Booth is charming in finish and effect, and his illustrations which appear from time to time in the magazines are worthy of careful study.

Make a pencil drawing suggesting color tones before doing the pen work. The form and spacing of the lettering is most important, while the balance and proportions of the other parts of the design must be carefully observed. Two pens, one fine and the other coarser, Zanerian ink will be needed. Bristol board or heavy drawing paper with a smooth surface is recommended for pen drawing for reproduction.

Study color values and note the distribution of the lights and darks, and aim for harmony between the light, half tones and darkest areas. Add dark areas first, following with half tones leaving the white paper for strongest lights. The background should be uniform in tint and consist of short, broken parallel lines. The white flecks indicate snow although the moon is smiling quite brilliantly behind the stately spruces. Oh, yes, we've seen it snow when the moon was shining, we've also seen it rain when the sun was smiling upon us. Use the coarse pen for dark parts of spruces, and the fine pen for snow or trees, mountain and foreground. The letters in words "The Educator" should be outlined on right by a heavy line; the curves were made free hand, the straight lines were ruled.

The best work sent in last month was that of Otis Sked, Jr. of Wilkes-Barre, Pennsylvania.

We are waiting for an opportunity to help you in the way of criticism and suggestions. It's up to you.

Mr. Rafael Angel Maldonado, P. O. Box 1333, San Juan, Puerto Rico, is a skillful ornamental penman. Of the Educator he states, "The Educator helps me a lot because of the inspiring work of the great masters. We young people really appreciate your efforts."

B. G. Johnson of College Place, Washington, is still writing a very beautiful ornamental hand as shown by the cards received from him. As part of his duty in the Walla Walla Business College he teaches penmanship.

This beautiful page of lettering and drawing is a product of M. Shinada, Yokomachi-Niizu, Niigata-ken, Japan.

Tamblyn Studio Changes Ownership

Dear Lord, in the battle that goes on through life.

I ask but a field that is fair,

A chance that is equal with all in the strife

A courage to strive and to dare;

And if I should win, let it be by the code,

With my faith and my honor held high;

And if I should lose let me stand by the road,

And cheer as winners go by.

C. W. JONES

You have been enjoying the masterful pages of pen work furnished The Educator each month by C. W. Jones, Brockton Business College, Brockton, Mass. Few of you, however, realize just how much Mr. Jones has been doing for you. He has gone to a great deal of expense in having these plates engraved and he is also offering our readers some unheard of offers in the way of books. Having published books for years we know it costs a great deal to have penmanship books published. If you are interested in fine penmanship books you will never regret having some of his books in your library.

Mr. Ira Short, 503 Marshall Ave., St. Paul, Minn. has made decided progress in his Ornamental Penmanship. His work is full of snap and skill.

Some very skillfully executed ornamental cards are hereby acknowledged from **E. Benguria,** Manrique No. 2, Apt. No. 7, Habana, Cuba.

About the first of September Stephen A. Ziller purchased the F. W. Tamblyn Studio, Kansas City, Mo. Mr. Ziller is a young man of excellent qualities, with a very promising penmanship future.

We first met Mr. Ziller in 1930 when he came to Columbus to specialize in penmanship and engrossing. The quality of his pen work and his progress were remarkable. He is exceedingly painstaking and accurate and has a good foundation from the standpoint of business training.

In taking over his new duties he assumes responsibilities which naturally would tax the ability of an older man, but knowing him as we do we have confidence in his ability and predict

Roger T. Ellzey

Stephen A. Ziller

that he will become a very prominent figure in the penmanship world.

Roger Ellzey, who was employed by the studio, has been retained by Mr. Ziller. Mr. Ellzey is also a young man of unusual ability in penmanship and engrossing. He, too, came to Columbus where he studied pen work. The progress of Mr. Ellzey, like that of Mr. Ziller, was unusually rapid. These two young men make an excellent team and their work which appears on the opposite page bears out our prediction that these young men have a very bright future.

We are proud of these boys and are delighted to see them safely embarked in the penmanship business.

Love birds by that talented penman, A. J. Williard, Harrisburg, Pa.

29

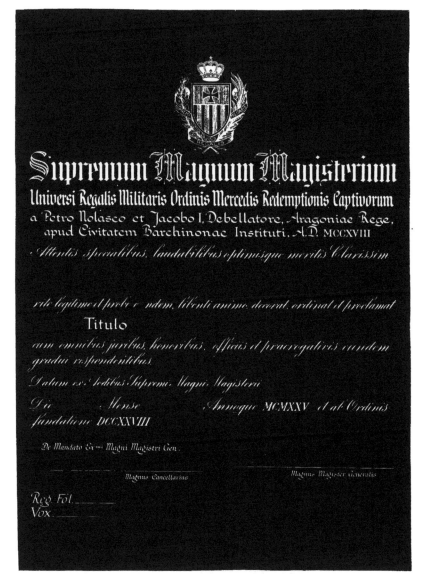

Supremum Magnum Magisterium
Universi Regalis Militaris Ordinis Mercedis Redemptionis Captivorum
a Petro Nolasco et Jacobo I, Debellatore, Aragoniae Rege, apud Civitatem Barchinonae Instituti. A.D. MCCXVIII

Attentis specialibus, laudabilibus optimisque meritis Clarissim

rite legitime et probe e ndem, libenti animo, decerat, ordinat et proclamat

Titulo

cum omnibus juribus, honoribus, officiis et praerogativis eumdem gradui respondentibus

Datum ex Sedibus Supremi Magni Magisterii

Die   Mense   Annoque MCMXXV et ab Ordinis fundatione DCCXXVIII

De Mandato Ex.mi Magni Magistri Gen.

Magnus Cancellarius   Magnus Magister Generalis

Reg. Fol.
Vox.

This beautiful page of engrossing was done by Stephen A. Ziller and Roger Elizey, of the Tamblyn Studio, Kansas City, Mo.

These inimitable signatures were prepared by Rene Guillard, Box 234, Evanston, Ill.

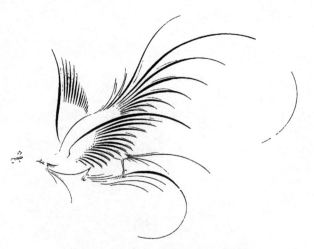

A simple effective flourish from the pen of H. S. Blanchard. The original was
loaned to us by Rosario Babin, Berlin, N. H.

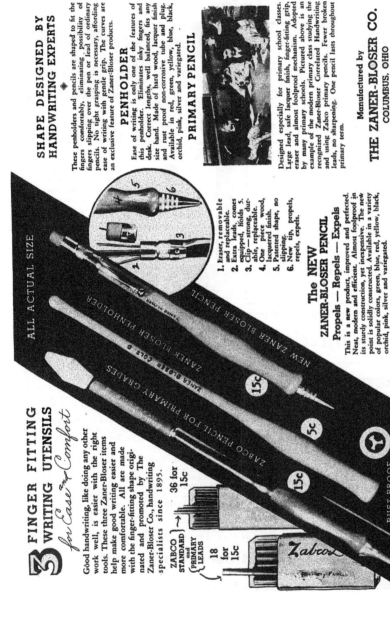

EDUCATOR

THE ZANER-BLOSER COMPANY
COMPANY
COLUMBUS, OHIO

Published monthly except July and August at 612 N. Park St., Columbus, O., by the Zaner-Bloser Company. Entered as second-class matter November 21, 1931, at the post office at Columbus, O., under Act of March 3, 1879. Subscription $1.25 a year.

Summer School

You can attend the Zanerian any time during the summer and take special work in

    Methods of Teaching

    Supervision

    Blackboard Writing

    Business Penmanship

    Professional Penmanship

    Ornamental Penmanship

    Engrossers' Script

    Text or Diploma Lettering

    Engrossing

    Illuminating

    Commercial Lettering

Come and spend a profitable summer and prepare for something better.

Whether you are a student, teacher or professional you are urged to come to The Zanerian where you can improve your penmanship, your teaching, and your earning ability.

The Zanerian has trained thousands and has helped them to secure good positions.

Prepare for the future.

The Zanerian College of Penmanship

612 N. Park St.   Columbus, Ohio

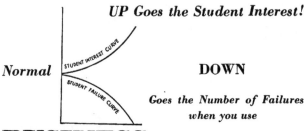

Volume 42   COLUMBUS, OHIO, MARCH, 1937   No. 7

The National Association of Penmanship Teachers and Supervisors

Announcement of the Eighteenth Annual Meeting, Wardman Park Hotel, April 29, 30, May 1, 1937.

The Eighteenth Annual Convention of the National Association of Penmanship Teachers and Supervisors will be held at the Wardman Park Hotel, Washington, D. C., April 29, 30, May 1, 1937.

The change in the meeting place for the 1937 convention from that voted upon last year was made in response to numerous requests received from members in various parts of the country that the convention be kept in the United States.

Washington offers the most alluring climate of any city in the country at this time when our association is holding its convention in Washington. The scenic beauty of Washington in the spring is noted throughout the world. All who have ever been in our capital city at this season invariably resolve to return for a second visit and those who have never been here will now have a twofold incentive to plan a visit to Washington and attendance at the National Association of Penmanship Teachers and Supervisors Convention in the same tour.

A very attractive and comprehensive program for these three convention days is being arranged. Outstanding speakers from various walks of life, educational, civic and business have been obtained to present addresses at the convention together with outstanding Handwriting Directors representing various parts of the country who will discuss modern views on Handwriting in Education. A detailed program of convention speakers and activities will appear in the April issue of the leading educational magazines.

Exhibits of handwriting representing all states will be on display in the spacious corridors of the convention hotel. These exhibits will represent work from the largest to the smallest

President
D. Francis Harrigan
Director of Handwriting
Peabody, Mass.

school communities throughout the country.

Special tours are being planned for sections of two days of the convention to provide opportunity for those attending the convention to visit the many places of historic and governmental interest in which Washington and its immediate vicinity abound.

On Thursday evening April 29, the President's Reception will be held for all officers, committee members, members of the association and friends. This occasion will provide opportunity for those attending the convention to become acquainted and enjoy an evening of social pleasure together.

On Friday evening, April 30, the annual banquet will be held in the Continental Room. A gala program with music and entertainers is being planned for this occasion.

Ralph E. Rowe
First Vice President
Portland, Maine

Miss Charlotte E. Barton
Second Vice President
Newark, N. J.

Miss Doris E. Almy
Secretary
Fall River, Mass.

F. J. Duffy
Treasurer
Duluth, Minn.

Membership committees are at work throughout the country zealously competing, state by state, to bring in a banner total membership.

Membership for superintendents, principals, and teachers $1.00, Penmanship directors and supervisors $2.00.

Many groups are working earnestly to make the Washington Convention both pleasant and profitable for all those who attend.

It is sincerely hoped that every state will be represented by delegates at the convention.

Begin to plan now to attend the convention. If you cannot prepare your exhibit before the week of the convention bring it with you and a committee will help you display this on the evening preceding the convention in exhibit space which will be reserved for you if application is made for this space and sent the secretary Miss Doris E. Almy, 337 Walnut St., Fall River, Massachusetts, before April 26, 1937.

Pleasure and profit await you in Washington on April 29, 30 and May 1.

Do your best to be present with us and help us to make this convention a success.

THE EDUCATOR

Published monthly (except July and August)
By THE ZANER-BLOSER CO.,
612 N. Park St., Columbus, O.
E. A. LUPFER............................Editor
PARKER ZANER BLOSER............Business Mgr.

SUBSCRIPTION PRICE, $1.25 A YEAR
(To Canada, 10c more; foreign, 30c more)
Single copy, 15c.
Change of address should be requested promptly in advance, if possible, giving the old as well as the new address.
Advertising rates furnished upon request.

THE EDUCATOR is the best medium through which to reach business college proprietors and managers, commercial teachers and students, and lovers of penmanship. Copy must reach our office by the 10th of the month for the issue of the following month.

Modern Handwriting

By E. A. Lupfer, Zanerian College, Columbus, Ohio

No. 7

The runner measures his speed with a watch.

Write the sentence and keep it for future comparison. From it select the weakest letters for further study and practice.

Ten Texas Four Fr Hamilton
T T T T T T T H H H

See how uniform you can make the beginning loops, also see how uniform you can get the hooks at the base line.

B B B B B B lllllb bbbb

Before working on the B review the exercise given for the P. If you have mastered the P the only difficulty you should find is with the bottom oval. See that the little loop is in the center of the letter and notice the direction it slants. Stop at the hook before making the final stroke. The ovals are made with a free rolling motion.

b b b b b bbbbbbb bbbbbb
limb limb limb limb limb limb
bumblebee bumblebee bumblebee bu

There is very little similarity between the form of the capital letter **B** and small letter **b**. The down strokes of the **b** should be straight. See that the loop is full and open and three times as high as the small letter **i**. Give special attention to the bottom part. Check the motion on the retrace.

Make line after line of single and connected **b**'s, then practice the words striving especially for freedom of movement and graceful lines.

Movement
Be sure that the hand slides along the line easily.

One of the important things in getting free movement is to have the hand slide. Therefore, point the knuckles toward the ceiling, letting the weight rest on the fingers rather than on the side of the hand. Too much finger movement makes laborous looking lines.

Business communications should be so constructed that their meaning cannot be mistaken.

After writing the above sentence examine each letter to see that it is absolutely unmistakable. Cut a hole in a piece of paper or card and use it for covering up the letters. In this way you can see only one letter through the hole in the card and not depend upon context for legibility.

B B B O O E es ot wh bl gor

The B and E upon close observation will be found to be very similar. Turn the B upside down and you have a very good capital E. The same is true if you turn the E upside down you have a good second part of the B. Therefore, try to get the bottom of the B and top of the E the same in roundness. Practice them by reversing your paper. That is, make a line of B's, turn the paper upside down and see if they make good E's. Get the loops in the center of the letter and of about the same size.

Practice the combination of letters. Above all, work for a neat page.

General's General's General's General's
G G G G G G G G G G G
G G G G G G G G G G G
G G G S F G F Georgia Ga.

Here is an excellent copy for study. Notice the proportion of the small letters and capitals. The small letters are about one-fourth of a space between the two blue lines, while the capitals should be three-fourth of a space. Be careful to make punctuation marks. Draw slant lines on your down strokes. All of the down strokes should be made in the same direction. Your writing should have a uniform appearance in size. That is, the minimum letters should be one-fourth of a space high. The extended letters are one-half space high, while the loops are three-fourth of a space high. Draw lines touching the tops of your letters and see if your letters line up as they should in size. Do some of your beginning letters in words extend too high? If so, reduce them in size. Others may have trouble in getting the small e too tall.

After working on the individual letters and exercises make the last line of mixed capitals. Notice the arrows pointing to the similar finish of the G, S and F. Study the direction of the final stroke. It is about horizontal and has a slight curve. You should always stop on the hook before making the final stroke.

R R R R R R R R R R

The R is similar to the P and B. Give special attention to the compound curve and to the finish. Unlike the B the little loop should touch or loop around the stem. The R finishes like K. The final stroke should be parallel to the bottom stroke of the top oval.

R R R R R R R R R R R R R R R
R R R R R R R R R R R R R R R R
Repetition fixes good and bad habits.
Practice intelligently and persistently.
P.B.Rightmire and B.R.Penman

Practice the different exercises mixing them in with letters, then practice the individual letters and finally work on the sentence and names.

Reported   Reported   Reported

These copies are made with the intention of showing you how to study. All of your down strokes should be on the same slant. Get your paper in front of you and pull all of the down strokes towards the center of the body. So many make the capital letters too tiny and weak that it is well for each class to watch the proportion of capitals and small letters. Anyone can check his own writing in the mechanical parts, slant, size and spacing.

Spacing is a little more difficult, although you should be able to see if there are big wide spaces or if the letters are crowded together. One letter should not step on the other's toes. Notice the arrows pointing to spaces which are about equal in size.

R R R R R R R R R R R

Make this row of **R**'s checking particularly to see they are three-fourth of a space high.

Contractions

George doesn't like to dance.
Louise hasn't any book.
You've often heard me say that.
They've never been late.
We've sung that song many times.
Don't forget your rubbers.
G G G G G gggg D D D hhhh

This copy contains excellent material for practice. It reviews many capitals and small letters. It also contains some beautiful easy words for individual practice.

You should also give considerable attention to the beginning words of sentences so that you can write capital and small letters together fluently.

This is the most popular style of r and will give you very little trouble from the standpoint of legibility if you get the top wide enough to make it distinct from the i. Check the motion on the shoulder indicated by the check marks. Curve the upward stroke and make the r slightly higher than the i. Get the downward stroke the same as in the i. In fact, the finish of the r should be exactly the same as in the i with the exception that the i is a little taller than the straight part of the r. The word, **runner** is especially appropriate in practicing the r because you should not have so many difficulties and can therefore spend most of your time on the r.

The word **reports** is a more difficult word and therefore needs special practice and study. Practice the spacing, the height, and slant. Check your writing as indicated by the copy.

A review of P, **B** and R. Write the names of boys and girls in your class or acquaintances whose names begin with P, **B** and R.

It is necessary to frequently call attention to position. You should sit up and not stoop over too close to the writing. The teacher should constantly inspect the position of the pupils. The teacher who perseveres in getting good position may expect a higher average of writing.

To develop a fluency to the right use wide spacing between letters.

Practice the retraced **K** large. The **K** should come down to the base line rather straight. Therefore, retrace the straight stem. In making the stem come down to the base line straight, stop, then raise the pen. Do not raise the pen at the base line while it is in motion. You will find the retracing of the compound curve good practice. Keep on the line in making the **K**. Notice how even the spaces inside the **K** are above and below the loop.

Stimulating Handwriting in the Grades

By Helen Marie Printz

Supr. of Handwriting, Wyomissing
and Mt. Penn, Pa.

Given before the Pennsylvania State
Education Association.

The development of civilization has been a record of progressive changes and education has been no exception. The program in the elementary school has undergone greater changes than any other level. Here the child is of primary importance. The entire curriculum has been reorganized; subject matter has been integrated; we find free creative expression, the child-centered school and creative youth activities. The secondary school has not yet made equal advances.

The teachers must be aware of the major function of the school and place in society today. Each teacher should know the psychological factors in their various stages and manifestations that enter into and condition the growth of our girls and boys.

Many of us are supervisors of both handwriting and art. We all know that art enters into every subject in the curriculum enriching it and making it more worthwhile. The art department was the first to relate its work to other subjects. This was not a selfish idea, at any rate art has lost nothing but education has gained a great deal.

We have the theory of growth activity and pupil activity opposing the doctrine of formal discipline and dictated education. A new method therefore was advocated giving more freedom, spontaneity and vivid self-expression. This gives rise to social instincts to children, constructive impulses, expressive instincts and the impulse toward inquiry. The aim is to draw out the possibilities from within the pupil on the one hand, and on the other to aid him in making effective adjustment toward the world in which he lives.

Hugh Mearns says that the natural creative impulses are always at work when the pupils are alive, active, inventing, organizing original ideas, assembling materials and carrying out enterprises. Pupils grow in capacity to govern themselves to organize materials for handling their collective affairs as well as a capacity for creative expression.

The desire to express thoughts and feelings is common to all normal adults and with little children it is impulsive if not instinctive. How does this relate to handwriting? Art and handwriting we me are closely akin. Both enter into every subject in the curriculum and are of vital importance. In this new progressive education movement have we, in handwriting made the strides they have in art?

There is a shifting of the fulcrum in the sea-saw of education; but that is good for us. It awakens our interests, it makes us take account of stock and get away from the thing we have been doing—we open new ideas and avenues of approach.

Where do we stand? Do we have informal work—dictated lessons or do we have both? In my estimation in some dictated lessons the content is too often unrelated to the natural needs of the child. Sometimes there is too often a break, a broken circuit between the teacher's enthusiasm and

the pupils. Well how are we going to have an informal writing period in which the basic principles are taught? I think by stimulating the pupils at the right time a teacher can do anything with the children whom she understands.

Please do not think that I do not believe in formal writing periods because I do—very much so; and the writing manuals should be in constant use so that the child has the correct formation of letters before him.

The various handwriting companies have given us excellent methods and ways of stimulating pupils. Each community is different and must work out their own problems to fit their needs. The stimulant that works in one section sometimes is a failure in another. I would like to tell you of some of the stimulants used by some of my teachers.

Shortly after school opened this fall my 1B grade in Wyomissing started to build a merry-go-round, large and strong enough to accommodate four. It was an outgrowth of our county fair. The 1B grade children write only on the board. While making ovals one day, someone suggested that it was like going around on the Merry-go-round. They worked out their rhythm and made believe that

they were on the Merry-go-round. Later on they composed several songs that they sang while writing. As the project was going on new words were taught and numbers as they counted tickets, etc. And so it went on each day something new was suggested by the children. The handwriting period was very popular and the Merry-go-round idea was continued until the pupils decided to make a change.

This fall, Bozo, a trained dog, visited Wyomissing just as he did in many other schools in this state. After Bozo's performance the children were all keyed-up; each group reacting in a different way. The fourth grade decided that they wanted to write a story about Bozo. Since the children were so fully saturated and stimulated, the teacher thought it would be an opportune time. As a result, the stories were excellent examples of good, free, spontaneous expressions written in the best legible writing because every pupil was putting forth his best effort to create a good impression.

One of my sixth grades has a splendid method of evaluating their written work. Each row has a checker and at the end of the writing period they pick out the best paper in the next row. These papers are taken to the front of the room and judged by the checkers. This is continued for a week—then the checkers change but the honor list is kept for the year. One of the most beneficial things here is the pupils' frank criticism of the papers. A criticism from a pupil goes farther than that of the teacher. This carries over in all their other work.

Another sixth grade has a little posture game. If the pupils take their writing position without any mistakes the pupils get four counts; but if, by chance, someone forgets to sit up straight, or turn his paper at the correct angle, etc. then those are counters against the pupils. I have found that this has caused keen rivalry between teacher and pupils.

We had a rather large hospital class in one of my fifth grades last year. Many devices were used but with no avail. The teacher was getting very much discouraged. Just about that time, there was good coasting and one of the pupils suggested that the teacher should go coasting with them. But the teacher said, "We cannot go coasting when our work is unfinished and some of it must be rewritten." Much class discussion followed and finally the children decided to have a Writing Club—members were eligible

(Continued on page 25)

Fortieth Anniversary Convention Eastern Commercial Teachers Association

HOTEL STATLER; Boston, Mass.

March 24, 25, 26, 27, 1937

TOPIC: **Measuring for Vocational Ability in the Field of Business Education.**

WEDNESDAY, MARCH 24

9:30 A. M.   Sight-seeing trips and visits to schools and business offices.

2:00 P. M.   Arrangement of exhibits

7:00 P. M.   Meeting of the Executive Board

THURSDAY, MARCH 25

10:00 A. M.   Registration of members.
Educational, sight-seeing and shopping trips. Secure specific information regarding trips at the Hospitality desk. The committee will be glad to assist members and their friends in arranging trips. Sale of banquet tickets. Tickets cost $3.00 and must be purchased before 3:00 P. M. Thursday. Visits to the exhibits.

11:30 A. M.   Official tour of exhibits by the Executive Board and chairmen of the local committees.

1:15—3:00 P. M.   Machine Instruction Demonstrations at the exhibitors' booths.

THURSDAY, AFTERNOON, MARCH 25

3:15 P. M.   Music

3:30 P. M.   OPENING OF CONVENTION—Ballroom
Platform Guests: Officers and members of the Executive Board.

> Address of Welcome
>
> Response to Address of Welcome—Mrs. Agnes C. Seavey, Vice-President, Auburn, Maine.

President's Address:
> Nathaniel Altholz, Director of Commercial Education, Board of Education, New York City.

Address: "Vocational Ability Testing from the Standpoint of the Employer."
> Dr. Robert P. Brecht, Executive Secretary, National Office Management Association, Wharton School, University of Pennsylvania, Philadelphia.

THURSDAY EVENING, MARCH 25

6:30 P. M.   40th Anniversary Banquet reception and dance.

FRIDAY, MARCH 26

8:30 A. M.   Breakfast for State Chairman Membership Committee.

GENERAL MEETING—Ballroom

9:30 A. M.   Music

10:00-12:00   Platform Guests: Past Presidents of the Association.
Chairman: J. N. Jackman, Kendall Company, Walpole, Mass.

Address: "The Business Education Council's Plan for Improving Methods of Measuring the Results of Teaching in Terms of Occupational Requirements."
> Prof. Frederick G. Nichols, Graduate School of Education, Harvard University, Cambridge, Mass.

Address: "A Fundamentals Test for All Vocational Commercial Graduates."
> Katherine W. Ross, Boston Clerical School, Boston, Mass.

Address: "A General Background Test for All Vocational Commercial Graduates."
> Prof. Phillip J. Rulon, Graduate School of Education, Harvard University, Cambridge, Mass.

Address: "A Personality Rating Schedule for Use with Commercial Students."
> Harold E. Cowan, Secretary, Business Education Council, Director of Commercial Education, Dedham, Mass.

12:30-1:45 P. M.   Luncheon meeting—National Council of Business Education.

2:15-3:00   GENERAL MEETING—Ballroom

Address: "The Challenge of the New Federal Vocational Act which Provides Training for Commercial Distributive Occupations."
> Dr. Norris A. Brisco, Dean, School of Retailing, New York University.

Address: "Cooperation by the Retail Merchants in Carrying Out the Provisions of the New Federal Vocational Act."
> Daniel Bloomfield, Manager, Retail Trade Board, Boston, Mass.

3:15-5:00   SECTION MEETINGS

"Vocational Ability Tests"—A series of vocational ability tests will be presented at the various section meetings by representatives of the Business Education Council with statements as to their distinguishing characteristics, plans for giving and rating them, and results of their use experimentally."

Secretarial Section

Under the Direction of Prof. Catherine F. Nulty, University of Vermont, Burlington, Vt.

Chairman—R. F. Webb, State Teachers College, Indiana, Pa.

The Stenographic Ability Test Presentation:
> Frank A. Phillips, Director of Commercial Education, Medford, Mass.

Critical Appraisals of the Test
> James J. McKinley, Aetna Life Insurance Company, Hartford, Conn.
> Margaret McGinn, Bay Path Institute, Springfield, Mass.

Discussion

The Typewriting Ability Test
Presentation: Raymond C. Goodfellow, Director, Commercial Education, Newark, New Jersey.

A Critical Appraisal of the Test
> Mrs. J. H. Quinlan, Simmons College, Boston.
Discussion

Eastern Commercial Teachers Association

Bookkeeping Section

Under the Direction of Mrs. Agnes C. Seavey, Principal, School of Commerce, Auburn, Maine.

Chairman—Prof. Atlee L. Percy, Chairman, Division of Commercial Education, Boston University, Boston, Mass.

The Bookkeeping Ability Test

Presentation: W. R. Catton, Burdett College, Boston, Mass.

Critical Appraisals of the Test

J. L. Holtsclaw, Director, Commercial Education, Detroit, Michigan.

L. H. Brigham, Office Service Manager, American Optical Company, Southbridge, Mass.

Discussion

Measurement of Ability on the Accounting Level

Presentation: Prof. William F. Shors, Rider College, Trenton, N. J.

A Critical Appraisal of the Test

Prof. Alfred D'Alessandro, Northeastern University, Boston, Mass.

Clerical Section

Under the Direction of Dr. Peter L. Agnew, School of Education, New York University.

Chairman—Clyde B. Edgeworth, Director of Business Education, Baltimore, Md.

The Filing Ability Test

Presentation: N. Mae Sawyer, Educational Director American Institute of Filing, Buffalo, N. Y.

A Critical Appraisal of the Test

Harriet I. Flagg, Teacher of Filing, Waltham Senior High School, Waltham, Mass.

The Calculating Machine Test

Presentation: Mary F. Ward, Principal, Boston Calculating School, Boston, Mass.

A Critical Appraisal of the Test

C. H. Katenkamp, Forest Park High School, Baltimore, Md.

Discussion

The Dictating Machine Transcription Test

Presentation: Genevieve A. Hayes, Co-ordinator, Julia Richman High School, New York City.

A Critical Appraisal of the Test

Lena B. Pool, Head, Commercial Department, English High School, Lynn, Mass.

Discussion

Testing for Clerical Ability

Mrs. Dorothy M. Holdredge, Secretary to Personnel Director, Dennison Mfg. Co., Framingham, Mass.

Discussion

Distributive Trades and Social Business Section

Under the Direction of Sadie L. Ziegler, Rider College, Trenton, N. J.

Chairman—Dr. Joseph W. Seay, Director of Admission, Rider College, Trenton, N. J.

The Development of a Program for Vocational Training for the Distributive Occupations.

Prof. Neal B. Bowman, School of Commerce, Temple University, Philadelphia, Pa.

The Development of a Composite Test for Economic Intelligence and Social Understanding Essential to Occupational Effectiveness.

Dr. Harald G. Shields, Director, School of Secretarial Studies, Simmons College, Boston, Mass.

Penmanship Section

Under the Direction of John G. Kirk, Director of Commercial Education, Philadelphia, Pa.

Chairman—Bertha A. Connor, Director of Handwriting, Boston Public Schools, Boston, Mass.

What are the Values of Penmanship in the Successful Operation of a Business?

(Speaker to be announced)

What is the Quality of Penmanship Actually Used by Employees in Different Business Positions? (Illustrated by lantern slides)

H. M. Sherman, State Teachers College, West Chester, Pa.

What Teaching Methods and Devices are Needed to Meet the Vocational Standards in Penmanship?

Harry Houston, Supervisor of Handwriting, Public Schools, New Haven, Connecticut.

Private Business School Executives' Section

Program Arranged by the Chairman, P. J. Harman, Director, Strayer College, Washington, D. C.

What the Private Business Schools Can Do to Obtain Recognition from Public School Principals, State Departments of Education and School and College Officials Generally.

D. C. McIntosh, Dover Business College, Dover, N. H.

Coordinating Tests and Measurements of Skill Subjects with Standardized Units of Measure (A necessary and logical follow-up of the subject discussed at the New York meeting last year).

E. G. Purvis, Dean, Strayer College, Washington. Essential Machine Equipment for Instruction and for Business Purposes.

P. S. Spangler, President, Duffs-Iron City College, Pittsburgh, Pa.

SATURDAY, MARCH 27

9:30-11:00 QUESTION BOX SESSIONS

Theme: Classroom Problems of the Teacher. There will be eight sections, namely, Bookkeeping and Accounting, Clerical Practice, Distributive Trades, Junior High School and Ninth Year Business Subjects, Penmanship, Private Business Schools, Secretarial Subjects and Social Business Studies. The purpose of these conferences is to afford an opportunity to teachers who have questions about instructional materials, classroom procedure, etc. to have them answered by a group of well qualified teachers of the subject under discussion. QUESTIONS SHOULD BE SUBMITTED IN WRITING EITHER SIGNED OR UNSIGNED TO CLINTON A. REED, STATE EDUCATION DEPARTMENT, ALBANY, NEW YORK, NOT LATER THAN MARCH 15 SO THAT THEY MAY BE DISTRIBUTED TO THE TEACHERS WHO WILL ANSWER THEM.

Bookkeeping and Accounting Section

(Bookkeeping, Accounting, Business Arithmetic)

Under the Direction of Mrs. Agnes C. Seavey, Principal, Auburn School of Commerce, Auburn, Maine

Discussion Leaders:

Prof. Paul Salsgiver, Department of Commercial Education, Boston University.

Prof. H. A. Andruss, Director, Department of Commerce, State Teachers College, Bloomsburg, Pa.

Eastern Commercial Teachers Association

William C. Wallace, Chairman, Department of Accounting and Law, George Washington High School, New York City.

Clerical Practice Section

(Filing, Calculating Machines, Dictating Machines) Under the Direction of Dr. Peter L. Agnew, School of Education, New York University, New York City.

Discussion Leaders:
C. H. Katenkamp, Forest Park High School, Baltimore, Md.
James Meehan, Hunter College, New York City.
Mary Stuart, Brighton High School, Brighton, Mass.

Distributive Trades Section

(Marketing, Merchandising, Salesmanship, Retail Selling) Under the Direction of Sadie L. Ziegler, Secretary, Rider College, Trenton, N. J.

Discussion Leaders:
Dr. O. P. Robinson, School of Retailing, New York University, New York City.
J. W. Miller, Secretary, Goldey College, Wilmington, Delaware. Prof. Lloyd Jacobs, Head, Department of Business Education, State Teachers College, Trenton, N. J. Dr. Leslie M. Davis, Head, College of Business Administration, Rider College, Trenton, N. J.
Grace Griffith, Central Commercial High School, New York City.

Junior High School and Ninth Year Business Subjects Section

(Introduction to Business, Junior Business Training) Under the Direction of John G. Kirk, Director, Commercial Education, Philadelphia, Pa.

Chairman—Charles W. Hamilton, Assistant in Secondary Education, Department of Public Instruction, Trenton, N. J.

Discussion Leaders:
Frank H. Ash, Bureau of Teacher Preparation, Teachers College of Connecticut, New Britain, Conn.
Clyde B. Edgeworth, Baltimore, Md.
Catherine Freimann, Forest Park High School, Baltimore, Md.
Frederick W. Riecke, Chairman, Commercial Department, South Side High School, Newark, N. J.
Dr. F. W. Loso, Director, Department of Business Education, Elizabeth, N. J.
Charles E. Cook, Director of Business Education, Rochester, New York.
Howard White, Junior High School No. 3, Trenton, N. J.
B. F. Jeffery, Principal, B. F. Brown School, Fitchburg, Mass.

Penmanship Section

Under the Direction of John G. Kirk, Director of Commercial Education, Board of Education, Philadelphia, Pa.
Discussion Leaders:
Harry Houston, Supervisor of Handwriting, New Haven, Conn.

Henry G. Burtner, Peirce School of Business Administration, Philadelphia, Pa.

K. C. Atticks, Head of Commercial Department, Brookline, Mass.

Michael A. Travers, State Teachers College, Trenton, N. J.

D. F. Harrigan, Jr., President, National Association of Penmanship Teachers and Supervisors, Peabody, Mass.

Private Business Schools Section

Under the Direction of P. J. Harman, Director, Strayer College, Washington, D. C.

Discussion Leaders:
Charles E. Zoubeck, Associate Editor Gregg News Letter, Gregg Publishing Company, New York City.
Dr. James M. Thompson, School of Commerce and Finance, New York University.
Katherine M. Snyder, Strayer, Bryant-Stratton College, Baltimore, Md.
K. M. Maukert, Principal, Duffs-Iron City College, Pittsburgh, Pa.
J. P. Alexander, New England District Manager, Westinghouse Manufacturing Company, Boston, Mass.

Secretarial Studies Section

(Shorthand, Typewriting, Business English, Secretarial Studies) Under the Direction of Prof. Catherine F. Nulty, University of Vermont, Burlington, Vt.

Discussion Leaders:
Prof. Roy Davis, Head, English Department, College of Business Administration, Boston University, Boston.
Prof. D. D. Lessenberry, Director of Courses in Commercial Education, University of Pittsburgh, Pittsburgh, Pa.
Mrs. Frances D. North, Western High School, Baltimore, Md.
Teresa A. Regan, Assistant Professor, Teachers College of the City of Boston, Boston, Mass.
Eleanor Skimin, Northern High School, Detroit.
Mrs. Esta Ross Stuart, Associate in Education, Columbia University, New York City.

Social Business Section

(Economic Geography, Economics, Business Law) Under the Direction of Harold E. Cowan, Head of Commercial Department, High School, Dedham, Mass.
Discussion Leaders:
Arthur Ross, Head of Commercial Department, Framingham, Mass. High School.
Raymond Dower, Head of Commercial Department, High School, Wakefield, Mass.
Mabel Marr, Head of Commercial Department, Bassick High School, Bridgeport, Conn.

11:15 A. M. BUSINESS MEETING
Awarding of prizes.

(Continued on page 25)

"Mr. Meadows Says"

BY GEORGE A. MEADOWS

Pres. Meadows-Draughon
Business College, Shreveport, La.

Good Health: Everyone should take good care of his health, for, unless one can keep well, he cannot stay on the job or be at his best.

So, watch your diet, get plenty of exercise, sunshine and fresh air, and you will get along a lot better.

BE TEMPERATE: Both young men and women are admonished to be temperate in their habits—not to smoke to excess, if you must smoke—avoid drinking all forms of intoxicants, at least when you are going to come into contact with business people or where alcohol on the breath might hurt your standing, and especially while you are on the job!

It never did anyone ANY GOOD to smoke or drink — just imaginary pleasure—but if you MUST do it, do it in such a LIMITED way, and at such TIMES, that it will not interfere with your work and will not get you "in bad" with those who may resent it.

Dependability: There is nothing more important to a young man or woman starting out in the business world than a reputation for BEING DEPENDABLE.

The best way to establish that reputation is to be on the job all the time. Better still, be a little AHEAD of time, and don't RUSH to get away as soon as the bell rings, or the day is over, officially.

If at any time you cannot be on hand, by all means communicate with your teacher or employer, as the case may be, advising as to the REASON why you cannot be present.

Another way to establish a reputation for being dependable is to take care of your obligations promptly; never allow them to run over a single day. If you cannot pay on the date due, see the person you owe and explain just when you will take care of the matter.

George A. Meadows

Get into the habit of regarding your obligations RELIGIOUSLY. Nothing will give you a better standing with business people—the people you expect to be associated with and do business with all of your life.

Thoughtfulness and Appreciation: Nothing will win more respect or consideration for a young man or woman than evidence of his or her being THOUGHTFUL and APPRECIATIVE of the things that are done for him or her by others. It doesn't matter how small the favor may be; ANYONE likes to know that it is APPRECIATED!

It doesn't cost anything or take long for anyone to say "Thank you," "I appreciate so-and-so," or the like. If it is inconvenient to express one's thoughtfulness or appreciation in person or over the telephone, it doesn't take but a little while, or cost much, to write a note.

Thoughtfulness and appreciation

not only attract favorable attention, but usually pay handsome dividends. So, above all, let's never fail to show our THOUGHTFULNESS or express our APPRECIATION, when people show an interest in us, or try to help us, no matter how insignificant the matter may appear or seem to be.

Personality

It has been said, "Personality is the outward expression of one's inner self." Someone else said, "We are a part of all that we have met or come in contact with." Another has said, "Education is EXPERIENCE"—our own experience plus the experience of others, which we get from books and personal contact.

Another person of experience and ability said, "One of the secrets of success is the ability to adapt ourselves." Still, another said, "Ambition is the driving force in one's life." Another said, "The way to achieve success is to find out what our obstacles are and then secure the necessary equipment to overcome those obstacles." In the case of a young man or woman, the equipment would mean securing the necessary education or training. In the case of a business organization, it might mean the securing of certain machinery or other facilities.

As for the actual value of PERSONALITY, it is said, "It represents at least sixty per cent, as against forty per cent for training and ability, when it comes to making a success in life." Personality wins friends and inspires confidence. That's the reason it is easy for some people to secure positions and get along well from the beginning—they have a pleasing, forceful personality!

If a student does not have this kind of a personality—if his personal appearance is not all that it should be, if he doesn't make friends and get along with others easily—he or she should start trying to IMPROVE or DEVELOP his personality AT ONCE. It isn't always easy, but IT CAN BE DONE! The main thing is to observe others and not be afraid to go ahead or express ourselves.

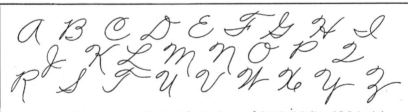

Written by Bertha Huth, a student in the Emporia Business College, Emporia, Kansas. J. E. Hawkins is President and C. D. Long is the penmanship instructor.

Masterpieces

From the Private Collection of C. W. Jones, Brockton Business College, Brockton, Mass.

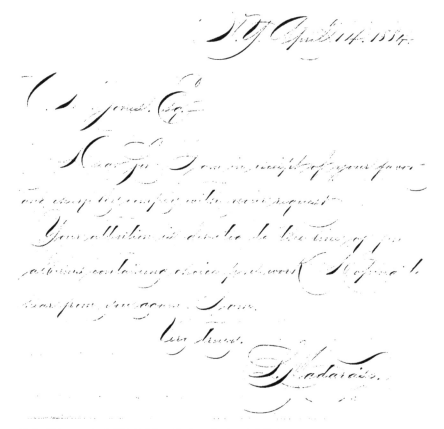

This beautiful letter was written in 1884 by L. Madarasz. The plate was loaned to us by C. W. Jones of Brockton, Mass.

Notice the delicacy of this work. The shades are not as heavy and bold as they were in more recent work by Madarasz. Many think that Madarasz reached his highest degree of skill in the nineties. This, however, contains some of the best work he ever produced. The small letters in the letter deserve your special attention.

Thousands have been moved to improve their writing by merely seeing specimens of Madarasz's work. His influence on those who admire fine penmanship was equal to that exerted by great musicians whose skill commands both inspiration and admiration.

Ornamental Penmanship

No. 17   **Script by the late A. M. Wonnell**

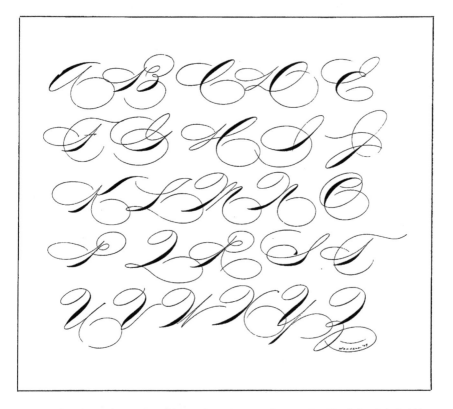

You have been working on individual capital letters in previous lessons so that this set of capitals should be easy. In making a set of capitals, or for that matter any body work, see that there is uniformity in the size of the various letters. Pick out letters according to groups and try to make them appear the same in size, slant, height, and the shades of uniform thickness.

Check through your alphabets to see how nearly the ovals are all the same in size.

Swing the capitals off with a free, easy motion. If your lines are shaky increasing the speed will improve the quality of line.

Study your position. Do you keep the tin of. your oblique holder turned up so that both nibs of the pen press evenly on the paper? Don't grip the holder, and see that your pen is not sprained by forcing it into the oblique tin. It should fit snugly but not too tight.

The Educator will be glad to examine your practice work if you will enclose return postage.

How to Draw a Perfect Ellipse of Predetermined Dimensions

By Daniel W. Hoff

DIRECTIONS.

1. Cross two straight lines at their centers, and at right angles to each other, one equal to the length and the other to the width of the proposed ellipse. These represent the two diameters. See lines A-A, and B-B in the accompanying diagram.

2. On either side of the intersection, place dots on the long diameter, at a distance equal to one-half its length, from the end of the short diameter, point B.

3. Drive a strong pin at each dot, and at point B.

4. Tie a nonstretchable thread, or string, to one of the pins on the line; pass it outside the one at point B; then tie it to the third pin, drawing it taut.

5. Remove the pin at point B; place the point of your pencil against the string at point B; and move sideward to the ends of the long diameter for one-half of the ellipse, repeating the process to complete the figure.

If your string has not stretched; if the pressure of your pencil against the string has been uniform throughout; and if neither pins nor knots have yielded, the result will be a perfect ellipse.

To draw an ellipse in ink, first outline in pencil on thin cardboard, and cut it out. Then cut a slightly smaller one, and paste this smaller one beneath the larger, to prevent ink running under the edges. Finally use this form as a guide for your ruling pen.

The oblique lines in the diagram show how the string appears as the pencil passes the different points on the rim of the ellipse, in traveling from pole to pole.

The same string, without changing the knots, was used for ellipses No. 1, No. 2, and No. 3, by simply shifting the pins from points 1-1 to points 2-2 and 3-3.

If you wish to outline a flower bed in the form of an ellipse simply substitute two strong stakes for the pins, a small rope for the string, and a sharp stick for the pencil.

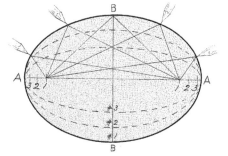

THE COVER PAGE

The cover page this month is the product of W. LeRoy Newark, an engrosser in the Zaner-Bloser Studio. Mr. Newark laid the foundation for his skill with the pen by first mastering flying figure eights, swinging circles and cutting other fancy capers on the ice in good old Pennsylvania. That is where he developed poise, grace, good nature, balance, and learned to glide with freedom and grace. Since that time he has covered acres and acres of paper with fancy pen capers.

How many can remember the Old Mill Pond or Mill Dam? The first country school which we attended was located in the hills of Pennsylvania along the Sherman Creek within a block of an old grist mill where the students spent many noon hours playing hide and seek, skating on the ice and watching the wheels go round and round.

Many times we went home with skinned shins from playing shinny. The ball usually consisted of an old battered tin can. In those days we may not have been able to cut such skillful words in the ice but we did many skillful things and had a grand and glorious time. Those were the "good old days" when we had few responsibilities and could take life easy. We skated miles up and down the stream, dodging holes and gliding swiftly over the smooth stretches. Playing "ticklish" was an interesting pastime. This consisted of seeing who could skate on the thinnest ice, nearest a hole or over broken ice. We dried our feet and clothes at the welcome fire (welcome if you supplied your share of the wood). Our main worries were how to conceal our wet feet upon our return home in the evening. Yes, the wood or coal box and our meals were neglected, but those were the "good old days."

Skating is a healthy, well balanced exercise and is easily mastered. Penmanship, too, is easily mastered when pursued with as much zeal as displayed by the skaters.

WHICH ONE IS YOU?

Eleven little typists
  Eager to begin:
One watched his fingers,
  Then there were ten.

Ten little typists
  Lookin' mighty fine.
"Your position's incorrect!"—
  So there were nine.

Nine little typists,
  Not a one was late;
One couldn't concentrate,
  Then there were eight.

Eight little typists
  (Wish there were 'leven);
One made a "Strike-over,"
  Then there were seven.

Seven little typists
  Up to funny tricks;
One sprained his shoulder,
  Then there were six.

Six little typists
  Very much alive;
One loafed his practice period,
  Then there were five.

Five little typists
  (Once there were more);
One struck "N" for "M"
  Then there were four.

Four little typists
  Typing merrily;
One stopped to erase,
  Then there were three.

Three little typists—
  Lots of work to do!
"Your arrangement's very poor!"—
  So there were two.

Two little typists,
  One was chewing gum,
Teacher made him leave the room;
  Then there was one.

One little typist—
  All his work is done
Big Business called him
  Now there are none—

—Katie May Ivey, High School,
  New Albany, Mississippi.

Ornamental signatures by J. W. Hepburn, Principal and Proprietor of Hepburn Business College, Calgary, Alta., Canada.

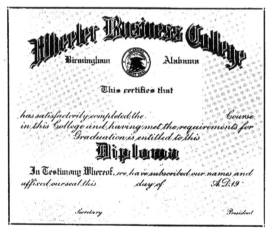

Spencerian

Advertising script prepared by Rene Guillard, Box 234, Evanston, Ill.

Real success is often achieved after many failures, an active man builds success upon a foundation of failures.

Written by T. Yoshida

Written by T. Yoshida, Shimonogo, Haruhimura, Nishikasugai-gun, Aichiken, Japan.

Wheeler Business College

Birmingham   Alabama

This certifies that

.... has satisfactorily completed the .... Course in this College and, having met the requirements for Graduation is entitled to this

Diploma

In Testimony Whereof, we have subscribed our names and affixed our seal this .... day of .... A.D. 19 ....

Secretary   President

A diploma prepared by E. H. McGhee, Trenton, N. J. Study the beautiful lettering and the accurate and effective shading.

Lessons in Card Carving

By J. D. Carter, Deerfield, Ill.

Lesson No. 6

In Lesson No. 6 I shall use the sharpened pen for cutting.

The design may be cut with knife but I have chosen to demonstrate that very high grade work can be done with the steel we find in a number of our better grade pens.

I have used with success pens sharpened in three different ways.

Possibly the easiest way for the beginner to sharpen would be to insert a used Zanerian Fine Writer, Gillott No. 1, or Gillott No. 170 in the holder in the reverse order from its use in writing.

Now without changing the general shape or contour of the pen use an emery stone or emery wheel and grind on the back of the pen until it is as thin as a razor; then finish by using a very fine finishing stone or hone.

When you have gotten a keen edge on the pen, proceed to cut by trying a few strokes until you have found the direction you can get good clean cut strokes by pushing pen to or from you or to one side.

I hold the penholder in my hand between the thumb and the first or index finger and have the small end of the penholder protrude between the third and fourth fingers. This gets the cutting edge low and aids in cutting on very thin paper or cardboard without cutting through the material.

Our lesson designs can be cut with a sharp knife if you prefer.

There are many designs that may be cut and used for decorations and occasions for pleasure and profit; such as place cards—greeting cards—wedding anniversary cards—cards for graduations—cards with gifts, etc.

Let's get busy and see what fine work can be made with the card cutting tools.

I will be pleased to see the progress of a number this month.

Criticism on your work for return postage.

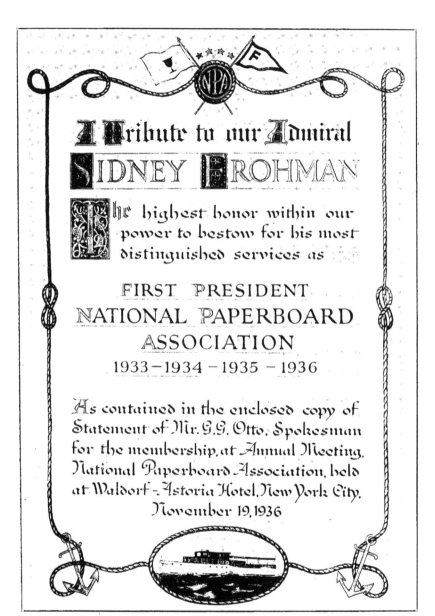

A Tribute to our Admiral
SIDNEY FROHMAN

The highest honor within our power to bestow for his most distinguished services as

FIRST PRESIDENT
NATIONAL PAPERBOARD
ASSOCIATION
1933 – 1934 – 1935 – 1936

As contained in the enclosed copy of Statement of Mr. G.G. Otto, Spokesman for the membership, at Annual Meeting, National Paperboard Association, held at Waldorf – Astoria Hotel, New York City, November 19, 1936

This beautiful piece of engrossing was done in the Harris Studio, 140 S. Dearborn, Chicago, Ill. You will do well to study the lettering, the beautiful initial letters, etc.

MEET
ARNOLD C. GORLING

Arnold C. Gorling, 530 Maryland St., Winnipeg, Man., Canada, who teaches penmanship and bookkeeping in the Success Business College.

At the present time Mr. Gorling has approximately three hundred students in his penmanship classes. He recently sent us some of his beautifully written cards. He is the proud possessor of The Educator Professional Certificate.

P. H. O'Hara is a busy man in the Maury High School, Norfolk, Va. He is also one of the most skillful business writers in the country. In fact, we doubt if any high school teacher can excel Mr. O'Hara in skill.

A dash from the pen of E. C. Enriquez, Pineda, Pasig, Rizal, P. I.

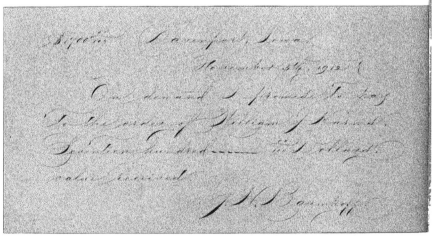

Graceful curves by the late H. B. Lehman.

Eastern Commercial Teachers Association

(Continued from page 15)

OFFICERS and EXECUTIVE BOARD

NATHANIEL ALTHOLZ, President, Director of Commercial Education, Board of Education, New York City.

MRS. AGNES C. SEAVEY, Vice-President, Principal, Auburn School of Commerce, Auburn, Maine.

HARRY I. GOOD, Secretary, Associate Superintendent of Schools, Board of Education, Buffalo, N. Y.

ARNOLD M. LLOYD, Treasurer, Principal, Banks College, 1200 Walnut St., Philadelphia, Pa.

JOHN G. KIRK, Director of Commercial Education, Board of Education, Philadelphia, Pa.

P. J. HARMAN, Director, Strayer College, Washington, D. C.

HAROLD E. COWAN, Head of Commercial Department High School, Dedham. Mass.

SADIE L. ZIEGLER, Secretary, Rider College, Trenton, N. J.

PETER L. AGNEW, Instructor in Education, New York University School of Education, Washington Square, New York City.

CATHERINE F. NULTY, Ex-Officio, Assistant Professor of Secretarial Studies, University of Vermont, Burlington, Vt.

CLINTON A. REED, Yearbook Editor, Supervisor of Business Education, State Department of Education, Albany, New York.

STIMULATING HANDWRITING IN THE GRADES

(Continued from page 12)

when they had passed all the writing requirements. This seemed to impress the pupils more than anything we had tried. Every child was interested. There were seven eligible members the first week, who went coasting with their teacher. The following week, more new members were added and that week they had an old-fashioned sleighing party. The club grew—and they had picnics, roller-skating parties, bird hikes and even a trip to Hershey Park (about fifty miles away.) This to me was one of the finest ways of stimulating this particular group—showing pupil initiative and pupil response.

There are hundreds of ways we can use in stimulating our pupils—especially in the integrated program. Sometimes I feel we are so busy we let good opportunities pass by.

I am going to repeat—that I do believe in formal lessons and we should always use the manual. I am not talking about the mechanics of writing but the stimulation. If a pupil has the right attitude, he cannot help but do his work joyfully. Each community must work out their own methods according to the individuals and environment. Handwriting to me is something like art. It is in everyone—(unless physically unfit)—a power within seeking for expression. It is the teacher's function to set it free and stimulate its growth and to prepare the child for rich and worthy living.

A. F. McIsaac, Bedford Chambers, Halifax, N. S., in renewing his subscription stated that he has had a great year during 1936 in document investigation work. He states that he had over 200 cases.

NEW ARRIVAL

Patricia Ann arrived January 23, 1937 at the home of Mr. and Mrs. Roger T. Elizey, Jr., 905 Tracy, Kansas City, Mo. Congratulations!

Lessons in Modern Engrosser's Script

Prepared in the office of The Educator

No. 7

This type of penmanship is one of the oldest styles in use today. It is also one of the most appropriate styles for use in engrossing. It has good reading qualities and therefore is very suitable for work which is intended for framing. It is used also on diplomas, resolutions, memorials and in hundreds of other ways.

One of the first requirements is a uniform shaped down stroke. One should practice on exercises and letters until a uniform pen pressure is developed.

In this lesson we give special attention to the lower loop letters. The lower loop letters should be the same in size as the upper loop letters. After making lower loops try mixing them with the upper loops to see that the upper and lower loops balance in size.

Study each letter individually, making line after line and comparing your work carefully with the copy. Intelligent practice is necessary. This work is done mainly with finger movement and of course a properly adjusted oblique penholder is necessary.

Send your practice work to The Educator with return postage for a few free suggestions and criticisms.

[Penmanship exercises: j j j j j y y y y y g g g g g g g g g]

joy joined judged yearling equality

Z Z Z Z Z quiz zigzaggy garage ƒ

laggard organizations grand yank

THERE WILL ALWAYS BE JOBS!

Any young person who wonders whether there will be a place in business for him need only remember that all around the business circle there are bookkeepers, stenographers, typists, clerks, secretaries, machine operators and other trained workers whose services will be needed as long as civilization is based upon a social system which demands that human wants and needs shall be adequately met.

Business is expanding all the time and as it grows it calls for more—and better—workers. But even if business should remain static so far as volume and number of persons engaged is concerned, there would be an enormous turnover due to incompetency, the ravages of old age, accidents, marriages, changes, etc. Business is expanding now!

Emporia Business College
Emporia, Kans.

A sketch of Johnnie Brown who failed to get a penmanship certificate. Drawn by D. J. Person, Carthage, S. D. Don't worry Johnnie you can try again.

J. W. MILLER IS HONORED BY NATIONAL COMMERCIAL TEACHERS' ASSOCIATION

Mr. J. W. Miller, secretary-treasurer of Goldey College, Wilmington, Del., was reelected treasurer of the National Commercial Teachers' Federation for the coming year. The meeting was held in December in Cleveland, Ohio. The meeting this year was one of the largest they have so far held.

The Goldey College is a member of the Accredited Commercial Schools Association which also met in Cleveland at the same time of the meeting of the National Commercial Teachers' Federation.

The school was represented at this meeting by Mr. Miller and Mr. W. R. Kiddoo, head of the Accounting Department.

DESIGNING AND ENGROSSING

By E. L. BROWN

Rockland, Maine

Herewith is shown a bit of lettering suitable for many purposes especially when legibility and speed are factors for consideration.

A drawing in detail is not necessary or recommended for this design. However, lay off very roughly the several lines of lettering for purpose of correct spacing, then letter in Zanerian ink, using a No. 2½ broad pen for all the lettering excepting words "The" and "Pioneer".

The background of start word "The" is one of many styles of tinting which can be quickly and easily executed. Use a coarse pen and thicken lines nearest letters. The relief lines on letters in "Sturdy Character" gives

a certain finish and variety which is always desirable. The effect is especially good when the relief lines are added in color tints or pale ink. Lines of lettering may be underscored with good effect by using ink diluted with water to give a pale grayish tone.

Try this design by using a different style of tinted background for word "The", either in line or stipple.

Send in your work for criticism. We want to help you; will you cooperate with us to this end?

CHARLES W. FOGARTY

We regret to learn of the death of Charles W. Fogarty, Principal of Brandon-Stevens Secretarial School, St. George, Staten Island, N. Y., through our good friend, R. E. Guth, 165 Broadway, New York City.

Mr. Fogarty was a native of Lyons, N. Y., and had lived on Staten Island since 1911. Shortly after he went to Staten Island he entered partnership with the late Joseph Stevens in the Brandon-Stevens Institute. Three years later he bought out his partner's interests in the school. The Brandon-Stevens School has enjoyed a splendid reputation as an institute

for the training of young men and women for commercial positions.

Mr. Fogarty credited penmanship with starting him on the road to success as a commercial educator. In 1905 he attended The Zanerian College of Penmanship, Columbus, Ohio, through the influence of that prince of penmen, A. W. Dakin, Syracuse, N. Y.

Mr. Fogarty was active in local community affairs. He was a Rotarian and it is said that he never missed a meeting for the past fifteen years.

He leaves a wife, a daughter and a son. Thousands of his students feel the loss of his friendship and counsel.

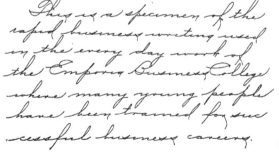

Written by a student in the Emporia Business College, Emporia, Kansas. J. E. Hawkins is President and C. D. Long is the penmanship instructor.

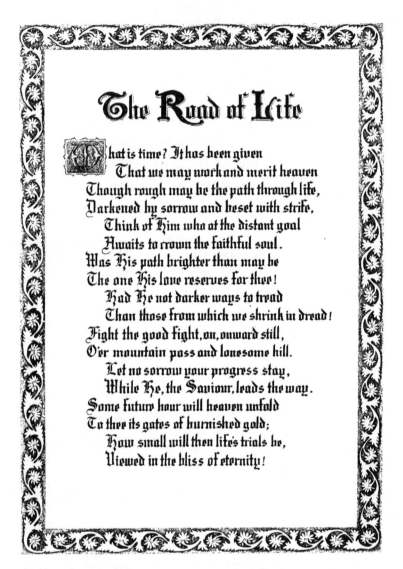

The Road of Life

What is time? It has been given
        That we may work and merit heaven
Though rough may be the path through life,
Darkened by sorrow and beset with strife,
        Think of Him who at the distant goal
        Awaits to crown the faithful soul.
Was His path brighter than may be
The one His love reserves for thee!
        Had He not darker ways to tread
        Than those from which we shrink in dread!
Fight the good fight, on, onward still,
O'er mountain pass and lonesome hill.
        Let no sorrow your progress stay,
        While He, the Saviour, leads the way.
Some future hour will heaven unfold
To thee its gates of burnished gold;
        How small will then life's trials be,
        Viewed in the bliss of eternity!

A poem engrossed by Sister Mary Bronislava, Felician Sisters, Coraopolis, Pa.

BOOK REVIEWS

Our readers are interested in books of merit, but especially in books of interest and value to commercial teachers including books of special educational value and books on business subjects. All such books will be briefly reviewed in these columns, the object being to give sufficient description of each to enable our readers to determine its value.

Federal Tax Course, 1937 Edition, published by Prentice-Hall, Inc., 70 Fifth Avenue, New York, N. Y.

This is an annual publication issued in November of each year. It is used by thousands of lawyers, accountants, bankers, business men and others who are called upon to prepare tax returns.

The 1937 edition of the Federal Tax Course brings you:

1. Editorial Explanations of the Law and Regulations.
2. A Set of Filled-in Returns.
3. Problems and Solutions.
4. The Treasury Department Regulations.
5. The New 1936 Federal Tax Law.
6. Explanation of Changes.

Specific Uses of the 1937 Tax Course include:

1. It shows you how to prepare accurate returns to secure all legitimate tax reductions.

2. It answers hundreds of questions concerning the Federal Income Tax that you may have to answer.

3. It gives you a convenient source of tax information when tax matters are under consideration.

The cost of the course is $10.12—a small fraction of what it may save in the preparation of your tax returns for next year.

Nature Magazine's Guide to Science Teaching, by E. Laurence Palmer, Director of Nature Education of the American Nature Association and Professor of Rural Education at Cornell University. Published by the American Nature Association, Washington, D. C. Cloth cover, 128 pages.

This book is written to guide those who teach science in the first ten years of school, not to dictate what should be taught there. It is prepared on a philosophy that science is not only a series of organized facts but more important than this, it is concerned with the method by which facts are established. Accordingly the program consists not of a survey of areas of content but rather of an exploration of different realms of experience. These experiences have been selected with care and organized in such a way that they are accumulative, and while each offers more or less immediately significant experience it adds to previous or leads to subsequent experiences.

The suggestions are directed towards the solution of pertinent problems and involve activities suitable to the abilities of the children to learn not solely from books but from real sources which are immediately available for study. While the initial experiences should be largely of a sensory exploration of the immediate environment these experiences may be enriched by materials such as are to be found in NATURE MAGAZINE and other suitable sources of reference.

Business English, by J. Walter Ross. Published by South-Western Publishing Company, Cincinnati, Ohio. Cloth cover, 397 pages.

The aim of this book is to provide a complete course of instruction and exercise material to fit the student to speak and write readily the clear, correct, forceful English required in the transaction of present-day business. The three main topics are Word Study (grammar), Sentence Study, and Business Communications. They are presented in the order named.

Being a teacher still in the service, the writer is fully aware that even the word "grammar" is unpopular with secondary school students; but, by the same criterion, he is fully aware also of students' deficiencies and their need for not merely a hasty review but a systematic, intensive study of the fundamentals of grammar. An earnest effort has been made to co-operate with the teacher in impressing upon the student the fact that a readily usable knowledge of these fundamentals is, regardless of his likes or dislikes, indispensable if he is

to fill satisfactorily the kind of position he will likely obtain on completing a business course.

1. It is made clear at the beginning and throughout the course that the use of technical terms is only a convenience in the discussion of the subject of English.

2. A practical reason is given at the beginning of each chapter for learning the principles presented therein. The student is shown the very definite connection between his study assignments and the work for which he is preparing.

3. There has been substituted for lengthy academic discussion an ample amount of exercise or problem material of nature and vocabulary within the average student's comprehension. The student is asked to apply rules rather than to talk about them. The frequent composition assignments in this edition emphasize this feature.

4. The parts of speech are presented in an order that makes possible the complete mastery of each (definition, classification, properties, and syntax) before leaving it, and the avoidance of the confusion usually experienced by the student of grammar.

5. Purely theoretical questions and hair-splitting technicalities have been purposely avoided. Only those principles, a thorough knowledge of which is essential to the user of forceful and effective English, are presented.

In the section on Sentence Study, the student is drilled in the recognition and the use of the various types of sentences and is familiarized with the application of the rhetorical principles of unity, coherence, and emphasis, in the sentence, the paragraph, and the entire composition.

In the section on Punctuation, the paragraph rather than the sentence is used in many exercises for the development of sentence sense and a review of the full stop marks.

In the chapters on Business Composition, which are greatly amplified in this edition, the student not only is familiarized with mechanical forms but also is led by easy steps from the writing of the simple types of letters to the composition of the more difficult types. Through the study of an ample number of models (actual letters), he learns not only composition styles but also much of business routine, practice, and policy.

Obviously, the teacher who desires to do so can conveniently start classes in letter writing or in the rhetorical principles and use the other chapters for reference and review as the needs of the students are indicated by the work submitted.

The material used in illustrations and exercises has been gathered from so many sources that the author must content himself with this general acknowledgment.

Business Executive's Handbook—By Stanley M. Brown. Published by Prentice-Hall, Inc., New York, N. Y. Leather cover, 1281 pages.

The BUSINESS EXECUTIVE'S HANDBOOK has been designed to provide within the covers of one handy volume, direct and practical answers to the business man's questions and problems.

The information contained in the Handbook will be found to be specific and to the point. Forms, tables, short cuts, listings of facts, outlines of procedure—these will save the business man time, trouble and expense. Whether the problem to be dealt with relates to Credits, Purchasing, Selling, Advertising, Insurance, Direct-Mail—to mention only a few of the subjects included—the Handbook supplies reliable information in the most concise form.

For assistance and advice in the preparation of the book, grateful acknowledgment is made to the hundreds of business men throughout the country who contributed very generously of their time and experience.

Here, for example, are a few of the pointers you will find—

—how to reduce your bill for telegrams and telephones

—how to prepare a simple, workable, money-saving budget

—how to cut corners in doing mathematical work of any kind

—how to increase the efficiency of your collection letters

—how to obtain the best results from your present personnel

—how to prepare advertising that will sell more products at a lower price

—how to cut insurance costs—fire, life, casualty

—how to purchase materials more economically

—how to write letters that will turn complaints into sales

—how to plan a fool-proof investment program for the future

—how to handle a corporate meeting from the sending of the notices to the proper writing of the minutes.

And these are but a few of the items covered in this extraordinary new book. No wonder that it has been called "the most valuable book ever offered to progressive business men."

Section	LIST OF SECTIONS	Page
1.	Business Mathematics	1
2.	Business Letters	133
3.	Selling by Direct-Mail	225
4.	Advertising	271
5.	Sales Contracts and Forms	405
6.	Purchasing Procedure	555
7.	Insurance	581
8.	Credits and Collections	673
9.	Dealings With Embarrassed Debtors	773
10.	Financial Statements	803
11.	Types of Business Organizations	893
12.	Partnerships	911
13.	Directors, Officers, Stockholders	947
14.	Corporate Meetings, Minutes, and Resolutions	1005
15.	Increasing Profits Through Budgetary Control	1085
16.	Life Insurance, Annuities, and Estate Planning	1113
17.	Telegraph, Telephone, and Postal Information	1159
	Glossary of Abbreviations	1211
	Index	1285

J. I. Kinman Elected President American Association of Commercial Colleges

"J. I.," as he is familiarly known, is perhaps one of the most aggressive, as well as progressive, school men in the United States. In a few short years, Kinman Business University has grown to be one of our largest commercial school institutions, with an enrollment of 700 in the day school and nearly 200 in the night school. He no sooner gets an idea than he immediately puts it into practice. He is said to be the originator of the amateur hour on the radio, having secured local talent from the surrounding communities to appear on a program given by the Kinman Business University over the radio. During the National Commercial Teachers Convention in Cleveland in December, he delivered a very interesting and worthwhile address on advertising before the Commercial School Section, of which he was elected Vice President for the year 1937. Another very successful plan apparently followed by his school, is that of agreeing to refund the first month's tuition to any student who is not satisfied at the end of thirty days. His school comprises the ground floor and second floor of a half block in the heart of the Spokane business district. His office seems to be a never ending machine for putting into effect various ideas, by which his institution is brought to the attention of the public.

J. I. Kinman

He has been for the past two years, president of the Spokane Chamber of Commerce and prior to that was president for two years of the Spokane Advertising Club. He is a senior partner in the Certified Public Accountancy firm of Kinman and Morris, with offices in the old National Bank Building.

He is a director in the old National Bank & Union Trust Company of Spokane, as well as director in the Fidelity Savings & Loan Association. A member of the Elks, Moose, Eagles, and a member of the Central Christian Church.

C. W. Woodward

Burlington College of Commerce, Burlington, Iowa.   Sec.-Treas. American Association of Commercial Colleges.

SCRIPT WILL DO

After falling overboard the captain yelled, "Drop me a line!"

The mate appearing at the rail shouted back, "What will your address be?"

A second grade spelling lesson from Meriden, Kansas. Mrs. Wilbur Morrison, teacher. The first specimen was written by Norman Lee Warner, the second by Clarence Koenitzer, and the third by David Tritt.

A unique flourish by H. S. Blanchard, loaned to us by Rosario Babin, Berlin, N. H.

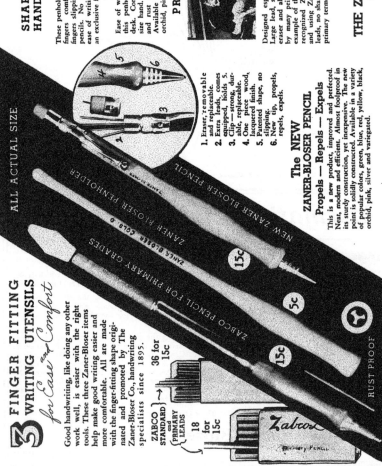

Vol. 42 APRIL, 1937 No. 8

The Educator

EDUCATION
PENMANSHIP
ENGROSSING

The Zaner-Bloser Co.
Columbus, Ohio

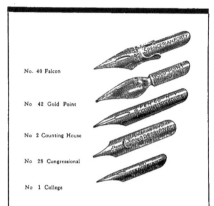

Volume 42　　　　　COLUMBUS, OHIO, APRIL, 1937　　　　　No. 8

The National Association of Penmanship Teachers and Supervisors

Eighteenth Annual Meeting, Wardman Park Hotel, Washington, D. C., April 29, 30, May 1, 1937.

Plans for the coming convention of the National Association of Penmanship Teachers and Supervisors are rapidly nearing completion and present indications are, that our convention will be one of the most successful in the annals of our association.

The officials of the Washington Board of Trade are planning a most royal reception for our delegates and are making every effort to show us the kind of hospitality for which their city is noted. Many government buildings, not ordinarily open to the public, will, by special arrangement made by the board, be open to us and their splendid cooperation gives every indication that we will long remember our stay in the city.

The school department of the city of Washington, has organized under Mr. Robert L. Haycock, Assistant Superintendent of Schools, Chairman of the Washington Hospitality Committee, and Mrs. M. M. Boling, Director of Handwriting, Chairman of the Washington Convention Committee and are planning exhibits, tours, entertainment and a most gracious reception for everyone in attendance.

The advance reservation for exhibit space gives evidence that the exhibit as heretofore will be one of the features of the convention.

This year the innovation of combining the president's reception with a round table discussion of current handwriting problems will give an opportunity for an evening of educational profit and social contact.

The tours which are being arranged for Friday would be well worth a visit to Washington, if none of the other features which are being offered were given. The opportunity to visit these Historic places in company with our friends and associates is one of which we should all avail ourselves. Group pictures will be taken at each place.

Friday evening the annual banquet promises to be a gala affair. It will be held in the beautiful Continental Room of the Wardman Park Hotel. A very prominent guest of honor will be present. Entertainment will be provided by a Washington Teachers' Committee and dancing may be enjoyed.

Send your membership at once to Mr. F. J. Duffy, Director of Handwriting, Duluth, Minnesota, Treasurer, and plan an exhibit of the work being done in your schools. Application for exhibit space may be made to Miss Doris D. Almy, Secretary, 337 Walnut Street, Fall River, Massachusetts.

Plan to be with us on April 29, April 30 and May 1 in the beautiful city of Washington, and we assure you that the officers of your association, the Washington Board of Trade, and the Washington School Department will do everything within their power to arrange a program which will be of pleasure and profit to all.

Very sincerely yours,

D. F. Harrigan, Jr.

President.

* * *

PROGRAM

Thursday

Address of Welcome

Hon. Melvin C. Hazen, President of Board, District of Columbia Commission.

Response to Address of Welcome

Mr. Raymond C. Goodfellow, Director of Commercial Education and Handwriting, Newark, N. J.

President's Address

Mr. D. Francis Harrigan, Director of Handwriting, Peabody, Massachusetts.

Address

Hon. George J. Bates, Member Congress.

Subject:　SCHOOL ADMINISTRATION FINANCE.

Address

Prominent Superintendent of Schools.

Thursday P. M.

SIGHT SEEING

Federal Buildings, City of Washington.

Address at Archives Building

Dorsey W. Hyde, Director of Archival Service.

Trip through New Federal Bureau of Investigation Buildings as guests of department.

Thursday Evening

President Reception:

Guests, Committee Members Washington Teachers, Friends.

Round Table Conference—Discussion.

Friday A. M.

Tours　Washington Teachers' Tours Committee

MOUNT VERNON
ALEXANDRIA
ANNAPOLIS
WASHINGTON UNIVERSITY
Others in Preparation.

(Continued on page 15)

THE EDUCATOR

Published monthly (except July and August)
By THE ZANER-BLOSER CO.,
612 N. Park St., Columbus, O.
E. A. LUPFER...Editor
PARKER ZANER BLOSER................Business Mgr.

SUBSCRIPTION PRICE, $1.25 A YEAR
(To Canada, 10c more; foreign, 30c more)
Single copy, 15c.
Change of address should be requested promptly in advance, if possible, giving the old as well as the new address.
Advertising rates furnished upon request.

THE EDUCATOR is the best medium through which to reach business college proprietors and managers, commercial teachers and students, and lovers of penmanship. Copy must reach our office by the 10th of the month for the issue of the following month.

Modern Handwriting

By E. A. Lupfer, Zanerian College, Columbus, Ohio

No. 8

SELF CHECKING CHART

If the student will check his own handwriting with this chart he will be able to discover many of his own weaknesses without the aid of his teacher. It will also help teachers to discover errors.

Students can profitably check each others papers.

When one first looks at a hand written letter he almost instantly forms an opinion of the handwriting. One gets a good or a poor impression from that first look and usually that impression is accurate and lasting.

Therefore, one of the most important things about handwriting is **General Appearance.** Let us consider your handwriting first from the standpoint of General Appearance; then try to discover the things which help or detract from good General Appearance of writing.

1. General Appearance
Good?
Fair?
Poor?
Neat?
Careless?

2. Margins
Even?
Crowded?
Wide & Irregular?

3. Quality of Line
Good, clean, free?
Heavy, labored?
Faint?
Shaded and uneven?
Blots and smeared places?
Mistakes and erasures?

4. Size
Uniform?
Too large?
Too small?
Irregular?
Alignment?

5. Slant
Uniform?
Uneven?
Backhand?
Too slanting?

6. Spacing
Uniform?
Uneven?
Crowded?
Scattered?

7. Movement
Good?
Slow and labored?
Wild and uncontrolled?

8. Forms
Good?
Legible?
Illegible in parts?
Loops?
Turns?
Angles?
Capitals?
Beginning strokes?
Ending strokes?

9. Position
Penholder?
Little finger?
Wrist?
Elbows?
Back?
Head?

10. Material
Good paper?
Smooth pen?
Good ink?

11. Attitude
Do you like to write?
Do you realize that good handwriting will help you in school and later in life?

Practice the retraced **K** large. The **K** should come down to the base line rather straight. Therefore, retrace the straight stem. In making the stem come down to the base line straight, stop, then raise the pen. Do not raise the pen at the base line while it is in motion. You will find the retracing of the compound curve good practice. Keep on the line in making the **K.** Notice how even the spaces inside the **K** are above and below the loop.

In making the small k care should be used in getting the finish like in **i.** Do not slur the last part but come down to the base line, then swing up gracefully. In order to help you we are giving you k with the under turn or u exercise. Make the five k's without raising the pen, but stop on the little loop each time before making the finish of the letter.

The **H** and **K** are similar. Practice them together. Also notice the similarity between the **H** and **K** loop and the loop in the **V** and **U.** Practice the large **U** exercise before making the **U** and **V.**

S s's's's ssssssss ssssssss

summons summons summons

sure sure sure sure sure sure

soar soar soar soar soar soar so

Trace the large **s** with a dry pen, then make one of your own very large and trace it. The **s** of course should be one-fourth of a space high. Close the **s** at the bottom and in the joined **s**'s swing through with a rolling motion without raising the pen. The word **summons** and **sure** are easy in that the movement should be fluent. There are very few pauses. The only pause seems to be on the **o** and **r**. The word **soar** is difficult in that you have a decided slowing up of motion at the top of **o, a** and **r**. If you write this word too fast it will become careless in appearance.

8 8 8 8 8 S S S S S S S

S S S S S S S S S S S S

Practice the compound curve or figure **8** exercise. Be sure that the top and bottom are equal. Slant the exercise so that the down stroke resembles the stem in the **S**. Practice the letter and exercise until you can make a good **S**. Be sure that you stop on the hook before making the final stroke. Make the letter **S** on the blackboard, erase all but the compound downward stroke and see if it is similar to the stem in the **T**.

September September Sept

Sept. Sept. Sept. Sept. Sept.

S Saturday Sat. Sunday Sun.

Write the words and the abbreviations watching the space between the capital and small letters. Are you curving the upstroke of your **S** and do you get a nice swing at the base line?

September pt pt pt pt pt pt pt

September mb be ber ber ber ber

b b b b b b bbb bbb b b b b

Practice the combination of letters found in the word **September**. This gives a good review of the small **b**. It pays to frequently review.

Place the hand so that it rests on the nails of the last two fingers.

See that the hand slides freely over the paper. A free hand is necessary for speedy writing.

The L contains two compound curves and two loops. The top loop should be larger than the bottom loop. The bottom loop should lay flat on the base line. Keep the crossing of the top loop rather low, making a long, full graceful loop. Curve the beginning stroke well and swing the finishing stroke gracefully below the base line.

In making the line of **L**'s see how nearly alike you can make the upper loops. They should all slant in the same direction and be about the same distance across.

Language Language Language

In writing the word **Language** keep the L and a close together. See that the two loops in the g's are the same in size as the upper loop in the l.

More mistakes are made on loops than any other group of letters. At least, loop letters when poorly made stand out prominently. Every loop should be open. The back should be fairly straight. Make the retraced exercise and five loops without raising the pen. It is a good plan to make several l's separately, then make the connected group of l's.

In making the line of l's see that the top and bottom turns are the same in roundness. Are your loops open or are they simply uncrossed t's? Cover the top part of the l and you should have a good i. Cover up the letter in the copy, then cover up your own. This comparison may help you.

language learning spelling ll

In the words above see how uniform in size and proportion you can make the loops. The loops above the line should be as large as the loops below the line.

Let your arm move when you write. Run your hand along the line.

Writing to be practical should be free. That is, you should be able to do it quickly and easy. Much attention should, therefore, be given to the manner of writing. Use arm rather than finger movement. Some finger action is permissible, but too much finger action will produce labored looking writing. The large muscles in the arm are not so easily tired as the small muscles of the fingers. Therefore, when writing with arm movement all day one is likely to tire less than if the small muscles of the fingers are used.

Let us continue our study so that the entire class shall have a perfect score in spelling.
Let Let Let L L L Laura Lorna
continue continue continue con
c c c cc cc on our ord
entire entire entire entire entire

An excellent copy for supplementary practice. Notice the check marks and other points to which we have called your attention in the copy.

reports reports reports reports
s s s s s r r r rs rs
sss sss rr rr

Review the word **reports** and give additional study and practice to the small letter **r** and **s**.

Q 22Q 22Q 22Q 22Q 22
2 2 2 2 2 2 2 2 2 2 2 2 2 2 2

The **Q** begins the same as the **W** and ends the same as the **L.** The body part is made from the indirect oval. Therefore, review the running oval exercise and the retraced exercise. Practice the retraced exercise in this copy along with the letter. Draw slant lines touching the edges of the loops.

An Evaluation of Manuscript Writing

By Frank N. Freeman
University of Chicago

Introduction of Manuscript Writing

Vertical Writing—In the last decade of the nineteenth century a new style of writing was proposed, backed by certain scientific facts and some convincing arguments. Physicians and students of school hygiene brought evidence to support the contention that the type of writing in vogue conduced to eyestrain and curvature of the spine. They advocated the substitution of vertical writing, written with the paper directly in front of the pupil and square with the desk, the pupil facing the desk with both arms resting equally on it. The arguments were widely accepted, vertical writing was widely adopted, and millions of pupils switched from slanting to vertical style.

Short Lived—The fashion did not last long. After about two decades nearly all school systems had turned back to slanting writing. School men had discovered that, while certain scientific facts favored vertical writing, other equally scientific facts were unfavorable to it. It was discovered by experience, and the discovery was confirmed by motion-picture studies, that a smooth, easy writing movement requires that the hand swing across the page with the elbow as a center and the forearm as a radius. This motion requires that the paper be tilted. It was further discovered that the essential demands underlying vertical writing, namely, that the paper be directly before the writer and that the writer face the desk squarely with both arms resting symmetrically on it, could be met with slanting writing. Consequently, in the return to slanting writing modifications were made to incorporate these conditions.

Disorganization—Meanwhile, a generation of children had had their handwriting habits uprooted and disorganized. The teaching profession had learned by the costly method of wholesale practical experimentation what might have been found out by systematic and comprehensive study and evaluation of all the facts in the problem. Some scientific study was made, to be sure, but it was too narrow and too one-sided to constitute a safe guide to practice.

The Analogy—The case of vertical writing has been described at some length because it furnishes a close analogy to that of manuscript writing. Manuscript writing is advocated by enthusiastic and progressive teachers and is backed by some scientific evidence. It has been adopted by some private schools and a few of the smaller public-school systems, but it has not up to now swept the country as did vertical writing. Mindful, perhaps, of the case of vertical writing and influenced, possibly, by the general scientific temper of the time, the educational profession has adopted a policy of watchful waiting until evidence could be assembled which would make possible a deliberate and balanced appraisal. A great deal of evidence has now accumulated, and it may be appropriate to undertake to evaluate the evidence and to judge whether manuscript writing has made good its claim to adoption or whether, perhaps, it

---

> When to change from Print to Script is a question uppermost in the minds of teachers of handwriting today. The consensus of opinion seems to be that the child should change to script before the habit of printing becomes habitual, and yet print should be used long enough to help in learning reading, spelling and expression.
>
> Dr. Freeman has done much scientific investigation and research. This article will be of special interest to you.

---

should be used in a limited way and some of its characteristics be incorporated into the conventional cursive writing. We may first consider briefly the claims made in support of manuscript writing.

Historical Arguments Advanced for Manuscript Writing

Two Styles—The first claim is based on historical argument. The basic historical fact is that modern handwriting is derived from an informal style of writing used for everyday communication which existed alongside the more formal and careful style of writing used for making books and permanent records. The existence of the two styles of writing from "time immemorial" is clearly brought out by the authority on paleography, E. A. Lowe:

From time immemorial there have existed the two kinds of script our specimens show: the set and the free, the formal and the unlabored, the painstaking book script and the quick, flowing cursive hand of everyday life. The two answered different purposes, their exigencies differed. What printing is to us, the formal script was to the generations before printing was invented. And the cursive of the notaries corresponded, roughly speaking, to our modern handwriting.[1]

[1] *Roger Fry and E. A. Lowe, English Handwriting, p.* 93. *S.P.E. Tract No. XXIII.* London: Oxford University Press, 1926

Cursive vs. Book Printing—Cursive writing, then, came into being in response to the demand for an easy, flowing style, and the fact that it existed parallel to the formal "book script" shows, so far as historical evidence can show, that it is better suited to informal writing than is the "book script," or manuscript writing.

The advocates of manuscript writing seem to imply that modern cursive writing was developed to meet the requirements, or at least the convenience, of copperplate engraving. There are two versions of the argument. One, given by Miss Wise,[1] traces "the probable causes which led to the de-

[1] *Marjorie Wise, On the Technique of Manuscript Writing, p.* xv New York: Charles Scribner's Sons, 1924.

velopment of our modern running hand" to the use of copperplate engravings for the preparation of copybooks for the teaching of writing after the "Revival of Learning." The influence of engraving led to the joining of letters, to the elaboration of capitals, and to the increase in slant. A somewhat less radical influence is attributed to the engraver's art by Professor James Shelley, who is one of the authorities cited by Miss Wise, in an article quoted in Manuscript Writing and Lettering:

When education became generally recognized as of national importance early in the nineteenth century, and handwriting became an important factor in such education, the printed characters of books were unsuited to the work of the pen, the traditions of manuscript writing in the Middle Ages had been practically lost, and teachers, when deciding upon the forms of the written letters, instead of inquiring into the basic principles upon which the art of handwriting should be developed, and attempting to determine the necessary conditions which should govern lettering, took over for imitation the results of another and quite different art which happened to be fashionable, namely, the art of engraving letters upon copperplate and printing therefrom.[2]

[2] *Manuscript Writing and Lettering, pp.* 29-30. London: Sir Isaac Pitman & Sons, Ltd. (second edition).

Professor Shelley does not attribute cursive writing as a whole to engraved copies, but only certain extravagances of the forms current in the nineteenth century. However, he somewhat inconsistently advocates going back not to a simpler cursive style but to the formal "bookscript," which never was used for informal writing. If it is true that the former cursive writing was corrupted by the art of the engraver, the logical remedy would seem to be to go back to the style which was so corrupted and not to return to a quite different style which was used for making books rather than for everyday communication. As a matter of fact, the faults which are complained of—the elaborate flourishes, extreme slant, and in some cases excessively long loops and angular forms—had already been eliminated from all modern writing, particularly from American writing, before manuscript writing came into fashion in the schools.

Correct historical interpretation, therefore, does not validate the claim of manuscript writing as a form to supplant cursive writing as a general style of writing. If manuscript has a valid claim, it will have to be based on other grounds.

Scientific Comparisons of Manuscript and Cursive Writing

Photo Analysis—To explain the historical fact that two styles of writing grew up, a formal style used in making books and the informal cursive style used in everyday communication, it is necessary to make an experimental analysis of the movement used in writing the two styles. Such an analysis was made by William H. Gray,[1] who took motion-picture photographs of a number of writers who wrote both manuscript and cursive with facility. He found several fundamental differences between the two. The most striking difference is that the pen stroke in manuscript writing is slower and more uniform

[1] *William Henry Gray, "An Experimental Comparison of the Movements in Manuscript Writing and Cursive Writing," Journal of Educational Psychology, XXI (April, 1930), 259-72.*

in speed than in cursive writing. In the cursive writing the pen stroke becomes much more rapid in the middle of the longer lines. It slows down, of course, at the sharp turns in the letters. To put the difference in another way, the manuscript writing is done with a rather slow, drawing movement, whereas the cursive writing is done with a more rapid and a more free, swinging stroke. This free stroke is made possible by the modification of the forms of the letters produced by joining them together. As a result there are fewer places where there is a sharp change in the direction of the stroke, with a consequent slowing-down or pause. Contrary to what might be expected, the actual lifting of the pen does not slow down the stroke itself. Slowing-down is caused rather by the form of letters, requiring numerous changes in direc-

tion. An example is the letter **e**. In manuscript writing the first stroke is horizontal and the circular stroke which forms the main outline of the letter meets this horizontal stroke at a sharp angle. In cursive writing no such angle exists.

Lines and Strokes—The lines and strokes of manuscript and cursive writing have been contrasted from the point of view of the movements used in producing them. A corresponding contrast is presented by their appearance. Because the strokes of manuscript writing are at more clear-cut angles to each other, the forms of the letters are more clearly defined. In cursive writing, on the other hand, as the movement of one stroke changes gradually into that of the next, so the forms of the letters tend to blend into one another. The consequence is that manuscript writing is more legible than is cursive, particularly if an attempt is made to distinguish the individual letters. **Legibility**—If it is necessary only to distinguish the word wholes in a familiar language, the difference in legibility is much less. It should be noted that the superiority in legibility of manuscript writing is marked only when the original or pure

---

Heard at N. A. P. T. S.

Our poor handwriting is not due to any lack of knowledge of the art among the teachers of penmanship. It is because our school authorities are not willing to recognize the importance of plain handwriting or to give a reasonable amount of time to the teaching of it.

---

manuscript style is used. When this style is modified to approach cursive writing by slanting it and changing the forms of the letters, greater speed can be attained but the superiority in legibility is lost.

Speed—As a final style of writing, then, cursive is more rapid and somewhat less legible than is manuscript writing. The superiority in speed is sometimes denied, and figures are given to show that manuscript writing is the more rapid. The contradiction is only apparent and is due to the fact that comparisons are sometimes made with younger children and sometimes with older children and adults. Kimmins,[1] for example, gives the results

[1] *Marjorie Wise, op. cit., p. xi.*

of tests of 9,264 girls who had written manuscript writing for two years or more. He finds that the younger children write the manuscript style the faster, whereas by thirteen years cursive writing becomes faster. The same contrast was found by Turner,[2] Gray,[3] and Gates and Brown.[4] It may

[2] *Olive G. Turner, "The Comparative Legibility and Speed of Manuscript Writing and Cursive Handwriting," Elementary School Journal, XXX (June, 1930), 780-86.*

[3] *William Henry Gray, op. cit.*

[4] *Arthur I. Gates and Helen Brown, "Experimental Comparisons of Print-Script and Cursive Writing," Journal of Educational Research, XX (June, 1929), 1-14.*

be accepted as a fairly well-established fact, then, that manuscript writing is faster in the writing of younger children and that cursive writing is faster in the writing of older children and adults.

Use of Manuscript Writing in Early Grades

Early Training—This fact introduces a new angle to the problem. Thus far in this discussion manuscript and cursive writing in general have been under comparison. It now seems that consideration must be given to the adjustment of writing to the capacities and the needs of younger and older children separately. The conclusions which have thus far been reached apply to the writing of older persons and may need to be modified in reference to young children. Since the emphasis in the early stages of writing is on learning to form the letters correctly and in the later stages on acquiring fluency and speed, it seems quite possible that manuscript writing may be better for one stage and cursive writing for the other.

Easier to Learn in Lower Grades—Examination will be made, therefore, of the evidence concerning the suitability of manuscript writing to the child in the early grades. It has already been noted that young children write the manuscript style more rapidly than the cursive. This fact indicates that it is easier for them to learn manuscript writing. Why manuscript writing should be easier to learn is not difficult to understand. Since the letters are separated, each letter stands out as a distinct unit of perception, and the unit of perception is smaller, being the letter rather than the word. The unit of movement is also shorter. Furthermore, the child does not have to learn to make the connecting strokes. These strokes, besides being additional elements to write, vary somewhat according to the letters which are being connected, whereas the separate letters are constant and invariable. Again, the connecting strokes change somewhat the appearance of the letters themselves. Finally, the manuscript letters resemble printed letters, and the child's familiarity with the printed letters is therefore a greater help in learning manuscript than in learning cursive forms.

Early Expression—The earlier acquisition of skill in writing the manuscript style gives the child an earlier facility in expressing himself in writing and therefore hastens the growth of ability in written composition.

Manuscript in Relation to Reading —The relation between manuscript writing and reading is mutual. Voorhis[1] has shown that the use of manu-

[1] *Thelma G. Voorhis, The Relative Merits of Cursive and Manuscript Writing. Lincoln School Research Studies. New York: Lincoln School of Teachers College, Columbia University, 1931.*

script writing in Grade I definitely hastens the growth of the ability to read. The gain is so pronounced as to be unmistakable. Because of the great importance of reading, this fact must be given due weight. It is reported by teachers, on the basis of observation rather than experiment, that manuscript writing also favors growth in spelling. This result seems very probable from the effect of manuscript writing on reading. It is also reported that children show more enthusiasm for manuscript writing in the early grades. This attitude may well be the consequence of the greater ease with which they learn it.

Manuscript For Young, Cursive for Older Pupils—If manuscript writing is better for the young child and cursive writing for the older pupil, can the problem be solved by beginning with manuscript and changing over to cursive writing? This plan immediately suggests the objection that such a change may entail serious difficulty and loss of skill. Fortunately, evidence is available on this point. Studies by Winch [1] and by Gates and Brown[2] show that, if the change is made not later than Grade III, it can

[1] *W. H. Winch, "Print-Script and Cursive-Script in Schools: An Investigation in Nervo-muscular Readjustments," Forum of Education, IV (June and November, 1926), 123-38, 206-22.*

[2] *Arthur I. Gates and Helen Brown, op. cit.*

be accomplished with little retardation in progress. If the change is delayed until the writing habit has been firmly fixed, the acquisition of the new style is more difficult. Goetsch's comparison of the writing in the later grades of children who started with manuscript and cursive writing respectively, while not altogether conclusive, indicates that the early use of manuscript writing has no detrimental effect on the later writing of cursive. [3]

[3] *Walter Robert Goetsch, "The Effect of Early Training in Handwriting on Later Writing and on Composition." Unpublished Master's thesis, Department of Education, University of Chicago, 1934. See also "The Effect of Early Handwriting Instruction," Elementary School Journal, XXXVI (December, 1935), 290-98.*

Reports Made by Primary Supervisors on Current Practices and Advantages and Disadvantages of Manuscript Writing

In addition to the evidence from scientific experiment which has been cited, it is also worth while to con-

sider the trend of practice and the opinion of teachers and supervisors. To get information on these points, the writer sent a questionnaire to 360 primary supervisors. Replies were received from 218.

The most pertinent facts concerning practice may first be summarized briefly. Of those replying, about a fourth now use manuscript writing. The large majority of those who use it introduced it during or before 1931, fewer than a quarter having introduced it since that date. Evidently those who were not convinced of its value during the early period of propaganda are either awaiting further evidence or have made up their minds negatively. About 10 per cent of those who tried manuscript writing have discontinued using it.

In Grades 1 and 2—Probably the most significant fact concerns the grades in which manuscript writing is used. The distribution given in Table I shows that of forty-nine reporting on this point, thirty-two teach manu-

script writing only in Grade I or in Grades I and II.

Opinions vs. Analysis—The opinions of the persons replying are given in Table II. It is significant to compare these data with the results of experiments and psychological analysis. The respondents were asked to list both the advantages and the disadvantages of manuscript writing based on their experience and conversation with other teachers or supervisors. It is evident that each of the first five advantages given by teachers coincide with the advantage found in the experiments. The sixth is obvious. It is clear also that the first three apply solely to writing in the early grades and that the fourth and the fifth apply more to these grades than to later years. So far as the disadvantages are concerned, it has been shown that the first, which is most often mentioned, is not serious if the change is made early. It is far outweighed by the advantages. The second is based on misinformation so far as the pri-

TABLE I

GRADES IN WHICH MANUSCRIPT WRITING IS TAUGHT IN 49 SCHOOLS USING THAT STYLE OF HANDWRITING

Grades in Which Taught	Number of Schools	Grades in Which Taught	Number of Schools
I	13	I-VI	5
I-II	19	I-VII	1
I-III	6	I-VIII	0
I-IV	0	I-IX	1
I-V	0	Special	4

TABLE II

ADVANTAGES AND DISADVANTAGES OF MANUSCRIPT WRITING REPORTED BY FIVE OR MORE SUPERVISORS USING IT

Advantages:

	Number Reporting
1. Easier to learn, less fatiguing, and gives better writing (more legible and neat), easier to teach	40
2. Helps in early reading because of similarity of written and printed forms	34
3. Enables children much sooner to use writing as a form of expression	15
4. Pupils like it and take pride in it, appreciate good writing	11
5. Helps in spelling	8
6. Is an aid to lettering in art and map work	5

Disadvantages:

1. Difficulty in changing to cursive	20
2. Slow or probably slow	8
3. Difficulty in transferring to schools which do not use it	7
4. Parents must be convinced	6
5. Less rhythmic and encourages finger movement and bad posture	5
6. Difficult to read cursive	5

mary grades are concerned, for investigation has shown that in these grades manuscript writing is faster. The third and the fourth are administrative difficulties which are not serious. The fifth can be overcome by proper methods of instruction and is not serious in the first two grades. The sixth does not apply to the primary grades, where the children do not need to read cursive writing. So far as these opinions go, then, the advantages of manuscript writing in the early grades far outweigh the disadvantages.

Time for Making Change to Cursive Writing

If manuscript writing is taught in the early grades and cursive writing in the later grades, the question arises: When shall the change be made? A consideration of all the factors leads the writer to recommend that the change be made in the latter part of Grade II. The reasons for this opinion are as follows: (1) The advantage of ease of learning would be lost if the pupils did not use manuscript writing long enough to be able to write it readily. (2) The advantage to reading probably extends into the second year. (3) The advantage in enabling pupils to express themselves freely in writing can be obtained only if the pupils write in manuscript style long enough to acquire some fluency. (4) The change should be put off until the pupil has become mature enough to have the skill to learn cursive writing easily; otherwise, there is no advantage in beginning with manuscript writing. (5) The change should be made before the habit of manuscript writing has become so firmly fixed as to make the change difficult. (6) The questionnaire sent to primary supervisors indicates that nearly all who begin with manuscript writing change to cursive writing in the latter part of Grade II, or at the beginning of Grade III. This fact shows that experience bears out the arguments given.

Conclusions

Finally—The conclusions and practical applications follow naturally from the facts which have been presented. They may be stated briefly: (1) Historical evidence, experiment, practice, and opinion indicate that cursive writing is better for the upper grades and for adult writing. (2) Experiment, the trend of practice, and the opinion of those who have used it indicate that manuscript writing is preferable for beginners. (3) The change should be made late enough to secure the advantages of manuscript writing as an initial style and early enough to minimize the difficulty of making the change. In the opinion of the writer, the point at which the change can probably best be made is the second half of Grade II.
Reprinted with permission of the Elementary School Journal, Feb., 1936.

N. A. P. T. S.

(Continued from page 7)

Friday P. M.

Address
D. Frank W. Ballou, Superintendent of Schools, Washington, D. C.

Address
Miss Bertha A. Connor, Director of Handwriting, Boston, Massachusetts Public Schools.

Address
Mr. R. T. Harbo, Administrative Assistant to J. Edgar Hoover.
Subject: Handwriting in Relation to Crime.

Friday Evening

Annual Banquet—Dragon Room, Wardman Park Hotel.
Entertainment—dancing.
Washington Teachers' Committee, Hosts.

Saturday A.M.

Address
Dr. C. E. Walters, Chief of Organic Chemistry Section, U. S. Bureau of Standards.
Subject: Government Analysis of School Inks.

Address
Mr. Bourdon W. Scribner, Chief of Paper Section, U. S. Bureau of Standards.
Subject: Government Analysis of School Paper.

Address
Dr. John G. Kirk, Director of Commercial Education and Handwriting, Philadelphia, Pa.

Address
Professor of Education, Georgetown University.

Address
Prominent Massachusetts Superintendent of Schools.

Saturday P. M.

Business Meeting.

By Curtis Hodges

One of the most interesting meetings in the history of the National Association of Penmanship Teachers and Supervisors will be held in Washington, April 29 to May 1.

The program which has been arranged by D. F. Harrigan, Jr., President of the Association, will be of outstanding interest. It will include an address by J. Edgar Hoover, Director of the Federal Bureau of Investigation, or one of Mr. Hoover's assist-

ants. The subject of this address will be "Handwriting in Relation to Crime." There will also be an address by Congressman George J. Bates, whose subject will be "School Administration Finance". Arrangements have also been made for a talk on the various qualities of ink and the way to determine the best ink for penmanship use. There will also be an address on the qualities of writing papers. These talks on writing papers and ink will be given by experts from the U. S. Bureau of Standards.

In connection with the meeting there will be an exhibit put on by the District of Columbia and many other states.

Mrs. M. M. Boling of the Washington Schools who has been appointed Chairman of the Convention Committee points out that not only will the convention have a chance to enjoy a wonderful program but also they will have an opportunity to see the most beautiful city in the world. One of the sights will be a trip through the new Archives Building which will be directed by Dorsey W. Hyde, Chief Archivist. Mr. Hyde will give a lecture in the lecture room of the Archives Building.

The visitors will also have an opportunity to see the other buildings in the Federal Triangle, all representing the cost of more than two hundred million dollars. Among other new sights will be the stately Supreme Court building, the new sixty acre Union Station Plaza, the broad Constitution Avenue leading from Union Station to the Lincoln Memorial, the Arlington Memorial Bridge erected at a cost of ten million dollars and the wonderful Mt. Vernon Highway leading to the old home of George Washington. These and many other sights will be at the disposal of the visitors.

This should prove to be one of the largest and most successful meetings the Association has ever held.

MRS. HANNA A. WESTROPE

Funeral services for Mrs. Hannah A. Westrope, 2215 Vine Street, Denver, Colo., a resident of that city for thirty years, were held January 9.

Mrs. Westrope died January 7 following a heart attack. She was 78 years old. She was born in Lancaster, Pa., where she spent most of her early life. She was married in Iowa to Perry A. Westrope. Mr. Westrope was a well-known penman. His fine specimens grace the pages of many scrapbooks. He was especially interested in penmen and did a lot to encourage and inspire young penmen. He died a year ago.

Mrs. Westrope is survived by a daughter, Mrs. Mildred M. Maier, of Denver, who lives at the above address.

Pres. Meadows-Draughon
Business College, Shreveport, La.

THE MOST PRECIOUS THING IN THE WORLD

Some one has said, "Time is the stuff life is made of." To put it another way, time IS life, and, therefore, it is the MOST PRECIOUS thing in the world.

Next to TIME, in importance, is the ABILITY to THINK. That's a broad statement, but THINK it over! The difference between an idiot and an outstanding industrialist, business or professional man is the ability to THINK RIGHT, STRAIGHT and CONSTRUCTIVELY.

The idiot was not endowed with that ability, whereas the industrialist, the business man, or the professional man was endowed with it from birth and has used it continuously to reach and maintain the position he now occupies.

The reason so many young men and women do not succeed in life is because they do not exercise their THINKING faculties enough. They do not stop to consider the VALUE of TIME.

The ABILITY to THINK can be developed by using the BRAIN CELLS the same as the MUSCLES OF THE BODY can be developed by exercise. It is largely a matter of HABIT, the same as exercise has to become a HABIT if we are to become an ATHLETE.

There are a great many STU-DENTS who get to a CERTAIN point and never develop BEYOND that point. Why? Because they do not APPLY themselves as they should. They do not THINK enough. They do not appreciate the VALUE of TIME.

Let's remember that God gives us only so much of that PRECIOUS thing called "TIME". Just how much, none of us can know in advance. But we CAN, if we will just THINK, USE the time, as it is meted out to us daily, to the BEST ADVANTAGE.

Suppose every student in school were to use his THINKING faculties all the time; that he fully realized the VALUE of his TIME and made the proper USE of it? Almost without exception, he would become far more EFFICIENT and would finish his training—or acquire the ability to hold a job—MUCH sooner. He would not only be BETTER qualified to hold a position, but he would advance much MORE RAPIDLY and his EARN-INGS, during the next few years, would be MULTIPLIED.

Of course, we do not expect students to be PERFECT, because we realize they are HUMAN the same as we; but we should like to see EVERY-ONE get into the habit of THINK-ING more and APPRECIATING the VALUE of his TIME. We believe that, if they would do this, they would NOT spend so much time talking to each other in the departments or in the hallways; they would not waste so much time in the rest-rooms; they would respect the rights of others and would not run wildly down the stair-ways; they would not "forget" and smoke in the hallway or in the study halls, etc.

We believe that, if they really STOPPED to THINK, they would MAKE EACH MINUTE COUNT—they would not SLIP AWAY FROM SCHOOL, unnecessarily; they would report to all classes on time and take all the subjects included in the course, enrolled for without having to be re-minded or rounded up continually. Yes, if students would really THINK, they would appreciate the value of time and would realize that rules and regulations are for their benefit and they would give their teachers and the management their fullest co-operation at all times.

PRESIDENT OF NATIONAL COMMERCIAL TEACHERS FEDERATION DIES

Leslie M. Hazen, president of the N. C. T. F. died at his home in East Cleveland, Ohio, on February 19. Mr. Hazen was head of the commercial department of the Shaw High School, E. Cleveland. He was born in the old Hazen homestead on the Limaville-Marlboro Road. Graduated from Marl-boro High School, from the normal department of Mt. Union College, and also was a graduate of the Canton Actual Business College. Received his Doctor of Science degree from Mt. Union College in 1903. Was active in the Federation for many years and held memberships in Sigma Alpha Epsilon fraternity, Linnean Literary Society, the Dynamo Association, and the Unionian staff while at Mt. Union. He was a 32nd degree Mason.

The Educator extends its deepest sympathy to his bereaved wife and two brothers.

50TH ANNUAL GRADUATING EXERCISES

We received an announcement of the fiftieth annual graduating exer-cises of Goldey College, Wilmington, Del. This program gives a brief his-tory of Goldey College and shows photographs of the officers and per-sonnel. The list of graduates con-tained over ninety names. This would indicate that Goldey College is enjoying a very good enrollment.

WINTERING IN FLORIDA

From our good friend, F. L. Faretra of Boston, we learned that Fred S. Heath, the well known penman of Concord, N. H., has been in St. Peters-burg, Fla., since January. Mr. Heath went to Florida on account of his health. We join his friends in wish-ing him a very speedy recovery.

Mr. Faretra is teaching some classes in penmanship at Boston University.

Candor is the seal of a noble mind, the orna-ment and pride of man, the sweetest charm of woman, the scorn of rascals, the rarest virtue of sociability.

This specimen was written by Lucy Danby, a student in Beacom College, Wilmington, Del. H. F. Hudson is the penmanship instructor. Beacom College is turning out some very fine writers.

The ornamental alphabet above is one of the finest ever written by L. Madarasz. Each letter deserves your careful study. The two plates were loaned to us by C. W. Jones, Brockton, Mass.

Ornamental Penmanship

No. 18   Script by the late A. M. Wonnell

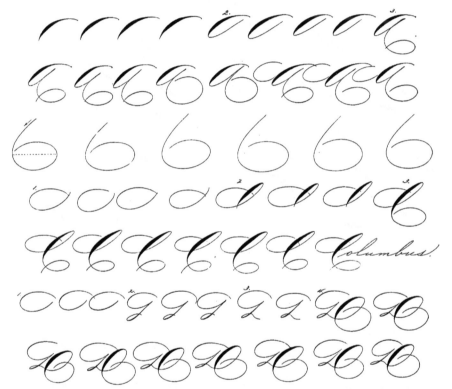

Review Work. Each time you review a letter you see something new and acquire additional skill. Study the letters in parts then apply them to words.

Columbia 5   *Doris Rawdin*

Kite Time

I like the blustery wind of Spring
That whips the tree with glee;
It carries high my colored kite
For all the world to see.

Just see it sway and then away—
A bird upon the breeze;
Oh that I too could sail away
Above the earth and trees!

This easy, free business writing by a fifth grade student is a credit to much of the writing done in many business offices. Doris Rawdin is to be complimented on what she has accomplished and we hope that she will always use care in all of her writing. She is a pupil in the Columbia School, Champaign, Ill., Ethel Kesterson, supervisor.

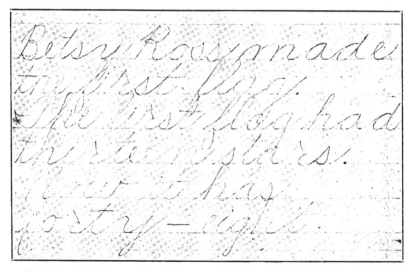

This free flowing, effective writing was done by Sue Rae Wascher, a second grade pupil in Lincoln School, Champaign, Ill., Ethel Kesterson, supervisor. Pupils who learn to write large, free writing such as the above are able to do it with ease and without any strain. The forms are large and easily visualized and mastered. Large pencil writing for primary grades is always preferable to small, cramped writing.

The Auto Game

An interesting way to secure good position

By J. A. Savage

Supervisor of Handwriting, Omaha, Nebr.

Here is an Automobile Game that I have been using for many years to help children to get correct position and movement in their writing. It never fails to create interest in the class.

Each child may name the kind of automobile he prefers. The muscle of the upper arm is the engine that propels the car. The muscle of the forearm is the hind wheels. The fingernails of the last two fingers are the front wheels. The wrist is the body of the car and should never drag. The pen or pencil is the steering gear. It should always point up toward the driver and never lie against the running board (thumb). If the thumb is kept well bent with only the end touching the pencil (steering gear) on the underside, opposite the first joint of the index finger and pushing the pencil up against the finger, the door of the car (space between thumb and pencil) will be wide open back of the steering gear and above the running board. If the automobile is now kept turned far enough to the left to keep the running board near the pavement (paper) the hand will be in good writing position. Both the front and rear wheels should, of course, be kept on the pavement. The foot levers are always in front, and the feet should be kept in readiness to be placed on the levers at all times. Now go to the filling station for a supply of gas (ink) and you are ready to drive. Crank the car by rolling on the muscle (hind wheels) without touching the pen to the paper. After the engine is going well, drive (write) down the street. (Space between blue lines on paper is street, blue lines are sidewalks.) Driver should be very careful not to skid across the sidewalks except at regular crossings (lower loops of y, g, etc.) Driver should be careful to keep engine tuned up and running and not to ride a bicycle (writing with fingers). Children should be required to keep cars adjusted properly and to drive carefully in all written lessons. Variations may be made in some of the details of presenting the Automobile Game but I am sure that you will get much good from its use.

Attractively written cards by J. R. McAllister, Struthers, Ohio.

TRI-STATE COMMERCIAL EDUCATION ASSOCIATION

The spring meeting of the Tri-State Commercial Education Association will be held at the William Penn Hotel, Pittsburgh, Penna., April 23 and 24. The exhibitors' dinner in the Adonis Room Friday, April 23 will be followed by a Reception, Dance and Cards in the Urban Room. The chairman in charge of arrangements is Miss Edith M. Winchester of Carnegie Institute of Technology. Dr. Elmer G. Miller, chairman of the exhibits, has reserved more space this year and promises a regular "Business Progress Fair" with prizes for attending members. Members will register Friday P.M. and Saturday 8;30 A.M. on the 17th floor. Mr. G. R. Fisher, the president, announces the tentative program for Saturday as follows:

Business meeting and election of officers

Speakers:

Dr. Glenn Frank
University of Wisconsin

Dr. Frederick G. Nichols
Professor of Commercial Education
Harvard University

Dr. J. Meyers
Western Reserve University
Cleveland, Ohio

Mr. George Taylor of Fifth Avenue High School is chairman of the following luncheon committee:

Miss Elsie Mares of Arsenal Junior High School

Mr. Curtis Taylor of Donora High School

Miss Amanda Gordon of Union High School, Turtle Creek

Mr. Theodore Woodward of Langley High School

Mr. Bernard J. McCormick of Oliver High School

This committee has arranged for the group's entertainment by the nationally known editor and speaker, Thurman (Dusty) Miller of Wilmington, Ohio. Due to the increased membership of the organization, preparation is being made to accommodate 1500 commercial teachers and friends.

CHESTER L. COOK

Chester L. Cook, an engrosser in the Harris Studio, Chicago, whose magnificent work has graced the pages of The Educator from month to month, was born on a farm near Golden, Illinois, September 3, 1902. He studied penmanship at the Gem City Business College, Quincy, Illinois, under H. P. Behrensmeyer. He began working for the Harris Studio in 1922, this making his fifteenth year with the studio. Mr. Cook is one of the highest paid engrossers in the United States. He can paint miniatures, portraits, landscapes, or anything in oil or water color. His lettering and script are exceptionally fine. Some of his work has been sent to many countries in Europe and all over the United States.

Mr. Cook is happily married. He is a tall, handsome, good-natured, very dependable young man. He has visited the office of The Educator a number of times where he has greatly enjoyed looking over the fine specimens of pen work which grace the walls of the Zanerian.

If you ever go to Chicago be sure to look up the Harris Studio and meet not only Mr. Cook but the rest of the expert engrossers in that studio.

BELIEVE IN YOURSELF.

Are you one who mistrusts his own ability? It is true some have less confidence in themselves than others have in them. They may be correct.

If you don't believe in yourself, why should anybody believe in you? But if you find others do believe in you, doesn't it inspire you to merit their confidence, and help you to believe in yourself?

Self-reliance and reliability possessed consciously are life's greatest satisfaction. They beget success in any field of endeavor.

Look about you for someone who believes in you. You will find that some do. Then try to determine if you believe as much in yourself.

Dare to venture. Try something—something worth while. The world can't defeat you. You defeat yourself. The more unfairness and injustice there is; the more opportunity for those willing to study, to understand, and to oppose forces that cheat the weak, the ignorant and unsuspecting.

Business education is armor, shield and buckler in this war.

Business College is a specialty school—nothing else takes its place for offering business education.

Emporia Business College
Emporia, Kans.

Lessons in Card Carving

By J. D. Carter, Deerfield, Ill.

Lesson No. 7

In this lesson we are stressing another special feature in design cutting on the cards.

It is well for us to remember the cards that give the best work for a variety of designing are cut from large cardboard which are made up by pasting and pressing two, three, four or more sheets of paper together; thus we have two, three, and four ply cardboards.

This gives us a chance to cut through the first ply to form and raise the design in relief without cutting clear through the card.

In most designs it is sufficient to cut through only one ply so if one is skillful and has a sharp tool many beautiful designs can be worked on the two ply cardboard. For the beginner, however, I would advise the use of four ply cards of good stock.

I have used two ply cards in cutting the design to illustrate this lesson.

Before cutting this Lesson No. 7 on card I would ask each one of you to sketch a neat outline of the flower on good white typewriting paper or some good white paper with smooth surface not too much glazed; using a No. 2 or a softer No. 1 pencil.

When the sketch is made quite clear and heavy, fold the paper in a manner so this design will be face down on some other part of the same sheet of paper. When this is done rub the back of the design briskly with thumb nail; a short smooth stick of wood or similar smooth, hard substance, and you find the design transferred clearly in reverse order.

Now if you will go over this transfer outline with soft pencil, you can easily make 6 to 12 direct transfers like the original.

By this method you can make many transfers on cards for cutting.

If the design gets too dim; run over the transfer outline again with soft pencil.

This is known as the soft pencil method of transfer and is often used in the transfer of designs in many lines of studio work.

When the outline has been transferred to the card, cut through the first ply of card with point of sharp knife.

Now proceed to separate the upper ply in the design with the same knife until you get a clear cut raised relief.

I shall be pleased to see some of your work.

Criticism and instruction on your work for return postage.

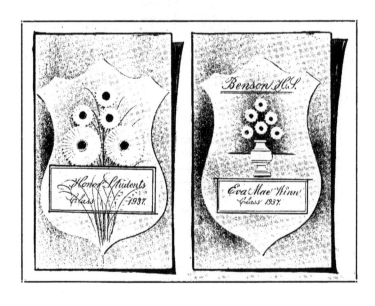

William J. Bogan
In Memoriam

Whereas, God in his infinite wisdom has taken from us our beloved leader,

William J. Bogan,

Be It Resolved that we

The Chicago Principals' Club,

extend to his family our deep sympathy in this hour of sorrow.

Be It Further Resolved that,

Whereas, the cause of education in state and nation has suffered an irreparable loss,

Whereas, the City of Chicago has lost not only its educational leader but a great and distinguished citizen,

Whereas, the teachers have lost their sympathetic counselor and inspiring guide,

Whereas, the youth of our city have lost their best friend,

Be It Therefore Further Resolved that these resolutions be spread upon the records of

The Chicago Principals' Club

and that an engrossed copy be sent to Mr. Bogan's family.

_____ _____
Secretary President
Engraved by The Zaner-Bloser Co.

Prepared in the Zaner-Bloser Studio by W. L. Newark. Mr. Newark is a skilled engrosser and an accomplished artist.

24

Whereas,

John Ames

having been an active
and loyal member of
this Association for
a period of more than
twenty years render-
ing an unparalled
service in the interests
of this body, we hereby
extend to him our

Thanks and Appreciation

Suggestion for an
Illuminated Album Page.

DESIGNING AND ENGROSSING
By E. L. BROWN
Rockland, Maine

(See Opposite Page)

Suggestion for an album page is presented in this connection. The decorative initial "J" will require more time and study than rest of design, and is an example of color values in line and stipple. Remember that a dark object requires a light ground, in other words, light on dark and dark on light is a general rule but not always observed to the letter, however.

Scroll work is rather difficult, and is a real study. It is a good plan to master a certain style and stick to it, until you evolve an individualized style by which you will be known. Gather ideas here and there from others but by no means become a copyist. Changing and adopting other's designs is tolerably permissible but the making of exact copies is inexcusable.

A pencil sketch is the first step and it is better to make a carefully executed drawing before inking. A color scheme must also be worked out in advance of the pen work. Outside of the words, "Whereas" and "John Ames" the lettering is all free hand. A No. 2½ lettering pen was used for the smaller lettering excepting that in last two lines. Study spacing and arrangement carefully.

We will repeat, use only India ink for pen drawing—Zanerian is excellent. An Engrossers outfit should include a drawing board, T-square, and ruling pens, a color box and brushes of different sizes, assorted sizes of lettering pens, etc.

Again referring to lesson will call your attention to the stippling used to obtain the color tones. The upper and lower part of panel the dots are quite uniformly spaced, whereas, on the darker portion random dots closely spaced are used for the desired effect. The scroll work must be lighter in value for contrast. Aim for gradation of tone from dark to light, and avoid a "spotted" appearance. Outline panel with a thick line. The upper part of letter "J" may be either solid black or finished like copy. This initial would look nice in color and we would recommend the use of the three primary colors, red, blue and yellow, mixed with Chinese white for this purpose. If you can find a sample page of illuminated work it would help you greatly in obtaining proper color and tone values.

State your problems and enclose your work for criticisms and suggestions.

GIVING HIS BEST

Fred Richardson, Ottawa, Ontario, in sending in a club of subscriptions enclosed some work from his students. George Jackson is his star left-handed penman. This young man submitted some specimens which are of a professional quality. In fact, we have received many specimens from professional penmen which were not nearly so skillfully executed. There was also some skillful ornamental work from Jean McGregor.

Mr. Richardson is one of those good hearted, efficient teachers who has spent a lot of time and effort in getting his own writing up to a high standard. He has made several trips to Columbus, Ohio, and spends part of his noon hours teaching interested pupils how to learn Old English and do other styles of pen work. Some day when Fred is gone his pupils will look back and say, "There was a man who was interested in his pupils and who was willing to give more than his salary called for."

"House Boat" at Edgewater, N. J. Painted in oil by J. B. Hague, of the Haring Studio, New York, N. Y.

BOOK REVIEWS

Our readers are interested in books of merit, but especially in books of interest and value to commercial teachers including books of special educational value and books on business subjects. All such books will be briefly reviewed in these columns, the object being to give sufficient description of each to enable our readers to determine its value.

Ideas for Letter Writers, by Guy W. Battles. Published by Rieger's, Inc., 319 Third Ave., Pittsburgh, Pa. Paper cover, 123 pages.

The material in "Ideas for Letter Writers" has been assembled from addresses, sales talks, and interviews given by the author; from letters written in response to requests for information pertaining to sales promotion and processes involved in duplicating and mailing; from actual cases with which the author has come in contact, and other sources he has reason to regard as authentic.

Experience gained during more than thirty-three years in merchandising, sales promotion, and advertising have provided opportunities to observe successes and failures; and in this presentation the author has endeavored to discuss matters of interest to those engaged in many lines of business.

Letters are prominently featured, as the author has been especially impressed with the potential sales possibilities of this helpful medium during recent years, in which millions of letters have passed through his duplicating establishment. Many have proved successful, but it has been his purpose to explain why others have not fulfilled their mission; and also to suggest applications for many lines of promotional activity.

Analysis of a product or service, its application and the potential market, will impress the reader with the possibilities of increasing business through consistent advertising; and the author trusts that the reader may arrive at a fuller appreciation of its value in sales promotion . . . and put the letter to work.

Modern Business Letter Writing, by Anne Boone. Published by The Ronald Press Company, New York, N. Y. Cloth cover, 251 pages.

. Even on busy days when correspondence is heaviest, the tested methods given in this book will help you produce good letters every time. Each letter clear, definite, direct—disposing of every matter and effectively accomplishing its purpose.

Miss Boone's successful work as supervisor of correspondence for several nationally known concerns has attracted wide attention. In this volume she shows just what methods are used by these important business organizations to obtain results they demand. Using "Modern Business Letter Writing" is a good deal like having Miss Boone add her efforts to your staff, defining what must be done; showing those who handle mail exactly how to increase their efficiency.

Anyone who really wishes to do so can write good business letters, says Miss Boone. Here she gives the kind of instruction that warrants such a statement: how to make letters concise but complete; how to develop speed in handling. Treating everything specifically, she gets down to the actual details of sentences, phrases, even single words. Important points are stressed in samples of well-planned work; highlighted by faulty correspondence offered in contrast.

A Teacher's Manual Designed for Use With "Man and the Motor Car," by Herbert James Stack, Ph.D., Director, Education Division, National Bureau of Casualty & Surety Underwriters, Lecturer, Teachers College, Columbia University. Published by National Bureau of Casualty and Surety Underwriters, New York, N. Y. Paper cover, 48 pages.

The traffic accident situation has produced a demand by the public that automobile drivers be educated instead of being allowed to get their driving habits through hit or miss methods, and that the high schools of the country assume the responsibility for doing the job. The fact that it is the young drivers who have the worst accident record adds urgency to the need for such an undertaking.

Automobile driving is one of the anticipated de-

lights of every Twentieth Century youngster. He looks forward with eagerness to the time when he can sit behind the wheel of a car and control its powerful machinery. The school could, therefore, find few subjects more intimately related to the desires and interests of students than the study of the motor car. Here is certainly one point at which education and life run along together. The indications are that the high school will accept this mandate; several thousand schools are already doing work in this field.

To meet these conditions, the National Bureau of Casualty and Surety Underwriters has published a book entitled "Man and the Motor Car." This was primarily designed for use in high schools. Since, however, the subject is so new, it has seemed particularly desirable to follow it with something that would help teachers in the use of the book.

In addition to a section on methods of teaching the course, guide materials are supplied. These are divided into sixteen units, which follow the chapter divisions of the text. With each unit there is a series of discussion questions. These questions are designed to lead the class into the consideration of problems that are related to the text material; they are not review questions or examination questions such as are contained in the appendix to "Man and the Motor Car."

Supplementing the discussion questions are short lists of problems. These are simple research projects designed to present in a more concrete and dramatic form some of the particularly important matters that are treated in the text.

Steps for further enlisting the active interest of the class are suggested in the activities recommended for each unit. These activities are intended to bring the students into close touch with the actual situations that they may expect to encounter. In most cases, these activities call for projects requiring the co-operation of all members of the class.

Educators in a recent conference of the National Safety Congress agreed that it is most important that schools emphasize good driving attitudes; of the three teaching fundamentals involved, namely, knowledge, skill and attitudes, the latter is by far the most important. Some of the questions and activities included in the manual, which may at first seem irrelevant are especially designed for the development of such attitudes.

The pamphlet lists supplementary readings, visual materials, and tests which may be used in connection with the course. Many of these publications may be obtained without charge.

The Secretary-Stenographer's Desk Book, by William Allan Brooks, Author of The Student's Handbook, A. B. C. Shorthand System, with an introduction by Andre Maurois. Published by The National Library Press, New York, N. Y. Cloth cover, 160 pages.

The Secretary-Stenographer's Desk Book is a complete guide to correct business usage for the entire office staff. It is a book that will help you to solve at once hundreds of questions of correct form usage and sound business practices—points the way to better jobs and better pay by showing you how to raise yourself to the standard of the highly skilled, highly paid secretaries of big business executives. It contains hundreds of personality hints; efficiency suggestions; lists of words often misspelled and confused; how to build a vocabulary; rules for correct capitalization; accurate punctuation; all about letter writing; sources of useful information; postal information; patents; copyrights; passports; weights and measures; special terminology and information about advertising; publishing, insurance, real estate, etc.

Thompson Business Practice Test, by James M. Thompson, Instructor in Management, School of Commerce, New York University. Published by World Book Company, Yonkers-on-Hudson, New York.

The Thompson Business Practice Test provides junior and senior high schools with an objective measure of achievement in general business practice. The test covers the major functions of business as presented in various junior and senior high school textbooks and courses of study, known by such names as Junior business training, Introduction to business, elementary business training, or every-day business.

1937 GEMS

1937 Gems, assembled and published by D. L. Stoddard, R. R. 4, Box 141, Indianapolis, Ind., cardboard cover, 100 pages.

D. L. Stoddard has spent the greater part of his life studying, admiring and producing pen work. His little book, Gems, which is 3½ in. x 5½ in. contains a collection of beautiful pen work from many of America's leading penmen. The size of the book permits one to carry it with him in his pocket. It is truly a vest pocket collection of Gems and inspiration. We congratulate Mr. Stoddard upon this excellent book.

Office Economies, by Eugene J. Benge. Published by The Ronald Press Company, New York, N. Y. Cloth cover, 151 pages.

This complete efficient guide to greater savings in office maintenance can show you exactly how to stop obvious but obstinate leaks and how to eliminate dangerously hidden wastes, through better organization, more efficient forms and more adequate equipment.

Representing years of varied and practical business experience, "Office Economies" offers on every point from the purchase of rubber bands to the training of employees, specific, remarkably effective "1-2-3-4" directions you will apply to realize savings that will pay for the book many times over. Each of its fifty money-saving sections point out good ways and warn you against poor ways to go about making any changes you decide are necessary. Costs of different items are broken down to show you what runs into money and what is of relatively small importance. Lists of questions put the spotlight on what needs correcting, show you where to concentrate your effort. Every corrective device and method prescribed has proved successful in application by the author and other recognized personnel directors and management engineers.

Eugene J. Benge is widely known among office executives for his cost reducing abilities. He has gone through the mill of thorough training as an office manager, personnel director, editor of the page of office tips in a famous business magazine, statistician, designer of office systems, and a management engineer for several nationally known concerns.

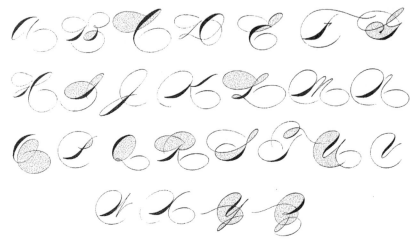

This alphabet was made by R. M. Maugans, Statesville, N. C. Mr. Maugans has followed correspondence work in ornamental penmanship and engrossing. He has whipped the writing into fine shape.

Whereas, An all wise Providence has seen fit to call from our midst our beloved employer and loyal associate

Thomas J. McDonnell,

Recorder of Deeds of
Lackawanna County, Pennsylvania.

Whereas, while we bow in humble submission to the will of an all merciful Creator, we deeply regret his untimely demise, therefore be it,

Resolved, By we, the employees of the Recorder of Deeds office that his passing has deprived us of a faithful and efficient employer, and a man who possessed a rare gift of gracious geniality that won and endeared him to all, and be it further,

Resolved, that as a mark of respect to his sterling worth as a man and of our love as a friend and associate, that these resolutions be engrossed and presented to his mother and beloved ones who have lost a loving tender companion, and devoted son.

We, the Employees of the Recorder of Deeds office subscribe to this act by our hands, this twenty-ninth day of January in the year of nineteen hundred and thirty seven.

John L. Finn

Thomas J. Connors   *Richard Harrison*
May Mullen   *Edward Rathbch*
Edward A. Munley   *George O'Bushka*
Winfield Borosky   *Andrew Pinselli*
Howard Seddon   *Vincent Seddon*

A beautiful piece of engrossing from Joseph W. Costello, Scranton Real Estate Bldg., Scranton, Pa., son of the late P. W. Costello. We are certainly delighted that the engrossing studio which P. W. Costello established many years ago is continuing to prosper and turn out such high class work. The above specimen resembles, to a large extent, the work of the illustrious father.

KARLEN

D. L. Stoddard

"GEMS"

WE USE

Cathedral Parchment

MADE SPECIALLY FOR

Diplomas, Certificates, Deeds, Charters

Guaranteed by the Mill

100% Rag-content meeting all Government Test requirements

Martin Diploma Company

Excellent Surface for Plate Printing, Lithographing and Engrossing

A page of gems selected from **D. L. Stoddard's 1937** edition of "Gems". It is
a very beautiful page and typical of the work to be found in this handsome
little penmanship book.

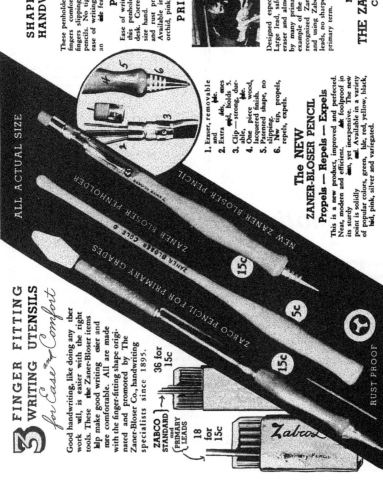

Vol. 42　　　　　　　　　　MAY, 1937　　　　　　　　　　No. 9

ZANER-BLOSER CO.
COLUMBUS, OHIO

W. J. JARVIS

Published monthly except July and August at 612 N. Park St., Columbus, O., by the Zaner-Bloser Company. Entered as second-class matter November 21, 1931, at the post office at Columbus, O., under Act of March 3, 1879. Subscription $1.25 a year.

Volume 42   COLUMBUS, OHIO, MAY, 1937   No. 9

Fortieth Annual Convention Eastern Commercial Teachers' Association

Was held in Boston, Mass., March 24, 25, 26 and 27 with an attendance of around 3,000. The meeting was pronounced the biggest and best in the history of the association.

"Forty years ago the Association was founded by a group of educators, who, with the spirit of true pioneers, struggled valiantly to win for the commercial curriculum acknowledgment of its rightful place in the general scheme of education. Their work was not in vain. With each passing year, the Association grew in numbers, strength and influence. It extended its sphere of service and won merited distinction for its leadership in the field of business education. It was instrumental in gaining recognition for commercial education as an integral part of the educational programs of state and local communities. We have just cause for celebration.

"Following its established policy of devoting its educational program to topics of professional and business significance, the Association selected for its discussions the theme, 'Measuring for Vocational Ability' in the Field of Business Education.'"

Experienced business executives and leaders in commercial education participated in making this program an outstanding one. The E. C. T. A. is noted for its cooperative spirit of service and good fellowship. It would be hard to find an organization whose various committee members served more loyally. Every committee seemed to function perfectly.

The program was one every commercial teacher should have heard. We wish that we had space to comment upon each talk. The Yearbook may

W. E. Douglas
Goldey College, Wilmington, Delaware
Pres. E. C. T. A.

be secured from A. M. Lloyd, 1200 Walnut St., Philadelphia, Pa.

The penmanship section was under the direction of John G. Kirk, Director of Commercial Education, Philadelphia, Pa., and Miss Bertha A. Connor, Director of Handwriting, Boston, chairman. The penmanship section is always given a prominent place and we hope that penmen and persons interested in teaching handwriting will continue to give this department their support.

The March of Time, a pictorial retrospect of persons and events in the life of the E. C. T. A., was presented at the Banquet by Arnold M. Lloyd, Banks Business College, Philadelphia.

The next convention will be held in Philadelphia, April 13-16, 1938.

New officers are: President, William E. Douglas, Goldey College, Wilmington, Delaware; Vice President, Mrs. Susette B. Tyler, Thomas Jefferson High School, Richmond, Va.; Harry I. Good; Nathaniel Altholz; Arnold M. Lloyd; Peter L. Agnew; John G. Kirk; Sadie L. Ziegler; Clinton A. Reed; Edward P. Jennison.

WHAT ABOUT HANDWRITING?

W. S. Gray, a national authority on reading, gave a report in the Journal of Higher Education on an investigation of reading deficiencies of college students. He found: "Limited mental ability, limited vocabulary, inappropriate attitudes and ineffective habits of thinking, persistence of immature habits of early reading, and visual defects." In other words, he found the reading of many college students far below standard, and that it hindered their educational progress. After the investigation a remedial program designed to improve the reading was developed.

We need not ask the results of a handwriting investigation. The report would show much illegible handwriting.

Good handwriting like good reading is a valuable tool to any student in securing an education. Where a student of any school cannot write legibly, he should be given work to improve his handwriting.

It's funny that adults don't find out that they can't write and prescribe some remedial program. The ability to write so others can read it is one qualification of an educated person.

THE EDUCATOR

Published monthly (except July and August) By THE ZANER-BLOSER CO., 612 N. Park St., Columbus, O.
E. A. LUPFER..Editor
PARKER ZANER BLOSER................Business Mgr.

SUBSCRIPTION PRICE, $1.25 A YEAR (To Canada, 10c more; foreign, 30c more) Single copy, 15c.
Change of address should be requested promptly in advance, if possible, giving the old as well as the new address.
Advertising rates furnished upon request.

THE EDUCATOR is the best medium through which to reach business college proprietors and managers, commercial teachers and students, and lovers of penmanship. Copy must reach our office by the 10th of the month for the issue of the following month.

Modern Handwriting

By E. A. Lupfer, Zanerian College, Columbus, Ohio

No. 9

Each pupil should keep his paper in front of him.

Form and movement can be taught together. Slow labored writing is of little value, while scrawly illegible writing is of no value. Try to do your writing so that it looks free and actually is written free and is unmistakably readable.

Study the similarity between the q, a and f. The q begins the same as the a and ends the same as the f. The loops in the two letters should be the same size. Cover up the loop in the q and you have a good a providing the letter is properly made. Make a row of a's, then add the q loop to them. Compare this line of q's with a line of q's which you have made in the ordinary way. This may help you in form study.

A copy with plenty of review material in it. It is well worth mastering each exercise if you have not already done so.

A good review lesson on the lower loops—master them.

Spelling

although   continue   journey
busy   entire   laid
choose   forward   lose
measure   surprise   wear
does   tear   though
answer   enough   through

balance   deposit   movement
educate   favor   pavement
memory   victim   apartment
surround   growth   treatment
recent   quarrel
college   type   prevent
general   progress   prefer
                        precede
calendar   holy   prepare
quest   inquire
prompt   regret   interlace
central   queer   interlock
hence   route   interest
patient   require   interstate
natural   strength

One of the best places to put handwriting into actual use is in the spelling lesson. Never permit scrawly work in the spelling lesson. Many poor grades are received in spelling on account of poor writing. Practice each word given above individually and as a group, and remember always to write carefully during the spelling lesson.

(handwriting practice: Z forms — "Zaner")

Another lesson on the **Z**. We believe in constantly reviewing letters. There are times when you should force yourself to stick to one letter if for no other reason than self discipline. However, there is not a great deal gained in practicing on a letter after you once lose interest in it. It is better to go on and come back to it.

The capitals **X** and **Z** begin the same. The first part of the **X** is the same as the top of the **Z**. The loop in the capital **Z** is the same as in the small **z** with the exception it is slightly larger.

(handwriting practice: Z exercises)

This exercise will develop the rolling movement necessary in making the lower loop in the **Z**. Study the direction of the three loops in the **Z**.

(handwriting practice: "Zanerian College, Columbus, Ohio.")

Zanerians are usually good at making the capital **Z** because they write it so many times. Practice makes for perfection, especially if you do your best each time.

(handwriting practice: figures 1 4 6 9 7 2 3 5 8 0)

Study the figures by making them large and retracing them. It would be well for you to retrace the copy with a dry pen. Study the similarity and dissimilarity of the various figures.

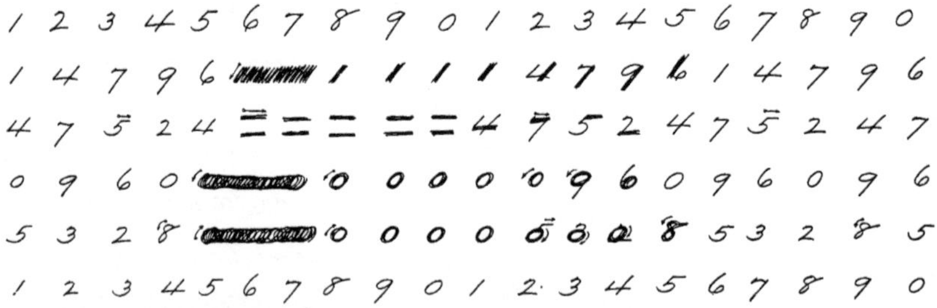

(handwriting practice: rows of figures)

This plate groups the figures according to formation and gives exercises to develop the various parts. The small push-pull exercise helps to develop the figures containing straight strokes. The **7, 5, 2** and **4** contain lateral strokes. Therefore the lateral exercise should help. The **9, 6** and **0** contain ovals. The **0** is the same as the body of the small letter **o**, while the **6** is the same as the last part of the capital **X**. The **9** is really an abbreviated **g**. The **3** and **5** finish the same. There is a similarity between the **2** and **4**. In making the **4** be sure to have the two strokes tied together, otherwise the **4** will look like 21. Notice particularly that the **5** is made in two sections. The top horizontal stroke is put on last and should be connected. Be careful to make your **7** and **2** distinct. Figures must be made absolutely legible. Many low grades are made in mathematics because of poor figures. Pupils sometimes cannot read their own figures.

In practicing this copy turn the paper so that the ruled base lines help you in making straight columns. This is an excellent arrangement for the teacher to count with the class. In the first three lines the teacher should count one for each figure and dash. In the 1 and 4 combination the teacher should count 1, 2, 3, 4. Try a little counting and see how much life you can put into the class in figure making.

Subtract:

10 lb. 5 oz.	12 ft. 4 in.	3 gal. 2 qt.
7 lb. 9 oz.	8 ft. 6 in.	1 gal. 3 qt.

6 bu. 1 pk.	2 qt. 1 pt.	10 yd. 2 ft.
1 bu. 2 pk.	1 qt. ½ pt.	5 yd. 2½ ft.

These different abbreviations should be thoroughly mastered. See that your figures fit in well with your writing.

Divide the following, timing yourself:

114 . 14	105 ÷ 35	424 ÷ 53	567 ÷ 81
136 ÷ 17	252 ÷ 63	497 ÷ 71	609 ÷ 87
216 24	125 ÷ 27	456 ÷ 57	432 ÷ 72
310 31	231 ÷ 33	219 ÷ 73	720 ÷ 90
175 ÷ 35	637 ÷ 91	641 79	372 ÷ 93
328 ÷ 41	405 ÷ 81	469 ÷ 67	490 ÷ 98

This copy makes good additional practice material.

Quality and speed both count.

In school and in business you should be able to write a large amount in a short time, and, of course, it should be readable.

Is Penmanship Important in Securing and Performing Clerical Jobs?

By Miss Ragnhild Johnson, Personnel Director, Kendall Mills, Walpole, Mass. (A talk given at the E. C. T. A.)

In the organization of a modern business, we have come a long way from the single proprietorship and the established family firm of fifty years ago which employed a clerk and a bookkeeper who kept meticulous ledgers in carefully written numerals and wrote letters in painstaking longhand. Today typewriters, bookkeeping machines, calculators, tabulating equipment, teletype machines are indispensable tools in turning .out the tremendous quantity of reports and correspondence essential to carrying on the activities of a present-day corporation which serves a wide territory rather than a local community.

The clerk and the bookkeeper have been supplanted by a vast number of clerks and bookkeepers, commonly referred to as our "white collar" class. In a recent report of the National Industrial Conference Board e n t i t l e d "Women Workers and the Labor Supply", some interesting data is presented regarding the growth of this clerical force from 1890 to 1930. Their analysis was based on data obtained from the United States Census of Occupations. They considered four major clerical occupations (1) clerks and copyists, (2) Stenographers and typists, (3) bookkeepers and accountants, (4) Telegraph and telephone operators. The total of men and women employed in these occupations in 1890 was 758,624 compared with 4,392,256 in 1930. The gain was distributed as follows:

	1890	1930
1. Clerks and copyists	557,358	2,398,991
2. Stenographers and typists	33,418	811,190
3. Bookkeepers and accountants	159,374	930,648
4. Telegraph and telephone operators	8,474	251,427

It is significant that the percentage of increase has far exceeded the growth in population. For instance, the gain is therefore attributed to the extraordinary expansion of this type of work. Among the clerks and copyists alone, there is an increase of 330 per cent, compared with a population increase of 98 per cent for the same period.

> Is it not discourteous to send a letter unless it is neat and perfectly clear, so that the recipient of the letter does not have to worry and puzzle over the contents?

The question that concerns us this afternoon is whether the machine method has completely absorbed the functions of our modern office or whether these clerical workers still rely to some extent on their ability to write legibly in order to perform their work satisfactorily. I have limited the discussion to the application of handwriting in business offices and therefore have not included at all the large number of people who are engaged in sales work where filling out order forms and sales slips legibly is always important.

There appears to be a widespread feeling among the public that handwriting is of slight importance today. Certainly the signature of many a prominent man is completely illegible but that does not mean he will tolerate figures he cannot read presented by one of his clerks. Most of us can probably call to mind an individual case where superior writing has been a distinct asset.

In a recent issue of Time Magazine is the story of Harrison Williams, a wealthy U. S. specialist in utilities finance, whose chief distinction may be that he' is 'the husband of Mrs. Harrison Williams, "the best dressed woman in the world". Time writes: "young Harry's penmanship got him his first job as a bookkeeper".

In order to present this subject objectively, we have gone to a representative group of eastern firms employing several thousand clerical workers with two issues:

1. The importance of handwriting in selecting employees.

2. The importance of handwriting in performing the job.

Every firm questioned stated that they preferred to have applicants fill out their application blanks in longhand. This may have two-fold significance:

1. That the specimen of handwriting so obtained is a criterion in the applicant's qualifications.

2. That employment managers still believe that they can read the character of the applicant in his writing. Most of us who are responsible for selecting people will deny the latter implication.

However, I think it is fair to assume that employment managers do consider legibility and neatness of handwriting when they are filling jobs where they know a certain amount of writing is required. Five companies reported they sometimes rejected applicants at once because of the quality of their handwriting and the majority of concerns indicated that other qualifications being equal, inferior penmanship would tend to eliminate a particular applicant in making the final selection, and certainly so if any amount of handwriting was required.

A large insurance company writes: "Most of our positions are filled with young people just out of high school. We are able to place year in and year out about one out of twenty-five. Picking that one impartially and fairly is quite a job. We must hope for more or less minute differences which gives one a superiority or apparent advantage. After picking out about a dozen applicants, the next step is to score them on a number of minor points. Penmanship is always included in this scoring plan".

Several other concerns confirmed this same viewpoint, insisting that in spite of mechanical equipment, they still use pen and ink.

No company reported using any formal method of scoring or rating of the applicant's handwriting. Either the personnel officer is not aware of the availability of such scales or he feels he can judge the quality of writing well enough for his purposes merely by looking at it.

For your interest, I have selected at random ten application blanks from our files that have been filled out by persons seeking clerical positions with us. I would be glad to have you, who are penmanship experts, examine them and pass on their legibility.

In analyzing the importance of handwriting in performing clerical jobs, we tried to find out on what types of jobs legible writing was a factor, whether both speed and legibility were considered essential, whether any style of handwriting was preferred, and finally whether any specific training was given to improve the worker's handwriting after he went on the job.

Among some 5,000 clerical workers reported, more than 50 per cent of the total were doing some work that called for legible handwriting. Bookkeeping and accounting jobs headed the list of those where handwriting is a criterion; there the importance of

> **Should not careless handwriting be considered a mark of disorderly, hit or miss mentality?**

good figures was emphasized again and again. As one organization pointed out, you can guess at a word but a figure must be read exactly the same way by every one. General clerical jobs, not more specifically described, were listed next in frequency, with other jobs such as payroll, order, inventory, invoice, schedule clerks, sales correspondents, telephone operators, and secretaries included.

Legibility was rated more important than speed except by two companies who paid on an incentive plan. No style of handwriting is preferred; legibility is the essential quality. None of the companies specified that they were giving specific instruction in handwriting on the job. However, in some cases, supervisors do criticize poor work. To me, it has always been noteworthy that bank clerks write neat, legible figures. If no specific instruction is given, the clerk himself must feel the pressure of keeping the books up to standard and acquire the skill himself. It is true, of course, that many of these clerks have had business school accounting where considerable emphasis is placed on the appearance of the ledger.

I hope the evidence presented confirms your own conviction as teachers of penmanship that there is still a real need for good writing and that you are performing an important service when you teach students to write neatly and distinctly. Undoubtedly good penmanship is one of the "plus" values every commercial student should aim to possess. It will promote favorable consideration of his application, which is of the greatest importance to him in seeking employment. If the job he goes on involves handwriting, he not only creates a favorable impression when data he presents is well written, but he saves his employer both time and money by reducing clerical errors.

Employment managers and office supervisors feel that the responsibility for developing this skill in students falls upon the schools. We expect good writing, but we are not willing to spend the time and effort to develop it among the people who come to work for us.

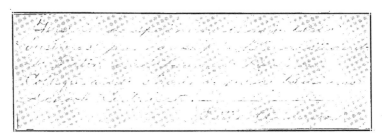

This specimen of easy, dashy business writing is from the pen of Esther Anderson, a student in the Eaton & Burnett Business College, Baltimore, Md. W. S. Chamberlain is the efficient penman and instructor.

The Write Right Club

Columbia School, Champaign, Ill.

Miss Blanche Cline—Principal

Miss Katherine Colyer—Writing
Chairman of Building

Miss Ethel Kesterson—Supervisor
of Handwriting

V. L. Nickell—Superintendent of
Schools.

The idea of organizing a writing club at Columbia School was the outgrowth of suggestions made by Miss Ethel Kesterson, our writing supervisor. Under the leadership of Miss Blanche Cline, principal, and Miss Katherine Colyer, writing chairman of Columbia School, this idea was first discussed with all pupils early in October. To each room it was explained that the chief purpose of the club was to encourage and recognize good writing not only in the writing class but in all written work. The name decided upon for the club was Columbia Write Right Club. The six rules to follow in order to become eligible for membership were set up and explained. They became known as the Write Right Recipe and are as follows:

1. Keep your arm on the desk.
2. Hold your pen right.
3. Keep your thumb still.
4. Keep your thumb near your paper.

5. Glide on the smooth part of the third and fourth fingers.

6. Be able to make easy exercises half way across the paper without picking up the hand.

Late in October the club was organized with 17 charter members. A large chart bearing these names and using the Columbia School colors of gold and brown was hung in the hall where everyone could view it. This honor served to interest children in acquiring sufficient skill to become members. Every few weeks a check-up is made in each room in order that any other children who are eligible may be added to the club or any members who have become ineligible may be dropped. In order to remain a member a child must have good writing habits, be able to write at least as well as the standard for his grade, and show evidence of a good "carry over" in the writing in all subjects. New members have been added until

in April there are 168 names on the roll of the club.

In recognition of the superior standard of writing attained by these children a white satin ribbon badge bearing a seal significant of good writing was awarded to each member of the Columbia Write Right Club at a special assembly of the children of the school.

As a special project to show one use for good writing the club members, working in small groups, bought and addressed valentines and gifts which were sent to the children at Huling Home, an orphanage in Rantoul. This venture proved so interesting to the children that many non-members became so desirous of joining the club that they began to exert added effort in writing well. The interest stimulated in good writing during the pursuit of this project was further evidenced by the improvement in the "carry over" or applied writing in all regular class work.

A few members of the large "Write Right Club" of Columbia School, Champaign, Ill. The sixth graders in this photo already have won Zaner-Bloser High School Certificates.

Another very important means of stimulating interest in good writing in the upper grades has been the plan of writing for Zaner-Bloser Certificates. Most of the pupils of the sixth grades have earned a Grammar School Diploma while some of them have the added honor of qualifying for a High School Diploma. Over half of the fifth grade children are also eligible for the Grammar School Diploma. A special list for each of these fifth and sixth grade rooms is kept posted in the hall. The addition of each new group of names always results in an excited group of children from all grades who are eager to see the names of the newly honored children.

Each week a different room in the building displays a writing exhibit in the hall. "Carry over" writing is stressed in these exhibits so that this plan serves to keep good writing ever before the children of Columbia School. All writing booklets, charts, and projects made by any room at any time during the year are also displayed on tables in the hall. The many parents, teachers, and university students who visit our school notice and comment on the writing that is being done. Columbia School is without doubt writing conscious this year.

COMMERCIAL SCHOOL MAN DIES

Mr. L. C. Spencer, president of the Spencer Business College, New Orleans, La., passed away on February 6 of heart attack.

As a commercial educator, L. C. Spencer was a pioneer and achieved greatness. In his younger days he taught in the Keachie College from which school he was graduated in 1888. He was, for a time, principal of Macodoches High School. His first business school was established in Shreveport and in 1897 he opened his school in New Orleans. Thousands of young men and women received modern commercial training in his schools.

As an author and publisher of commercial textbooks Mr. Spencer was very successful. His books on shorthand, typewriting, English and spelling were used widely throughout the South. Like many of the other business college pioneers he believed in practical education and, by his efforts, he has helped commercial education to attain a prominent place in our educational system today.

Mr. Spencer served perseveringly, intelligently and successfully.

INCREASED ENROLLMENT

Mr. A. D. Deibert, Principal of Deibert's Private School, Philadelphia, N. Y., in sending in specimens of his students' work, reports that his school is enjoying the largest enrollment since 1931.

Judging from the quality of the work submitted, his students are doing better work in handwriting than they have ever done. The standard, as a whole, is very high and a number of these students are considerably above the average for business college students.

SIGHT-SAVING CLASSES

Summer courses for the training of teachers and supervisors of sight-saving classes will be conducted in Western Reserve University, Cleveland, Ohio; Wayne University, Detroit, Michigan; and Teachers College, Columbia University, New York City. Those who wish to specialize in sight-saving work should write for detailed information to the National Society for the Prevention of Blindness, 50 West 50th Street, New York, N. Y.

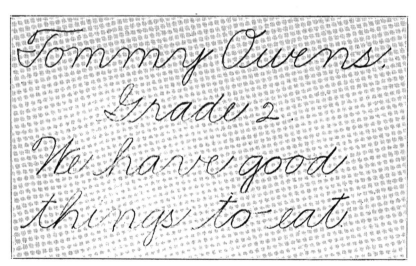

With large, free writing like the above Tommy can express his thoughts in an ideal way. Who can write more legibly? We compliment Tommy and his teacher Zula B. Marsh of Mole Hill, W. Va.

"Mr. Meadows Says"

BY GEORGE A. MEADOWS—
Pres. Meadows-Draughon
Business College, Shreveport La.

Roger W. Babson, the great Statistician, says: "Business men are learning how to invest their money, but they have NOT learned how best to invest their TIME. Time is a GREATER FACTOR in our success than either property or credit. TIME IS CAPITAL."

NO ONE has ever given sounder advice to anybody—young or old, men or women. Time is, by far, our—YOUR—greatest asset. It is the greatest factor in success. Indeed, time IS capital . . . The greatest difference between men and women who get somewhere and those who do not, is due largely to their differing appreciations of time. Some make the most of it. Others do not.

"Tempus fugit"—time flies—says a Latin proverb. This is misleading. Time is without limit. Time goes on forever. It is YOU who "fly". It is YOU who pass quickly. YOUR days of opportunity for a real start toward a successful future are limited. YOU are limited. So, if you are to make the most of YOU, you must know how to make the most of TIME.

Punctuality and regularity in attendance are absolutely essential to success. The student should feel it just as much his duty to be on time, and to be at his desk every session from Monday morning until Friday afternoon, inclusive, as if he had a position in some bank or business office. Too many students give "illness" as their reason for being absent. Remember, business men want HEALTHY young people to work for them.

You make your own record. Your school cannot recommend you unless you make a GOOD RECORD—unless you attend school regularly and get there on time, apply yourself well at all times, and master your course thoroughly.

Make every minute count! When you waste your time in school or fail to study outside of school, you are just hurting yourself. Don't loaf on the street, or elsewhere, after school and on Saturday; use your time on your books. You have only so much time; use it to the best advantage. Your future depends on how you use your time NOW.

Remember, you are as much a part of the school as any of the teachers. Help to make the school you attend as GOOD a school as possible.

Typewriting Certificate

This is to certify that

a student of the Lord Selkirk High School,

has written on the typewriter at a rate of

words per minute for fifteen minutes

DATED   TEACHER   PRINCIPAL

The above certificate was prepared by Mr. G. R. Brunet, Lord Selkirk School, Winnipeg. This certificate is appreciated very much by the students who win it.

Lessons in Modern Engrosser's Script

Prepared in the office of The Educator

No. 8

Make the capital letters as best you can, then compare your efforts with the copy. Try to discover which of your letters are the weakest and practice upon them individually. If you have not previously practiced capital letters take each letter by itself and work upon it until you have a good knowledge of form and until you have enough skill to make a row of good letters.

Arrange the letters according to similarity of form. For instance, the A, M, and N have similar beginning strokes. The compound curve in B, D, F, G, L, P, R, S, and T are similar. Notice also the similarity of the beginning stroke of the H, K, U, V, W, and Z. We have a similar beginning loop on B, F, P, Q, R, T, U, X, and Y. You will also notice the similarity of ending strokes like the C and E, H, K and R, Q and L. When mastering one letter you will be able to make part of some other letter.

After mastering the capitals, proceed with the figures. The figures presented are good, usable figures for quick, rapid work. Master one style well. Be sure that your figures are plain and carefully made. Devote most of your time to the capitals and figures since you have spent a great deal of time on the lower case letters in previous lessons. We will be pleased to examine your practice work.

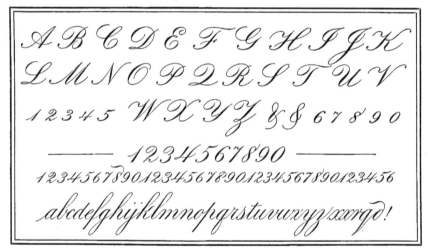

Ornamental Penmanship

No. 19   **Script by the late A. M. Wonnell**

Practice these letters and names, but if your name does not end in "er" do not become discouraged because Courtney, Brownfield, Faretra, Leslie, Fields, Baird, Jones, Smith, Thompson and a host of other fine penmen's names end in letters other than "er".

Review the difficult letters in previous lessons.

One can never do too much review work. Each time you review a letter you will see something new, something which you have overlooked.

Send your practice work to The Educator for suggestions.

This is a specimen of my plain business penmanship while a student in the Cannon's School of Business and striving for an advanced Business School Certificate.

Elsie Kaoru Uesato

January 26, 1937

Strong practical business writing by a student of C. W. Cannon, of the Cannon School of Business, Honolulu, Hawaii. Mr. Cannon is securing similar results from his large class of students. We congratulate him upon his efficient teaching.

HONOR SOCIETY ADOPTS "60 UNIVERSAL" AWARD

"60 Universal" is a new feature of the awards to students of typing in business schools and high schools offered by the International Honor Society for Business Education. "60 Universal" is a new award given for a net typing speed of 60 words a minute or more and carries with it a gold pin similar in design to the "70 International" pin awarded by the Society for 70 words a minute typing speed.

The purpose of the Society is to meet the ever increasing demand of the business world for higher skill in the techniques of business. The "70 International" and "60 Universal" typing awards are designed to inspire teachers and students to strive for outstanding results in speed and accuracy. The keynote of the plan is to stimulate the motive of rivalry and to give recognition for outstanding performance. Any student, teacher, typist or stenographer who can meet the requirements of the Society's tests is eligible to win either the "60 Universal" or "70 International" awards. The Grand President of the International Honor Society for Business Education is J. I. Kinman, President, Kinman Business University, Spokane.

HOMER O. WARREN

Homer O. Warren, principal and one of the proprietors of the Troy Business College, Troy, N. Y., for the past thirty years, died on February 19.

Mr. Warren occupied a very prominent position in commercial education throughout the United States and especially in New York State. He was identified with commercial education since receiving his early education in Ashtabula, Ohio, where he was born in 1874. He took work in commercial education in the Grand River Institute at Ostenburg, Ohio, Spencerian College, Cleveland, Ohio, and several other commercial schools. He established a business college in Ashtabula and in 1905 went to Troy, New York, as principal of the commercial department of the Troy Business College, which he later purchased in connection with William H. Aderhold.

Mr. Warren was a very skillful penman and took pride in the penmanship department of the Troy Business College. Mr. Warren received his penmanship training in the Zanerian College, Columbus, first attending in 1896 and later returning in 1909 for additional work. Through his influence his partner, Mr. Aderhold, attended The Zanerian.

Mr. Warren for years was a very active worker in the N. C. T. F. He was very active in various local and national organizations and was identified with the Church of Christ. He was a man of strong personality and conducted a very thorough school.

He is survived by his wife and four children.

G. Laurens Atwill has been employed by the Troy Business College, Troy, N. Y. He began his work with that institution last September.

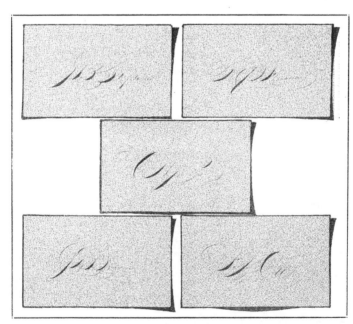

Cards written by M. Masuda, Muroran Middle School, Muroran, Hokkaido, Japan.

PENMANSHIP

Only a very wise man could say which, of all the inventions of the ages, was most important. A good case might be made for the invention of writing. It was a memorable day for the world when some man or men figured out a series of symbols which by common consent were to represent certain ideas, because that one invention made possible the capture of the great thoughts of the past and their transmission to the most distant ages.

Writing was known and practiced many long centuries before the printing press and the typewriter were dreamed of. Skill in the art of writing was a coveted accomplishment and scribes, as they were called, occupied a high social position in the days when the copying of manuscripts was an exalted profession.

These men took as conscientious care that their writing should be beautiful as Rembrandt that his convases should be perfect, or Wagner that his operas should be magnificent. They set us an impressive example.

What is more irritating than to get a letter from a valued friend written so illegibly that not even a contortionist could decipher its message? A Hollywood beauty attired in filthy rags is not a more disappointing experience. What shall it profit a writer if his thought be celestial but his penmanship execrable?

Few skills of the hand will pay better dividends to a young man or woman than dexterity with the pen. Let him learn to write legibly, boldly, beautifully, and so plainly that a wayfaring man though a fool need not err therein, and he will have cause for gratitude for the rest of his days.

—The Columbus Dispatch.

HOWARD C. STRALEY RECEIVES PROFESSIONAL CERTIFICATE

We want to congratulate Howard C. Straley of the Marietta Business Institute, Marietta, Ohio, on his fine penwork which recently captured one of the Educator Professional Penmanship Certificates. Mr. Straley is making rapid strides in the penmanship profession.

Recently Mr. Straley brought his penmanship students to Columbus and took them through the Zanerian College, where they viewed the collection of specimens of master penmen of both the past and present.

Some of the daintiest specimens we have received lately have been received from H. J. Ennis, 2315 Northeast 40th Avenue, Portland, Oregon. The lines were so faint and delicate that the engraver was unable to make reproductions. Mr. Ennis is one of the skillful penmen of the Pacific Coast.

A charcoal drawing by David J. Person, Carthage, S. D. One who wishes to become a fine penman will never regret spending some time on drawing.

Lessons in Card Carving

By J. D. Carter, Deerfield, Ill.

Lesson No. 8

Sketch the design in pencil first, then ink in and cut the same as in previous lessons.

Make carbon copies of your designs, which may be traced on other cardboard a number of times before you are required to go over them again with pencil.

Keep your knife sharp. Study designs and persevere.

You will find it a lot of fun to make new designs, suggestions for which may be found in almost any magazine.

Send your work to me for suggestions.

The Amphion Chorus was on the air Saturday, March 27, over the Red Network. They broadcasted from Station WDAY at Fargo, N. D. This Chorus originates at Fargo, N. D., and Moorhead, Minn.

This group of singers has been honored by receiving several invitations to sing before the National Federation of Music Clubs and other musical organizations.

In this group of singers is our former penmanship pupil and friend, Frank A. Krupp of the Interstate Business College at Fargo. Mr. Krupp is a violinist of no little ability and he has entertained at some of our various school gatherings when he was in Columbus, Ohio.

A Very rich, well planned and well executed testimonial of appreciation prepared by E. H. McGhee of Trenton, N. J. who is one of our leading engrossers today. Mr. McGhee is conducting a very successful up-to-date studio.

SCRIPT IN ADVERTISING

Have you noticed in magazines, newspapers and other places where advertisements appear that script is playing a greater part today than ever before. Headings made in script seem to stand out and attract more attention than type. We are receiving a great many hand written letters which have been reproduced. In one of our newspapers we recently noticed an item regarding Charlotte S. Talcott, of New York City, who is following the career of writing advertisements in longhand. Surely this field is a very inviting one, and to those who are interested in penmanship it is worth trying. Few commercial artists are able to write good script. Penmen are able to write better script and can cooperate with commercial artists to good advantage.

LONG DISTANCE

CHARLES S. GILBERT

CHARLES S. GILBERT is a member of the faculty at the State Teachers College at Mansfield, Pennsylvania, where he has offered instruction in History and Handwriting since the fall of 1924. He is a graduate of the Nebraska Wesleyan University and the University of Alabama.

Before going to Mansfield, Mr. Gilbert was Superintendent of Nebraska City Schools for a number of years, and he was for a while Supervisor of Art and Handwriting in the City Schools at Atlantic, Iowa. He has taught in summer sessions at the Oswego, New York, State Normal School; the East Stroudsburg, Pennsylvania, State Teachers College; and at various other institutions in the middle-west.

Mr. Gilbert is an entertainer, crayon artist, and lecturer. For some time he appeared on the platform of the Associated Chautauquas of America. He makes many commencement addresses, and during the summer he is in demand for talks before educational gatherings throughout the country. He devotes considerable time to the filling of diplomas and to other pen work in general of a commercial character.

DESIGNING AND ENGROSSING
By E. L. BROWN
Rockland, Maine

COMMERCIAL DESIGNING

There is a large field for Commercial designs. Every kind of business, large or small, needs advertising designs of one kind or another. Attractive letterheads have a pulling power that ordinary type does not. Catch lines, trade marks, appropriate and distinctive designs are often required by business houses, and this means orders for one capable of doing such work.

First block in the masses roughly aiming for balance and color values. The story is about Diplomas, therefore this word receives more prominence than the others. Spacing is important in all lettering. The decorative features of this design do not affect the legibility of the lettering. Simplicity is a factor to consider in your designs. Too much ornamentation is worse than none at all. The lettering is all of the free hand type excepting that of word "Diploma" which was "ruled up" with T-square on drawing board.

The scroll work must be graceful, sweeping and symmetrical, and should be carefully outlined in pencil before inking. Two styles of stippling are shown in this design. Random dots closely spaced for background of scroll work inside of initial "D" and more evenly spaced dots are used elsewhere. Color values govern effects; study them critically. All work for photo zinc etching must be executed in jet black ink on white cardboard for best results.

Try color on a similar design, using red for initial "D", pale green for center scroll, etc.

Your work will be criticised if you will send it along—let us help you in your problems.

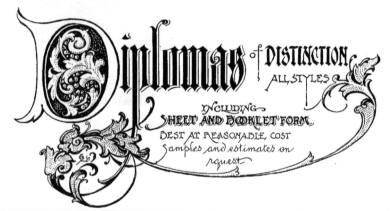

AUTHOR OF "THE THREE MUSKETEERS", A BEAUTIFUL PENMAN

We read in Winston Flashes that when Alexander Dumas went to Paris in 1823, he had but one accomplishment—beautiful penmanship. Dumas, you will remember, is the author of THE THREE MUSKETEERS, which is one of the most widely read titles in the public library today.

Those of our readers who have a flare for history will doubtless wish to find out just how well Alexander Dumas was able to write and how he learned to write so well. Judging from the marvelous books he has written, he must have been able to correlate his handwriting with the thought processes pretty well. What a shame it is that more people are not able to write and think at the same time as Alexander Dumas was able to do. We have every reason to believe, however, that present day students are improving in that respect, and we trust that this improvement may result in thousands of books even better than THE THREE MUSKETEERS, if such a thing is possible.

MANUSCRIPT WRITING DISCUSSED AT THE N. E. A. MEETING AT NEW ORLEANS

Our readers will be glad to know that the National Education Association now has a penmanship section. The first meeting was held in New Orleans, February 23, 1937. Miss Edith Conard, Teachers College, Columbia University, read a very excellent paper on manuscript writing and a very interesting discussion followed. Other phases of penmanship instruction were also discussed at this meeting, which was very well attended considering the fact that it was the first meeting of this section.

AMERICAN ASSOCIATION OF COMMERCIAL COLLEGES BECOMES NATIONAL SPONSOR OF PI RHO ZETA FRATERNITY AND SORORITY

J. I. Kinman, president of the Kinman Business University of Spokane, Washington, and president of the American Association of Commercial Colleges, announces that the American Association of Commercial Colleges will take over the national sponsorship of the Pi Rho Zeta fraternity and sorority.

Mr. Kinman is the national president, and C. W. Woodward, secretary-treasurer, of the College of Commerce, Burlington, Iowa, will become secretary-treasurer of the national sorority and fraternity. Other officers and the board of directors will be named in the very near future.

The Compass, the official monthly magazine of the American Association of Commercial Colleges, will also become the official magazine of the national Pi Rho Zeta fraternity and sorority.

The Grand Vice-President is W. C. Angus, Angus School of Commerce, Winnipeg, Canada. The Grand Secretary is Ramona Foster, American Institute of Business, Des Moines, Iowa.

Signatures by: Mr. M. A. Albin, 3823 S. E. 65th Ave., Portland, Oregon.

SAFETY AND HEALTH OF AMERICA'S SCHOOL CHILDREN—

This is the title of a pamphlet which is published by the Department of the Interior Office of Education, Washington, D. C. for free distribution. Some of the recent disasters of the public schools called for literature of this kind. Copies of this pamphlet may be secured by writing to the Department of Education. The pamphlet contains two hundred questions on safety and health of school children. We would suggest that Business College Proprietors secure a copy of this pamphlet. It contains some things of interest to any school concerned in the welfare of its pupils.

IMPROVING

The Department of Education in Washington reports that the educational level of our country is slowly rising. There is a long ways to go, however. If we may judge from the many letters which we receive daily, the standard of the handwriting of the country should be raised at least to the point of being easily read.

The cover page this month was made by W. J. Jarvis, Faribault, Minn. Mr. Jarvis has had considerable skill in art work. This cover page seems to be a little better than the previous one.

Written by T. Koike, Matsuida, Usuhigun, Gummaken, Japan.

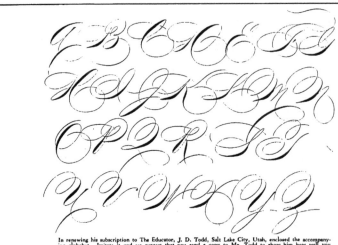

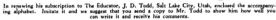

In renewing his subscription to The Educator, J. D. Todd, Salt Lake City, Utah, enclosed the accompanying alphabet. Imitate it and we suggest that you send a copy to Mr. Todd to show him how well you can write it and receive his comments.

A Dennis Flourish.

BOOK REVIEWS

Our readers are interested in books of merit, but especially in books of interest and value to commercial teachers including books of special educational value and books on business subjects. All such books will be briefly reviewed in these columns, the object being to give sufficient description of each to enable our readers to determine its value.

Fundamentals of Advertising, Third Edition, by Edward J. Rowse, A.M., Commercial Co-ordinator, Supervisor of Merchandising Instruction, Boston Public Schools, and Louis J. Fish, M. B. A., Director of Commercial Education, Boston Public Schools. Published by the South-Western Publishing Company, Cincinnati, Ohio. Cloth cover, 404 pages.

This textbook on advertising is an attempt to evaluate basic advertising principles and to present them to students in a simple, direct, and unornamented manner. The inspirational in advertising is too often intangible and without teachable content. The enthusiasm possessed by the creator of a successful advertisement is rarely transferable to the student in its entirety. Attempts to transfer to the student this very desirable but intangible trait too often complicate hopelessly the teaching content. There are, however, fundamental principles in advertising, which, when clearly outlined, provide a content that is teachable, educational, and vocational.

"Fundamentals of Advertising" represents an effort to perceive, distinguish, and recognize these basic principles and to present them logically to the student of advertising. To have high school or even college students attempt to create advertisements on a large scale is, to say the least, debatable and dangerous. To understand what is advertisement already in existence is well within the reach of all students.

This textbook presents a study of current, or existing advertisements with only a modicum of assignments requiring original advertisements. The authors are convinced that this approach to the study of advertising is better and less discouraging from the student's viewpoint than that requiring the creation of much advertising. From this basic presentation, however, the student may well experiment with simple creative projects. The authors are also convinced that a mere study of this textbook will not make an advertising expert. any more than a high school course in commercial law makes a lawyer.

If this textbook is successful in making the student appreciate the gigantic size of the advertising field, the enormous expenditures for advertising, the colossal power of advertising in commercial activities, and the necessity for thoughtful deliberation before even a modest advertisement is published, the authors will feel that the textbook has accomplished its purpose.

20th Century Typewriting, Third Edition, by D. D. Lessenberry, Director, Courses in Commercial Education, University of Pittsburgh, and Elizabeth A. Jevon, Teacher of Typewriting, Schenley High School, Pittsburgh, Pa. Published by South-Western Publishing Company, Cincinnati, Ohio. Cloth cover, 200 pages.

In the study of typewriting, the primary aim is the development of typing power for personal or vocational use. This is an all-inclusive aim. It must be broken up into its elements in order that materials of instruction and teaching procedures through which the aim is to be realized can be evaluated correctly. Some of these elements, which may well be ranked as secondary aims, may be summarized as follows:

1. The development of fundamental techniques for the control of the keyboard and the machine parts.
2. The development of the habit of accuracy in typing and in proofreading material.
3. The development of facility in the use of effective written speech.

4. The development of a familiarity with office forms and office procedures.
5. The development of a feeling for the correct spelling and syllabication of words.
6. The development of desirable social attitudes, business habits, and tact.

The problem of developing typing power is thus seen to begin with the technique of typing; but along with this development of skill must go the development of the individual in order that there may be intelligent use of skill. This broadened scope of typewriting instruction calls for teaching that will stimulate, guide, and challenge each student. It also calls for a textbook that will provide carefully planned and organized drills and problems through which typing power may be achieved. Thus the revision of typewriting textbooks keeps pace with progressive school philosophy.

In the revision of 20TH CENTURY TYPEWRITING, certain basic principles are retained from the former edition; other features are entirely new in typewriting-textbook construction. The organization of the teaching materials into specific blocks of work and the giving of an over-view of the problems of each block are features that will make for greater ease in motivating student practice. The use of all the letters of the alphabet in each paragraph of practice material provides for a steady improvement in the stroking of all letters and quickly leads from letter recognition to word recognition. The thought contents of the paragraphs will commend the book to all who appreciate the importance of developing attitudes as well as habits, of stimulating the growth of qualities as well as the growth of skills.

The use of the stencil drill to free students from the fear of making errors and the use of memorized sentences and paragraphs to build rapid and accurate stroking are teaching procedures that have been tested with marked success in experimental classes. Speed is no longer left to take care of itself any more than accuracy is expected to take care of itself. Through suggested practice procedures and specific practice materials, speed with control is developed from the beginning. The student is led to type on the word level with a minimum of waste motion and before his typing habits have been established on a low level of skill.

Fundamentals of Selling, by R. G. Walters, Personnel Officer, Grove City College; Co-author of "Fundamentals of Retail Selling." Published by South-Western Publishing Company, Cincinnati, Ohio. Cloth cover, 488 pages, third edition.

The same fundamental principles govern all types of selling, including retail selling, wholesale selling, specialty selling, advertising, and sales correspondence. It is desirable, therefore, that students who have had no previous training in selling be given a course in the general principles of salesmanship, and it is for such students that this book has been written. If desired, this course may be followed by specialized courses in retailing and advertising.

Many people believe that salesmanship, as taught in schools and colleges, is limited to the selling principles used by traveling salesmen. This, of course, is not the case; and in this textbook the student is taught to apply the general principles of selling not only to the work of the traveling salesman but also to retailing in all its forms, including retail store work, filling station work, and the selling of farm products.

The needs of the individual consumer and of society in general are emphasized throughout the text. The student is made to see that success in selling comes not only from an ability to make a sale but also from a desire to give permanent satisfaction to the buyer. High-pressure selling is frowned upon, and service and high ethical standards are stressed.

It is now generally recognized that selling requires skill and that skill can be acquired only through practice. To furnish such practice, one or more projects are given at the end of each chapter. These projects afford practice in all phases of the salesman's work, including the securing of prospects, the making of the preapproach, the preparation and delivery of the sales talk, and the clerical work incident to selling. Schools that give students practice through the use of the part-time, co-operative plan will find the text unusually well adapted to their needs.

ARE YOU AWAKE? by Florence E. Marshall, published by National W. C. T. U. Publishing House, Evansville, Ill. Cardboard cover, 96 pages.

"This book is entirely novel in temperance education for young people. It pokes good-natured fun at the gullible guzzler who, sheep-like, tags on unwittingly along in the wake of the liquor advertising. It challenges him to investigate, not by making himself an experimental guinea pig for the benefit of the liquor interests, but by a thoughtful consideration of what alcohol is and what it does, in order that he may protect his own interests. It makes one laugh and it makes one think. Although it educates for total abstinence, it is by no means dry reading. Some of the 'wet' newspapers have paid it the grudging tribute that it is actually interesting in spite of the subject."

The book is written in poetry and is very cleverly handled. It attacks the problem from the standpoint of education.

Our Business Life, by Lloyd L. Jones, M. A. Published by The Gregg Publishing Company, New York, N. Y. Cloth cover, 660 pages.

The primary aim of "Our Business Life" is to give the student a citizen's understanding of how business functions to supply the wants and needs of man, to make it clear that business plays an important part in the daily life of everyone, and to provide the student with the business information and consumer skill that will enable him to live more satisfactorily. This book deals with the effective and efficient use of the commonest business services. The foundation that it builds for businesslike living also serves as a foundation for further study of the business subjects and for work in the business world. The book is intended also to help the student understand the nature and principles of the business and economic community of which he is a part—to the end that he may be a better citizen. Business is studied as "man's best effort for meeting the needs of man."

Experience, study, and research have been called upon to make the text authoritative, practical, and teachable. The approach is natural and the student gets an understanding of business by applying business principles to his town life, and to family, school, church, and community life. Teachers realize that the secret of successful instruction in the beginning grades of the secondary school is pupil activity. "Our Business Life" recognizes that beginning students are not reflective thinking adults but "doing" individuals. The book, therefore, includes a wealth of activities that develop enthusiasm for a study of business on the part of both teacher and student. The optional feature of using a work book with the text gives added practicability to the program.

In recent years, junior business and economic citizenship courses have been adopted in many cities and states. Varying needs have resulted in one-, two-, and three-semester courses. Although "Our Business Life" was planned for one year, it is marked by an elasticity that will enable the teacher to make the course longer or shorter by the wise elimination or expansion. The teacher's manual recognizes these differences and provides helpful planning to that end.

The reader of "Our Business Life" will find that it discovers and holds to the middle of the road in its treatment of business and our economic society. Its mission is to present conditions and practices as they are and as they can be interpreted in the light of well-recognized trends.

We believe the fact that this book contains a work program for the student, thus making the use of the correlated Work Book optional, will be considered a constructive feature by school authorities, teachers, and patrons.

Colorado Association of Highway Contractors
Incorporated

Resolution

Whereas

G. W. "Bill" Hamilton

Has generously, faithfully and effectively served this Association since its inception; during the years of 1933 and 1934 as Vice-President and more particularly during the years 1935 and 1936 as President; and

Whereas, by personal sacrifice of time, energy and ability he has sought and achieved understanding, cooperation, and good will among the members and has effected better relations among those with whom the members transact business; and

Whereas, under his able leadership, the Association has firmly progressed, increased its prestige, enhanced its effectiveness; and

Whereas, each member feels a deep and sincere appreciation of these considerations, now, therefore, be it

Resolved

That in recognition of this splendid service, the members of this Association in Annual Convention assembled, Wednesday, January 20, 1937, extend to G. W. Hamilton sincere and heartfelt thanks together with best wishes for his future welfare and success.

Dated at Denver, Colorado, January 20, 1937.

President

A page by Norman Tower, Denver, Colo.

A Reed Page

A rather plain, attractive signature.

Well balanced, harmonious and beautiful.

Can you read it?

At a tender age.

R. R. Reed today

If you think that these signatures are easy, try to duplicate them.   Mr. Reed has a signature for every mood.

Mr. Reed is with the Platt-Gard Business University, St. Joseph, Mo.

Dear Mr. Stoddard

Practical Paying Pen Work is correct in every detail. It contains countless valuable suggestions and helps for making pen work pay, and is an indispensable aid to the penman. You have made a wonderful contribution to the profession.

Yours very truly,
H. P. Morgan

Dear Mr. Stoddard.

Thanks for the new specimen leaves from your most recent edition of "Gems from the Masters"

These additions more than double its value

2/26/37.

Yours Sincerely,

Springfield Mass
11-15-35.

Mr. Dear Stoddard
Penman

"G" New edition of Gems just received, approved and appreciated.— Truly a package of pep for practicing penmen. Hope you are well and happy. Sincerely,

What is more effective and more appreciated than a beautifully written letter. We receive many attractive letters every day. The above plates were loaned to us by D. L. Stoddard, R. R. 4, Box 141, Indianapolis, Ind.

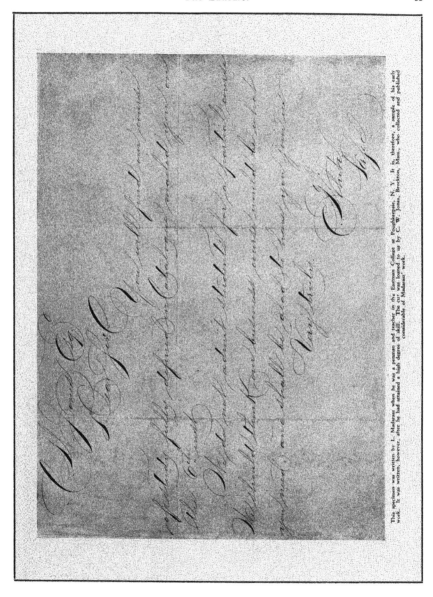

This specimen was written by L. Madarasz when he was a penman and teacher in the Eastman College at Poughkeepsie, N. Y. It is, therefore, a sample of his early work. It was written, however, after he had attained a high degree of skill. The cut was loaned to us by C. W. Jonas, Brockton, Mass., who collected and published considerable of Madarasz' work.

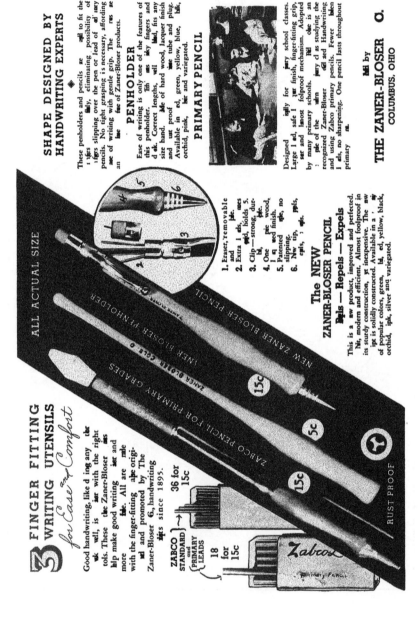

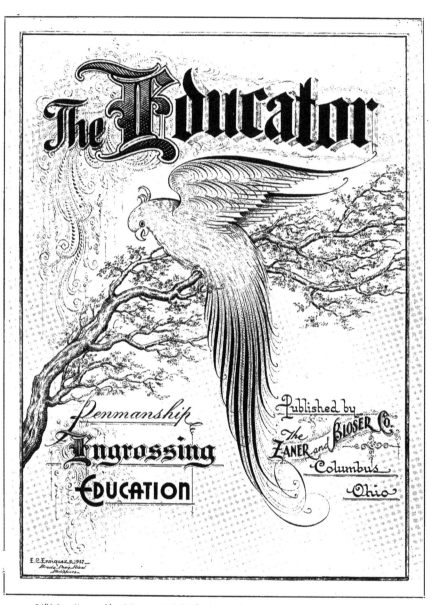

The Educator

Penmanship
Engrossing
EDUCATION

Published by
The ZANER and BLOSER Co.
Columbus
Ohio

E.C.Enriquez © 1937
Escuela Army Naval
Philippines

Published monthly except July and August at 612 N. Park St., Columbus, O., by the Zaner-Bloser Company. Entered as second-class matter November 21, 1931, at the post office at Columbus, O., under Act of March 3, 1879. Subscription $1.25 a year.

Volume 42   COLUMBUS, OHIO, JUNE, 1937   No. 10

The National Association of Penmanship Teachers and Supervisors

The eighteenth annual convention of the N. A. P. T. S. held in Washington, D. C. was exceptionally educational and enjoyable.

The members took advantage of Washington's unrivaled places of historic interest for sight-seeing tours.

EXHIBIT WORTH SEEING

The penmanship exhibit contained work from various parts of the country and was a splendid exemplification of the way in which the idea of correlating handwriting with other school subjects has been accepted generally by supervisors and teachers of handwriting.

A MEATY PROGRAM

Each speaker gave those who attended the meeting an abundance of inspiration and workable ideas to carry back to their classrooms.

A group of N. A. P. T. S. members on a sight-seeing tour at the side of the White House. (Reading left to right):

Ellen Christman, Womelsdorf, Pa.; Esther Nichols, Lancaster; Walter Ridgeway, Camden; Beulah P. Beale, Baltimore; Lucretia Cavanah, Cleveland; Lena A. Shaw, Detroit; J. H. Bachtenkircher, Lafayette; Genevieve Brown, Indianapolis; Mr. Ralph L. Myers (in rear), Bridgeton, N. J.; Mrs. Ralph L. Myers, Bridgeton, N. J.; Olive Mellon (in rear), Atlantic City; Margaret B. Toole, Wooster; Anna Lee Wolfe, Covington; P. Z. Bloser (in rear), Columbus; Sylvia Perkins, St. Louis; Mary M. Ashe, Rochester; Ida S. Koons, Ft. Wayne; Mary Curren, Wheeling; Eleanor D. McElroy, Fairmont; Mary A. Daniels, Lebanon; Katherine A. Turner, Philadelphia; Cora Major, Philadelphia; Anna L. Maginnis, Philadelphia; Emma Clammer, Troy; M. Otero Colmenero, San Juan, P. R.; Fanny J. Stout, Sellersburg, Ind.; Linda S. Weber, Gary; F. J. Myles, Nashville.

THE EDUCATOR

Published monthly (except July and August)
By THE ZANER-BLOSER CO.,
612 N. Park St., Columbus, O.
E. A. LUPFER..................................Editor
PARKER ZANER BLOSER..........Business Mgr.

SUBSCRIPTION PRICE, $1.25 A YEAR
(To Canada, 10c more; foreign, 30c more)
Single copy, 15c.
Change of address should be requested promptly in advance, if possible, giving the old as well as the new address.
Advertising rates furnished upon request.

THE EDUCATOR is the best medium through which to reach business college proprietors and managers, commercial teachers and students, and lovers of penmanship. Copy must reach our office by the 10th of the month for the issue of the following month.

Modern Handwriting

By E. A. Lupfer, Zanerian College, Columbus, Ohio

No. 10

Position

Always take the right position.

You should sit well back in your seat.

Bent backs are a sorry sight to see.

In checking the specimens from students in different grades in schools we find that many reach the end of a course and still do not have a good position or good movement. One should assume an easy writing position. We think that some who do not enjoy to write would enjoy it if they were able to write in an easier way. Check your position and have someone else watch you write. See that your fingers are not cramped. Above all do not grip the penholder.

P P P P P P P P P P P P

P P P P P P P P P P P P P

Penman Penman Penman

By this time you may have forgotten how to make the capital P, and this copy is therefore given to refresh your mind. If you have trouble with it go back to the previous copies on the P and study them.

Retracing exercises are good to develop free movement and also help one with formation of letters. Watch the size of your capitals. They should not be quite a space high. They should never touch the line of writing above. You should get from twelve to sixteen letters on the line. Occasionally you will see someone writing with as few as four to six letters on the line. This means that the work is sprawled out too wide and awkward. The remedy is to put more letters on the line.

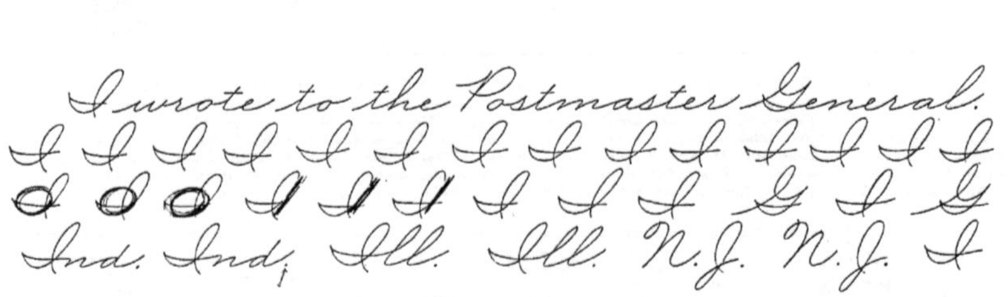

I wrote to the Postmaster General.

I I I I I I I I I I I I

I I I I I I I I I I I

Ind. Ind. Ill. Ill. N.J. N.J. I

A review of the I which is similar to the J. Compare the back of the I and J. The J and I start the same.

The J is made from the oval and straight line. Make the indirect oval and split it down the middle. In other words the top of the J is only half of an oval. The back of the J should be straight. The top loop should be slightly larger than the bottom loop. Never if possible run the loop of the J into other letters above or below the line.

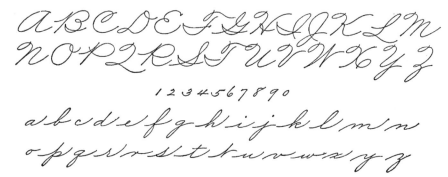

This alphabet was written by E. W. Bloser. It shows a beautiful swing. It will be well to study it carefully. Practice on each individual letter then make the entire alphabet. Watch the slant and proportions.

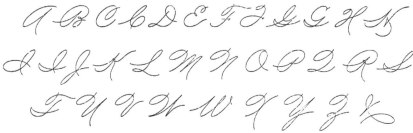

Here is another alphabet well worth your careful study. It is a very skillfully made alphabet. Notice the freedom of the lines and the beautiful curves.

This forceful looking business letter was written by E. W. Bloser in 1906. It shows a freedom and strength of line which is worth imitating.

A good handwriting will pave the way for success and get you started in life.

He most lives who thinks most, feels the noblest, acts the best. Patience is the key to contentment.

Written by F. B. Courtney, that skillful penman who has done so much for the penmanship profession. See if you can catch his style.

A FINAL SPECIMEN

We would suggest that you write a specimen similar to the one below and submit it to us for a certificate. Insert the name of your school and the kind of certificate you are working for. If you are in a business college you should substitute business college certificate. In preparing specimens of this kind watch the general appearance. Be sure not to get blots and smeared places on a specimen which you intend to send to anyone. Be careful with your writing at all times. You will then not have much trouble when you write for exhibition purposes. When you have written your specimen send it to The Educator for examination.

March 4, 1937 Penmanship Grade 8

A B C D E F G H I J K L M
N O P Q R S T U V W X Y Z
a b c d e f g h i j k l m n o p
q r s t u v w x y z 1 2 3 4 5 6 7 8 9 0

This is a specimen of my best penmanship while attending the Central School of Marysville, Kansas and practicing for a Grammar Grade Certificate.
Amy Ruth Griswold

Eighth Grade penmanship by Amy Ruth Griswold of Marysville, Kansas. The original was even more pleasing in appearance than the reproduction. The original was written in blue ink and was therefore a little difficult to reproduce. The teacher is Miss Mildred Kirkwood. Thirty-three of her pupils won Grammar Grade Certificates and twenty-two The Certificate of Excellence. We want to congratulate Miss Kirkwood on the splendid results she is securing.

ft, but penmanship is
tice.

Considerations for a Progressive Program in Handwriting

By Olive A. Mellon, Director of Handwriting, Atlantic City.

With the advent of the new era in education has come the tremendous task of reorganizing the school curriculum. This does not necessitate a complete tearing down of former procedures, but certain adjustments and adaptations are necessary in order to meet the immediate needs of modern education. This task of revision has fallen heavily on all administrators in the educational field. The director of special subjects has had to assume his portion of responsibility by contributing his thoughts relative to his special field.

The true purpose of modern education is to develop the child mentally, physically and socially so that he may become an acceptable citizen, loyal to his fellow man and to his country. With this objective in mind, every curriculum group should set about to make a study of the child—what will appeal to his interests and serve his needs;what will be of value to him as an adult; what is suited to his age and mental capacity; what will develop in him power and independence; and what will contribute to his physical and social growth? It has been through research, teacher training schools, demonstration schools, laboratory services, current texts and journals on modern educational procedures that progress thus far has been made.

The field of handwriting has not been exposed to the many changes nor explored in detail as have many other special fields. This is perhaps due to the fact that many of our educators are not familiar with its development sufficiently to advance many new thoughts or arguments. To be in full sympathy with the teaching of handwriting and to have a realization of its complexity, one must have training in its performance.

What a change in attitude we would see in many of our administrative officers if they had passed through the strenuous routine of training that many of us have experienced! However, a marked change in attitude has been evidenced in this respect during the past year or two. Only recently an investigation was made to secure the feeling of school superintendents toward handwriting. With scarcely an exception the prediction was for a bigger and better future for this in-

Olive A. Mellon

structional activity. Educators are now seeing the folly of its abolition during the lean days of economy. Many schools had abolished its supervision completely; others made certain adjustments which proved unsatisfactory and unfruitful; the result being a complete deterioration in the product.

If a superintendent were to sum up the values of good handwriting in his school system, he would find that it indicates a high standard of achievement; a well organized system; an efficient and conscientious corp of teachers; and a well disciplined group of children. This being true, is its contribution not worthwhile?

Should not one of our considerations for a new program in handwriting be to seek more wholehearted administrative cooperation?

More Adequate Teacher Training

Since handwriting functions in the majority of school activities, it is highly essential that the teacher be equipped to transmit knowledge pertaining to this art and be able to demonstrate in a clear, legible hand. She must also be familiar with the use of scales, tests, and standards for the grades. She must understand how to select and organize subject matter. She must be capable of training the child to do constructive

thinking. In addition to her special training, a well balanced general education is most essential.

The new educational movement carries teachers and supervisors into many unexplored fields. The supervisor of today does not know when she enters a classroom whether she will have to make a contribution to King Tut's Tomb or whether she will have to elucidate on the difference between hay and straw for the benefit of both teacher and pupil.

An unsatisfactory situation often arises in the Junior High School or in a departmentalized organization where each teacher is given a special assignment of subjects. If handwriting does not fall to her lot, she does not always support it. Whether her assignment is instruction in handwriting, or not, if it functions in her subject matter she should be broad enough in her thinking to see its value as a tool of necessity and lend her loyal support in the maintenance of a high standard of efficiency. Only when teachers and administrative officers give this subject their hearty support, will murmurings cease relative to poor handwriting in the upper grades.

As A Character Contributor

The search is on at the present time for ways and means of developing character. Can instruction in handwriting contribute any desirable character traits? Do you know of any better medium through which such traits as responsibility, accuracy, efficiency, loyalty, honesty, courtesy, pride, etc. can be developed than through instruction in handwriting? There is no more effective way of bringing forth character development than during the discussion period preceding the drill period. Opportunities should be given the child for expression of thought. It is through these expressions that the teacher guides the child in courtesy, tact, and consideration and develops in him an attitude of appreciation for the readers' time as well as his eyesight by encouraging him in his best attempts. The success of any lesson depends largely upon an interesting approach —setting the stage for the actual operation.

Safety Education

Through the same medium, the Safety Program may come in for its share of development. Training in safety now constitutes a major objective in education. Each year is bringing greater need for child protection due to the increase in traffic problems. It must be recognized as a fundamental condition of life and since it occupies a prominent place in the citizenship program, why not let it become a live part of the progressive program in handwriting?

The ingenious supervisor and teacher can find many interesting and valuable ways of aiding in the development of a safety conscience through this instructional activity.

Individuality in Handwriting

Individuality is an element which enters into handwriting regardless of age or ability and must receive a certain consideration. How often do we hear a poor writer exclaim, "But this is my individuality showing up. I should not want to destroy my individuality by training the hand in any definite set of characters." Does individuality in handwriting not need amelioration in many instances? Is it an asset if the product is such that the reader is delayed in the reading operation? Is it an asset if totally illegible?

On the other hand, can individuality be completely destroyed? Is not the above excuse given many times because of inability to produce better writing? Poor writing is the result of lack of opportunity, lack of knowledge, lack of practice, or lack of inclination. Individuality in handwriting needs to be encouraged, guided, and improved, then it is an enviable asset to any individual.

The new program in handwriting should provide for great flexibility so as to meet individual differences in interest, age, and ability. There is a tendency in handwriting instruction to cling to a program of extreme uniformity even in the face of recognized individual differences. Changes in methods have been meager even though fully cognizant of the social changes and individual variations.

To acquire skill in this art the child encounters new and varied experi-

> **Bad handwriting a mark of genius? Pshaw! It's much more apt to be a sign of dull, lazy intellect.**
>
> The Newark Ledger

ences as he progresses from the primary to the intermediate and on through the grammar grades. Each level has its goals of attainment and variation must be recognized in such factors as position of hand, movement, speed, size, degree of progress and capability of working with the group.

The problem of left-handedness arises in the first grade and requires much individual attention. It is here that the case must be investigated and a solution reached. A child showing a tendency toward left-handedness should be tested to determine which hand will yield the better results. The parents' cooperation should be enlisted and respected in such cases, as no teacher wishes to assume the responsibility of any disorder which might arise through changing the hand. In recent years there seems to be an increase in the number of left-handed writers, including those using an inverted position. This situation may be due to the informal instruction given, where not sufficient emphasis is placed on habits of position and pencil holding. It is a matter which calls for further study and investigation by progressive educators and handwriting specialists.

Subject Matter and Method

The foregoing considerations have been more general in nature. Now, let us enter the classroom and see how we can aid the teacher and child in the actual operation.

If the true principles of modern education are to be observed, all subject matter must be based on the activity or "center of interest" operating in the classroom. The activity which serves as a basis for instruction seems to be mainly in the social science area. It should be gathered by the child through socialized procedures and approved by the teacher. Assignments can be made to groups which will be responsible for certain phases of the activity. Through reading and discussion, rich informative material may be organized into various drill units and made ready for use for classroom practice.

These drill units should provide for practice on sentences, words, phrases, combinations, and single letters; and formal exercises may be employed in the development of the capital letters. To insure progressive teaching, a step in handwriting should be attached to each drill unit; as, in word

(Continued on page 21)

One of Miss Olive Mellon's rooms in action. Notice the excellent handwriting on the board.

Current Problems in Handwriting

John G. Kirk, Director of Commercial Education, Philadelphia, Pa.

(A talk given at the N. A. P. T. S.)

We are frequently forced today to change our philosophy of education because we live in a world in which social conditions and attitudes change rapidly. One notable change relates to the doctrine of the imposition of learning. This idea is giving way to the new doctrine of growth and adaptation. Educators today are thinking in terms of the child-centered school, child growth, personality growth, individualism, and creative learning.

Handwriting, perhaps even more than some other subjects, has felt the effects of this philosophy. Penmanship problems of today are widely different from penmanship problems of ten years ago. Handwriting instruction has broken away from the traditional procedures which aimed primarily to teach writing as an art. It is no longer considered a segregated subject and modern procedures aim not to teach subject matter, but rather to teach the child. Individual initiative, individual interests, individual needs and capacities form the basis of instruction now.

Just how strongly and firmly this philosophy is affecting the teaching of handwriting may well be understood by considering the opinions of a few of the educational leaders as expressed in current articles and in the newer books. For example, Lois Coffey Mosman, Assistant Professor of Education, Teachers College, Columbia University, says in her "Teaching and Learning in the Elementary School," that writing skill should be learned in relation to its use. Writing should begin by writing something which the children need to write in the course of their living together in the schoolroom. If children are writing what to them is important, they will want to do well those things which they need to write.

From a 1932 publication, "Directing Learning in the Elementary School," W. S. Monroe of the Bureau of Educational Research at the University of Illinois and Ruth Streitz of the University of Cincinnati, believe that recently there is a growing tendency to teach handwriting incidentally as a phase of activity units. The subject of handwriting is begun only when there is a readiness for writing and formal instruction is not given

until the need arises. Keeping this in mind, the authors say that material must be planned so that it can be adapted to meet the demands of all types of school organizations. In order to stimulate an interest and create a desire to write, there are many possibilities suggested for teaching writing incidentally. For example, labels for lockers, cloakrooms, and classroom libraries; invitations to other classrooms, to the principal, to parents; copying parts for school plays and posters.

NEW N. A. P. T. S. OFFICERS

President, Ralph E. Rowe, Portland, Maine

Vice President, Ida Koons, Fort Wayne, Ind.

2nd Vice President, Henry Garvey, Tuckahoe, N. Y.

Secretary, Ottie Craddock, Farmville, Va.

Treasurer, Doris E. Almy, Fall River, Mass.

Although reasonably satisfactory results may be obtained by incidental instruction, it is agreed that systematic teaching is desirable. It is to be remembered, however, that repetition does not insure learning and practice will not improve handwriting if there is no interest and desire.

In "Education of Children in the Primary Grades," (a 1935 publication), Horn and Chapman say that we must keep in mind the fact that the child comes to school not without experience. The teacher, therefore, must not analyze the writing skill into logical elements and have children begin with, strokes and letters. She must be guided by the children's interests and must teach the children to write words—and words they want to write. The authors feel that progress will be faster if the skill is taught through application rather than as an end in itself. The aim should be writing, not handwriting; written expression and not penmanship. Procedure should be

so organized that the child will manifest a real desire to write.

Paul McKee, Director of Teachers College and Professor of Elementary Education, State Teachers College, Colorado, discusses the teaching of writing in his book entitled, "Language in the Elementary School." It is Doctor McKee's opinion that writing is much more than a skill. It is essentially a tool rather than an end in itself. It is a means of expressing thought or meaning. This means that instruction in writing must take care of the meaning element and that the child should look upon writing as an expression of thought. Therefore, a good program in writing, according to Doctor McKee, will be concerned about both the meaning and the skill elements in writing. There will be practice exercises through which the child may hope to acquire skill in movement and form, and increase the speed and quality of his writing. Care will be taken, however, to see that most exercises are concerned with meaningful content as judged by experiences in other school work and that every exercise has a very definite purpose behind it in terms of the removal of discovered writing difficulties.

Another authority, George E. Freeland, Supervisor of Practice Teaching and Assistant Professor of Education in the University of Washington, Seattle, says that writing is a medium for expressing the English language through written words. The increased use of typewriters has decreased the conventional value of handwriting considerably in the last decade. However, the ability to write well is still worth while and necessary. The conventional reaction to good or poor writing is almost as strong as that for spelling. No child should be allowed to suffer unnecessary difficulties in social or vocational life because of neglect of this side of his education in elementary school. There is better reason for spending time in developing ability to write rapidly and legibly than there is for spending time in technical grammar or a great deal of our arithmetic. But it is to be remembered that legibility and a certain amount of speed are the only essentials in writing. Writing from an artistic standpoint should have no place in the elementary school curriculum of today.

In further support of this idea, Annie E. Moore in her book "The Primary School," chapter entitled "The Informal Approach to Writing," says: "Exacting and minutely detailed systems of teaching penmanship constitute a pernicious interference with the natural development of self expression through writing and with the normal development of handwriting itself."

In Philadelphia we are applying the principles of this "newer and more progressive" philosophy to our handwriting instruction in a most concrete way.

For the elementary schools, Grades 1 to 6, we have provided a new course of study which was officially accepted and introduced into our schools in March, 1936. Fundamentally, this new course is built on the integration and correlation of subject matter, individual analysis and remedial drill work, and the development of "writing consciousness." Great flexibility and provision for much individual initiative on the part of supervisors, teachers, and pupils are two important motivating processes.

The plan of integrating instructional materials with the other writing which a pupil wants or needs to do is taken care of, especially in Grades 3 to 6, by the provision of two types of lessons—namely, the drill type and the applied type. In the formal or drill type lesson, the content is determined by the needs of the group. It may be words, sentences, a paragraph (from English, reading, geography, history, or any other activity), or figures. The aim of the drill lesson is the development of correct handwriting technique and muscular coordination. Drill, therefore, is especially devised to care for individual needs.

In the applied type lesson, the content may be verses from poems, original paragraphs, letters, lists of spelling words, arithmetic, assignments, or notebooks. The aim of these lessons is to integrate handwriting instruction with other learning activities; to strengthen the theory that the ability to use correct writing habits and to produce a legibly-written product in all written work determines the success of the writing instruction.

In order to secure the desired outcomes, the course aims to develop:

1. The realization (on the part of both teachers and pupils) of the great value of facility and legibility in the writing of all written work.

2. The realization that self-analysis, self-criticism, remedial instruction, and consistent, intelligent practice are powerful agents in reaching a desired standard.

3. The realization that progress is most rapid when each pupil sets a standard for himself which is better than his best and yet attainable. By these procedures, it is hoped that upon achieving one standard, the pupil will be encouraged to aim at a higher one.

In some cases, schools provide in junior and senior high school no formal instruction in handwriting. This practice, however, is very much to the disadvantage of pupils, because while pupils have developed by the end of the sixth grade a minimum quality of 60 on the Ayres Scale and an approximate speed of 70 letters a minute, if the incentive to write legibly and with the desired speed is not maintained, deterioration in quality sets in immediately and soon becomes a serious fault. So far, the only opportunities provided in secondary schools for additional instruction and drill are in vocational business training courses. It will be at once appreciated by all who give thought to this problem that it is unwise to drop all provision for systematic instruction in handwriting beyond the sixth grade. Such instruction is essential in vocational business training courses and would be highly beneficial for all secondary school pupils. Instruction in handwriting in secondary schools should include the diagnosis of individual errors; practice in writing any of the pupil's daily work which is under criticism; a minimum of emphasis on formal drill; and insistence upon legibility with moderate speed in all written work should be the aims.

For pupils in vocational classes who need to attain higher writing standards, more intensive practice is necessary. This intensive practice will consist partly of the use of the special materials and forms which are used in business and partly of more extensive and strenuous drill. It is vitally important that these students realize that the important requirement for improving one's handwriting is the will to improve and the interest in studying to find ways of improving. A vocational motive or special interest will aid greatly in sustaining pupils in their efforts to gain greater skill and more efficiency. Necessary guidance in the correct diagnosis of errors, in the proper evaluation of writing, and in the selection and use of remedial measures makes necessary the provision for sufficient time in the junior and senior high school curriculum. These classes may be classified as regular penmanship classes, hospital or restoration classes, or handwriting clubs.

Certainly, no discussion on present-day handwriting problems, and particularly in the light of an "ever-changing philosophy," would be complete without some mention of manuscript writing. It is a topic which demands careful consideration by experts in the handwriting field for several very good reasons:

1. Because so many progressive and enthusiastic educators are advocating its use.

2. Because some private schools and public school systems are using it.

3. Because its use can be justified by a scientific and an historical background.

4. Because its advantages are accepted so readily and are exploited so widely.

Dr. Frank N. Freeman of the University of Chicago, after much scientific investigation and research, published his findings in the Elementary School Journal, February, 1936 in an article entitled, "The Evaluation of Manuscript Writing."

Some of the most interesting and pertinent of his conclusions are as follows:

1. From the replies of 218 out of 360 questionnaires sent to primary supervisors, about one-fourth were found to be using manuscript writing.

2. The large majority of those using it introduced it during or since 1931 and about 10 per cent of those who tried it have discontinued using it.

3. Historical evidence, experiment, practice, and opinion indicate that cursive writing is better for the upper grades and for adult writing.

4. Experiment, the trend of practice, and the opinion of those who have used it indicate that manuscript writing is preferable for beginners.

5. The change should be made late enough to secure the advantages of manuscript writing as an initial style and early enough to minimize the difficulty of making the change. In the opinion of the writer, the point at which the change can probably best be made is the second half of Grade 2.

The foregoing is a statement of some of the trends of the moment and progressive teachers welcome change because—Where there is no change, there is no life, no progress. We should also contribute as much worth while data on timely questions as possible for our contributions involve research and thought. Two important questions of the moment to which we might all give attention are: How should beginners be taught to write? Is manuscript writing better for Grades 1 and 2?

We may all add much valuable information to supplement Doctor Freeman's study of the value of manuscript writing by recording our own experience. Experiments should be well-organized and carried on in controlled classes under the direction of unbiased teachers, principals, and handwriting supervisors and under as wide a scope of varying circumstances as possible. Research of this sort is one of the surest ways of combating a common tendency to "gad about after the new things," to the neglect of older but often very much worth while methods.

"Mr. Meadows Says"

BY GEORGE A. MEADOWS
Pres. Meadows-Draughon
Business College, Shreveport, La.

Let's try to develop sweet dispositions rather than sour ones—let's try to cooperate rather than tear down.

Someone has said that we can catch more flies with honey than we can with vinegar. Let's remember that, and when we want something from someone else, let's approach that person in a nice, sweet, sensible way, rather than by starting out criticising and finding fault.

Try SMILING rather than frowning. It will get you a lot further. If things are not going right, instead of finding fault try to figure out how to improve the situation, and then offer your suggestions in a tactful sort of way.

Try to cooperate with your teachers. Remember, they know more than you do, or they would not be holding their positions. Remember,

too, they are human, and will likely come nearer helping you and giving you good reports if you are considerate of them.

Above all, remember to conduct yourselves as ladies and gentlemen at all times, bearing in mind that this reflects on you and your parents, as well as on the school.

Always be appreciative of things that are done for you, regardless of how much obligation the other fellow may be under to you.

In a nutshell, COOPERATE, don't fuss; be pleasant, not disagreeable; don't frown, but smile; work with the other fellow, and for the other fellow and he, in turn, will work with and for you.

Above all—don't waste your time, but make every minute count!

DEIBERT PRIVATE SCHOOL CERTIFICATE WINNERS

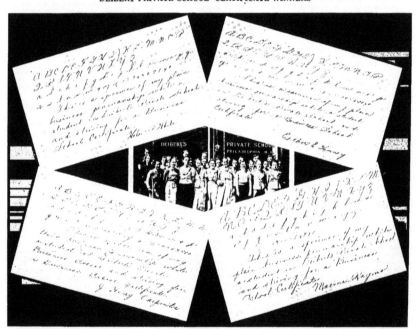

The above twenty-seven pupils won Zaner-Bloser Penmanship Certificates. The Deibert School is a select business training school in the northern part of New York State. All commercial subjects are taught and penmanship is given its proper place in this institution. Mr. A. D. Deibert is the President.

N. J. S. T. A.

The Handwriting Department of the New Jersey State Teachers' Association held its annual Business Meeting at Van Nest Hall, Rutgers University on Saturday, May 7, 1937. The guest speaker was Mrs. Ethel De Beck, Department of Research, Newark Public Schools. Her topic was "Measurements and Scales and their uses in the Classroom". Mrs. De Beck brought to the meeting a collection of scales and graphs to illustrate her very dynamic and interesting talk. Unfortunately, time did not permit discussion.

The Business Meeting was under the direction of the President, Miss Marjorie Flaacke and followed the usual routine, with reports of all committees. The committee on Research for the Handwriting Department reported through Miss Charlotte Barton, Elementary Supervisor of Newark Schools, a study on materials and equipment for the teaching of handwriting.

The organization is beginning a study of the handwriting problem from all its angles and Miss Barton's report is on but one division of the situation.

The Handwriting Department has so increased its membership that it has outgrown the capacity of the room assigned. Stimulated interest throughout New Jersey, which necessitates the appointment of special teachers and supervisors of Handwriting, has brought this situation about and the Handwriting Department is becoming a very important part of the State Association.

The officers of the year 1936-1937 were re-elected and are as follows:

President—Miss Marjorie Flaacke, State Normal School, Newark, New Jersey

Vice-President—Miss Olive Mellon, Supervisor of Handwriting, Atlantic City, New Jersey

Secretary—Miss Jennie Egan, Supervisor of Handwriting, Red Bank, New Jersey

Treasurer—Miss Clara Harrison, Supervisor of Handwriting, Burlington, New Jersey

Following the Business Meeting forty members remained for luncheon at the Blue Hills Plantation, Dunellen.

A PLEASANT VISIT

We had a pleasant visit with John H. Karr of the Karr School of Business, Van Wert, Ohio, who reports that his school is in a very thriving condition.

Mr. Karr is one of those school men who believes in good handwriting. He not only exacts good handwriting from his pupils but uses fancy penmanship in his advertising.

Cards by Arnold C. Gorling, 530 Maryland St., Winnipeg, Man., Canada, teacher in Success Business College.

Signatures by Mr. M. A. Albin, 3823 S. E. 65th Ave., Portland, Oregon.

Ornamental Penmanship by R. M. Maugans, Statesville, N. C., who has been taking correspondence instruction and following the lessons in The Educator.

Lessons in Modern Engrosser's Script
Prepared in the office of The Educator

No. 9

At this time of the year engrossers are busy filling diplomas. Script is used by them in writing dates, names of courses, and names. The accompanying names were written by E. H. McGhee, the engrosser of Trenton, N. J. They make an excellent lesson in script at this stage of our course. Practice on each name and send us your best work for criticism.

If you want to succeed in engrossing work financially, master script.

Maurice L. Guadagno *Richard C. Penrose*
Natalie D. Hutchinson
Julius Ervin Kovacs *William A. Quinn*
Virginia Frances Baumann
Zoemain Y. Techmechian *Olivia F. Landow*
Uriel Xergia
Trenton *New Jersey*

REEMPLOYED

Mr. O. G. Martz, was for quite a number of years Supervisor of handwriting in the Public Schools of Norwood, Ohio, but like a number of special teachers and supervisors was transferred to high school work during the depression. We are happy to report that he is now back in his old position as head of the Handwriting Department. We feel that many other schools will employ Handwriting Supervisors as financial conditions of the schools continue to improve.

HOW ABOUT YOU?

I have been a regular subscriber to "The Educator" for many years. I couldn't do without it.

Mr. C. W. M. Blanchard,
Supervisor of Penmanship
37 Winthrop Street,
Medford, Mass.

This beautiful writing was done by a second grade pupil of Miss Maude Schell, 40 South Main Street, W. Alexandria, Ohio.

By the late H. B. Lehman.

Bonaparle

The man of Destiny — the incarnation of energy — his name the byword of marvelous achievement; gigantic in intellect — adamant in civic honesty — magnanimous and sublime in victory, herculean in defeat.

Statesman, financier, educator, philosopher, litterateur, — a mystic fatalist polished by dire privation into the greatest of great men.

Fame has emblazoned Napoleon with the brilliancy of the mid day Sun.

Futurity alone may produce his equal.

P.Z. Bloser. 1937. — Madarasz

Written by P. Z. Bloser in imitation of one of L. Madarasz's famous specimens.

CONSIDERATIONS FOR A PROGRESSIVE PROGRAM IN HANDWRITING

(Continued from page 13)

practice, attention may be directed to uniform size of letters; or in sentence practice, spacing may be the objective. Any factor can be attached to a drill unit but there are certain ones which seem to make closer application than others. The child should be guided in the selection of his own weak factor and practice should be directed from that point.

Regardless of what the "center of interest" may be, the subject matter which is selected should be organized in such a way that the child will have varied practice and an opportunity for much repetitive drill if he requires it.

There is urgent need for more definite helps for teachers along this line. Very little has been developed along the line of new methods for the new program. Even though our texts are up to date in most respects, they fall short in advancing methods and indicating socialized procedures to fit the new program and meet the needs of the child. Without an organized procedure it would be necessary to "draw the reins to check the hoss" as the teacher may stray into by-paths by not directing her instruction toward a definite goal.

What knowledge does the child acquire through this procedure? He learns to seek sources of information.

To train with a group.

To assume responsibility.

To strive toward a worthy goal.

To make comparisons with former attempts.

To be cognizant of the fact that drill promotes skill.

To aid in diagnosing faults and supplying remedies.

To protect his equipment.

To measure results.

When directing h a n d w r i t i n g through the activity movement or a "center of interest", the teacher might profit by observing the following ten steps:

1. Direct practice toward a worthy goal.

2. Encourage desirable working habits.

3. Provide for pupil participation.

4. Create a consciousness of the purpose of drill and provide for varied types.

5. Attach a step in handwriting to each drill unit.

6. Provide for individual differences.

7. Encourage frequent comparisons.

8. Maintain a flexible handwriting program.

9. Foster health through correct posture.

10. Check up on accomplishments.

Knowledge Tests

A consideration for a new program in handwriting is the introduction of knowledge tests. A recent investigation in this phase of instruction revealed a decided need for testing the child's knowledge of writing as well as his skill. Surprising as it may seem, many sixth grade pupils did not know the number of letters in the alphabet; did not know the letters in sequence; could not distinguish between capital J and small j; capital Q and small q; did not understand the terms, upper loop, retraces, alignment; did not have a knowledge of the proper formations of many capital letters and could not explain the difference between direct and indirect movement.

Lack of knowledge is largely responsible for much of the poor writing in these grades and the inability to diagnose understandingly. A child must know before he can perform intelligently.

Progress Rating

Another consideration is ways and means of rating the child's progress. Individual differences enter the picture again. Not every child can reach the grade standard as children make progress at varying rates, but he may have shown progress since the beginning of the year. If progress is the goal, not grades, should he not receive credit for his gain thus far?

Progress books seem to meet this need fairly well, which is shown through specimens taken at the beginning, the middle, and the end of the year. Progress can be rated at the middle, and at the end of the year by comparing with the first specimen. A skeleton form may be set up to register yes for improvement and no for nonimprovement. The total in the yes column based on the number rated gives a class progress rating. The same scheme may be used effectively for rating the efficiency of the class—those reaching the grade standard as against those below standard.

Print or Manuscript Writing

Manuscript writing seems to be gaining considerable momentum during recent years, particularly in the primary school. Texts have been published recently by two prominent companies, and more adoptions are reported being made each year.

The originators of this movement, in enumerating its virtues, contend that satisfactory results can be attained with undue strain. It is well adapted to the left-handed child or one with a nervous disorder. It is an aid to early reading and spelling experiences. It is better adapted to the immature child than the cursive style.

Many school systems use it throughout the grades, while others recommend it only for the first and second, with the transition to begin the latter half of the second year. This movement, however, is still in the process of experimentation; and, like every new venture, it is subject to criticism and debate.

If at the end of the child's elementary training he has shown considerable gain in the product of his reading, writing, and spelling, due to his early training in this print style, then it is a worthwhile contribution to the educational field and should receive consideration when setting up a new program in handwriting.

To summarize:

(1) This is an opportune time for the revision of all courses of study in handwriting.

(2) The "center of interest" which serves as the basis for instruction seems to lie mainly in the social studies area.

(3) There is an urgent need for new procedures for the development of this tool subject based on a "center of interest".

(4) More adequate teacher training in handwriting is needed.

(5) Through handwriting many desirable attitudes and ideals are developed which contribute toward character training.

(6) Administrative cooperation is highly essential for a successful handwriting program.

(7) Individual differences and individuality in handwriting should be provided for in the new program.

(8) Manuscript or print writing is gaining momentum in the primary school, but it is still in the experimental stage.

These theories which have been advanced are not in criticism of any former plan of instruction in handwriting. They may not be entirely psychologically sound but they have been presented for the purpose of furthering the study of this art through the new educational program.

The ultimate aim is to so train the child in handwriting that he may go forth with power and independence and with a fuller realization of the value of good handwriting in business and society. Let us continue our exploration and experimentation in this instructional activity as it is only through such channels that progress is made in any line of human endeavor.

Lessons in Card Carving

By J. D. Carter, Deerfield, Ill.

Lesson No. 9

In lesson No. 9 I shall illustrate a combination decorative effect by using an India ink spray.

This simple spray method has been used by the artist in many different ways, and if rightly handled the quality of the work can be made to equal that of the air brush.

In making the designs I cut the forms for the shield, the rectangle for the place for the names, and circles for the flowers from paper.

After the patterns had been made I arranged them on the card then used the spray of India ink which left the portions protected by the patterns, white or light, depending on the arrangement and rearrangement of patterns.

After getting the design on card I proceeded to cut the designs with the carving tool as described in former lessons.

As stated above, artists have used this spray method in different ways; but I am describing below a method I have found very simple and effective.

First take a picture frame and neatly tack or secure a piece of door or window screen to it. (8 in. by 10 in. frame makes a convenient size).

After securely fastening the screen, proceed to make four legs, one for each corner by using screws 1 in. to 1½ in. in length. Dowel sticks or small blocks of wood can be used for the legs instead of the screws if desired.

This makes a frame that will rest at a convenient height above patterns and paper placed on the drawing board.

Our second step will be to get a sponge cup to hold a small sponge. Moisten the sponge with water then squeeze all the water from the sponge you can conveniently with the hand.

Next place the sponge into the cup and pour India Ink on the sponge until it is saturated with the ink. Don't get too much ink if a fine spray effect is desired.

Third, use a stiff bristle brush—(a nail brush or bristle varnish brush with the bristles cut off about half length will do) and press bristles of the brush on the sponge in the cup until brush is thoroughly moistened.

Now arrange the frame over your paper and design you have prepared to outline then move briskly the moistened brush over the prepared screen and you will notice a fine, soft spray is falling on the paper and pattern to form the desired designs.

If you succeed well with this perhaps later we may bring out something pleasing and more elaborate.

You can do spray work on wood, cloth and other materials, and this method can be used effectively in getting outlines of grasses, ferns and plant life as they develop in their seasons.

Let us see some of your work. Criticism for return postage.

From the pen of Rene Guillard, Evanston Township High School, Evanston, Ill.

When Mr. Bowes was in his teens he attended the British American Business College in Toronto, Ontario, where he received his first inspiration in writing from his instructor, Mr. Connor O'Dea, one of the finest penmen he has ever known.

After graduating from this institution and the Normal School he taught in ungraded schools for a number of years. One day he answered an advertisement in a city paper for a teacher who could teach bookkeeping, arithmetic and penmanship. His application was accepted and he remained with the Cornwall Commercial College for about ten years. Later he left there and accepted a position with Wood's School in New York City where he taught penmanship and other subjects. In subsequent years he taught in Drake School, Paterson, N. J.; Bank's Business College, Philadelphia; and Bryant & Stratton Commercial School, Boston. In all of those schools penmanship was his major subject.

For two years he was head of the commercial department in the Bryant and Stratton School in Manchester, N. H., the school in which the famous penman, G. A. Gaskell, once taught. Much of his skillful work adorned the walls of that institution when Mr. Bowes was there.

Mr. Bowes is married and has a family—two sons and a daughter.

He states: "The Educator has always been an inspiration to me and I possess copies of it which date back many years. Through it I have been able to see the work of the finest penmen of the present time and of the past also, and I owe much of my success in teaching penmanship to the matter contained in its pages."

Mr. Bowes is teaching penmanship and commercial work in Bay Path Institute, Springfield, Mass. This

school has about fifty persons on its faculty and administrative staff and occupies exclusively an attractive, modern four-story building. Two-year courses are offered in Accounting, Business Administration and Secretarial. One-year courses are also offered.

Penmanship is given four hours credit.

ROMANCE STARTED AT THE ZANERIAN

In 1916 two charming, ambitious, young people enrolled in the Zanerian College for courses in penmanship.

Those were memorable days when ambitions knew no bounds, and the W, X, Y and Z's were obstinate headaches. Dan Cupid, however, demanded his share of time, and the Edith H. Welsh of those happy days became Mrs. Lester L. Kerney.

Recently Mr. and Mrs. L. L. Kerney of Akron, Ohio, visited The Educator office force and the Zanerian. They are now teaching in the Davis Business College at Akron, Ohio.

We are always glad to have our old pupils and friends drop in to see us, and to tell us of their success and experiences.

THE CHILLICOTHE BUSINESS COLLEGE'S NEW DORMITORY

A $50,000 dormitory is being built by the Chillicothe Business College, Chillicothe, Mo. This is one of the most outstanding projects in commercial education. It is one of eight buildings on the Chillicothe Business College campus.

It is interesting to know that the stone used in the construction is being quarried on the school's farm and is being crushed in the school's own crusher. The building will be strictly fireproof and wherever possible student labor is used. The building will be 114 x 36 feet, with red mat face brick and concrete. It will have a large lounge, recreation room, laundry and trunk rooms, two rooms for matron, and 41 double rooms for students.

We congratulate the men back of this school.

FUNDAMENTALS

Dr. W. W. Charters, director of educational research at Ohio State University, in a broadcast stated that many time worn "fundamentals" are merely "frills". He urged discarding such old favorites as algebra, geometry, foreign languages and much of the history.

In the field of skills, Dr. Charters urges that reading, handwriting and arithmetic be retained as essential subjects. In his opinion, those subjects should be required in elementary and high schools which are of primary importance to all students and those should be elective which fit the needs of individual students and which finances will permit to be offered.

Dr. Charters argues that real fundamentals help one to live a wholesome and effective life as a child and later as a citizen. In making the above statement, Dr. Charters is mindful of the value of good handwriting to the student while in school.

Many persons overlook that good handwriting is an invaluable tool which helps the student in preparing other subjects. For this reason alone it pays every student to write well, freely and automatically as early as possible.

FORMER ZANERIAN BECOMES COUNTY SCHOOL SUPERINTENDENT

O. C. Anderson, who attended the Zanerian in 1925, is now County Superintendent of Schools, Clay County, Illinois.

It always gives us great pleasure to learn and to pass on to our readers information about accomplishments and attainments of our former students and friends.

Mr. Anderson is a fine young man and an enthusiastic penman. We predict continued success for him in Clay County.

THE DETROIT EDUCATIONAL NEWS SAYS:

"Michigan ranks 16th in the per cent of literacy, according to recent reports. There are 76,800 people in the state who cannot read or write. This represents 2 per cent of the 1930 population".

We wonder if they have included the bankers and school teachers in their survey.

The KBU CIRCLE is a very attractive four-page publication gotten out by the students of the Kinman Business University, Spokane, Washington. It is very attractively printed and well illustrated, containing photographs of schoolroom scenes, students, etc. It no doubt has had quite an influence in building up the school to its present large enrollment.

By E. L. Brown, Rockland, Me.

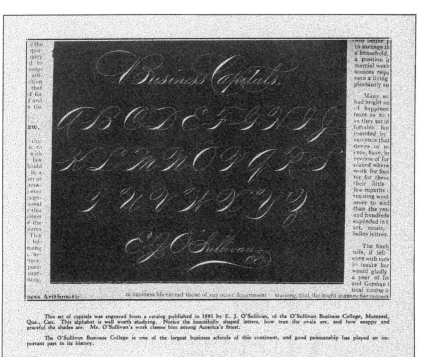

This set of capitals was engraved from a catalog published in 1895 by E. J. O'Sullivan, of the O'Sullivan Business College, Montreal, Que., Can. This alphabet is well worth studying. Notice the beautifully shaped letters, how true the ovals are, and how snappy and graceful the shades are. Mr. O'Sullivan's work classes him among America's finest.

The O'Sullivan Business College is one of the largest business schools of this continent, and good penmanship has played an important part in its history.

THE COVER

The cover page this month was made by E. C. Enriquez, Pineda, Pasig, Rizal, P. I.

The bird in the design is known as the "Catala", a native of the Philippines.

We congratulate Mr. Enriquez upon his skill in handling the pen, and his ability in designing such an attractive page.

AN OLD FRIEND

We were pleasantly surprised to receive a letter from our old friend and penman, L. E. Stacy. Many penmen will remember Mr. Stacy as author of the "Blue Book", a history of penmen. Mr. Stacy has for the past 25 years been with the Spirella Company of Niagara Falls, New York. While his interests have been in the selling end of the business, he states that he is still interested in penmanship and probably always will be. We are always glad to learn of the success of former penmen and old friends.

HONORED BY ROTARIANS

Harry M. Spamer, president of Eastman-Saratoga School of Business, Saratoga Springs, N. Y., was elected president of Saratoga Springs Rotary Club in April.

THE HANDLESS PENMAN

J. C. Ryan, the handless penman, is still writing cards. The last we heard from him he was in Seymour, Texas. His writing is of a very high professional nature.

It is always very instructive and helpful to watch Mr. Ryan write. He has a sunny disposition and is rendering the country a very great service in writing cards and in teaching patience and perseverance. If you ever get a chance to see J. C. Ryan, the handless penman, write, do so. Until you have seen him write you have missed something in penmanship which is really worth while.

BOOK REVIEWS

Our readers are interested in books of merit, but especially in books of interest and value to commercial teachers including books of special educational value and books on business subjects. All such books will be briefly reviewed in these columns, the object being to give sufficient description of each to enable our readers to determine its value.

Standard Handbook for Secretaries,

by Lois Irene Hutchinson. Published by McGraw-Hill Book Company, Inc., New York, N. Y. Cloth cover, 616 pages.

The big field of opportunity for women today is unquestionably secretarial practice. But, with the wide and constant demand for secretaries, stenographers and office assistants, comes naturally the call for a higher standard of efficiency. More and more executives are delegating to their secretaries duties and routines they formerly handled themselves. More and more the secretary becomes the executive's right-hand assistant. To enter this wider field of opportunity, the secretary today must be expert in secretarial technique.

Here is a book compiled by an experienced secretary during years of active work with prominent executives and professional men all over the country—written expressly for the purpose of providing secretaries with the handbook of reference facts, of procedures, of methods that will give them this finished training in secretarial technique.

The secretary confronted daily with hundreds of questions from how to spell "traveling" to the intricacies of foreign exchange will find in this thorough, comprehensive handbook the facts she needs—and she will get them in findable, clear, usable form.

Simplicity and clarity of statement are stressed. The book is unusually comprehensive, covering not only many facts to help in the production of normal stenographic and typing work, but also many useful items relating to diplomacy, efficiency and office procedure, legal matters, communication services, financial information, and tables and lists of many kinds.

Special attention is given to grammar, the book explaining such matters as grammatical rules and correct usage so clearly that the reader can readily grasp these frequently confusing aspects of composition. All the latest practices and points of usage and style are included, making the book strictly up-to-date in every way.

Tested Selling Ideas, from the files of

"Printers' Ink" and "Printers' Ink Monthly." Edited and compiled by Carroll B. Larrabee, Managing Editor, Printers' Ink Publications, and Henry William Marks, Manager, Readers' Service Department, Printers' Ink Publications. Published by McGraw-Hill Book Company, Inc., New York, N. Y. Cloth cover, 368 pages.

In this book are given the concise, boiled-down experiences of a number of successful manufacturers in solving important sales, merchandising, and advertising problems. This book is not a survey of current merchandising. It is not a success book built on glittering generalities. It is a case book based on the in-the-field experiences of a great many manufacturers during the toughest depression that American business has ever encountered.

In preparing this book we have not sought the showy or the tricky. Rather we have been interested in the practical and simple ideas that are capable of adoption in a great many industries.

One thing the reader must remember and that is that because a plan worked successfully in an industry somewhat removed from his own, this is no sign that it will not work in his industry. As a matter of fact, this book would never have been compiled were we not convinced that the simple, practical, usable idea which has worked efficiently in one industry in ninety-nine cases out of one hundred is adaptable to a dozen or one hundred other industries.

In planning each issue of "Printers' Ink" and "Printers' Ink Monthly," its editors are continually looking for factual experiences which comprehend the kind of ideas that are adaptable to the problems of many different companies. The compilers of this book were fortunate to be able to tap the large reservoir of ideas that are found in the back issues of the "Printers' Ink Publications."

Originally it was planned to divide the various ideas into subjects, each subject to be the heading of a chapter. It was soon found, however, that even the simplest ideas had a number of different applications or were compounded of several different merchandising or advertising ideas. Therefore, the conventional type of index was wholly inadequate to give a picture of the book's contents.

Consequently an index was prepared according to the specific problems touched upon by the contents. This index is designed to make this book a practical desk reference book, a miniature encyclopedia, if you will, of merchandising ideas. Thus there is hardly an item which is not listed under several index headings.

In using this volume we hope that the average reader will at least give it a more than superficial general reading. This will give him an idea of its contents and the possibilities of the book as a help to him in his daily work.

His next use of the book depends entirely upon the problems that he faces in his daily work. Suppose he wants to add a new fillip of interest to his company's plan of educating retailers. If he will refer to the index heading "Retailer—Education" he will find twelve references to twelve specific plans. Perhaps he, is thinking of a new sampling plan. By referring to the "Sampling" index heading he will find fifteen citations.

It is not our belief that most readers will adopt any idea in the whole cloth. It is hoped, rather, that the reading of how various problems have been solved will suggest methods by which the individual reader can solve his own problem by adapting rather than adopting ideas.

Each item has been made concise because it was our desire to get as many items as possible in the book. We believe that it in a general way covers pretty nearly the whole range of merchandising and advertising. As such we hope that it will be useful for many years to come.

Perhaps a word is needed here as to timeliness. Although the material is made up almost entirely of plans that have been put into effect since the depression, most of these plans are basically timeless in that they are as good today or tomorrow as they were yesterday. As a matter of fact, some of these ideas have been operating successfully in various forms for several decades. Therefore, this book is designed to be used for steady reference and not merely for the solution of one problem or other.

It is appropriate to remark that selling is selling and advertising is advertising—regardless of the commodity or the size of the company making or selling it. The tried-and-true fundamentals known and practiced by good merchandisers are basic. There is nothing essentially new; the newness can come only or mainly in methods of application.

Likewise the principle or the method employed by a big merchandiser is based upon the same fundamentals, the same framework, as are used by the small company.

Hence the businessman who is hunting for something new would be doing better for himself if he would try to make the best possible use of existing fundamentals that have proved themselves time and again.

Finally, it is our hope that the book itself will make interesting enough reading, with its fascinating stories of successful solutions to business problems, to reward the reader who may have no immediate use for it in his business.

The utmost credit, of course, is due to the management of the "Printers' Ink Publications," who have so liberally opened their files. It hardly seems necessary to say that this book would not have been possible without the initiative and inventiveness which are characteristic of American business. To the many business-men who have contributed freely of their ideas we wish to express our deep gratitude. Without their hearty cooperation this book would not have been possible.

Carroll B. Larrabee
Henry William Marks

Flourishing, by Kikuo Yamaguchi,

537 Daicho Ashikaga-shu, Japan, stiff cardboard cover, 32 pages, 6 x 8½ in.

An interesting collection of skillful flourishes, well printed on highly glazed paper. The flourishes show a masterful control of the pen, and a good sense of balance. The designs are distinctive, though they have been influenced by the pen flourishes made by American penmen. Rapid strides have been made in pen work in Japan as this book testifies.

Grapho-Analysis, published by the

American Institute of Grapho-Analysis, Inc., Kansas City, Mo., M. N. Bunker, Pres. Consists of ten pamphlets each containing 48 pages bound in cardboard.

This work on Grapho-Analysis is published in lesson form containing 20 lessons in 10 booklets.

The author, in a clear way, tries to show, by scales and examples, how the various conclusions are reached. Many examples of handwriting from people of various traits of character are shown.

Consideration is given to forgery identification, which the author states "in a purely mechanical sense is based on exactly the same variations of strokes as the character determination".

"Grapho-Analysis does not depend for its existence on the formation of letters. It takes such formations into consideration, but apart from the completed letter the parts of the letter are given an individual value when standing alone. In a mathematical way these individual strokes or parts with their independent values are considered in their relation one to the other, following out a new plan of study and presentation."

How to File and Index, by Bertha

M. Weeks, Director Chicago Bureau of Filing and Indexing. Formerly Director of the Standard School of Filing and Indexing of the Globe-Wernicke Company, St. Louis and Chicago. Published by The Ronald Press Company, New York, N. Y. Cloth cover, 261 pages.

Here is the practical filing book that will help you solve in detail the special filing problems and requirements of your business.

Are you following the most efficient routine for preparing papers for your files? Have you the best possible follow-up system? Would separated alphabetic and geographic files or an independent subject matter file give better service in your particular type of business? Do your individual needs call for a central or departmental filing system? HOW TO FILE AND INDEX will answer these questions and many more.

Miss Weeks, filing consultant to many large companies, covers the entire subject of filing from general principles to specific details as they apply to your business. Advertising agencies, hospitals, lawyers, engineers, accountants, and architects will find this an unusual and invaluable book. Special chapters discussing filing problems peculiar to their professions alone are an outstanding feature.

This book will give you an up-to-date filing system guaranteeing greater accuracy, quicker filing, faster finding, and space economy. It will help you to choose the most efficient equipment and the most competent personnel for your filing department. It will show you how to analyze and reduce filing costs. Everything from installing a complete filing system and keeping it running smoothly to filing a newspaper clipping is covered in detail. Numerous illustrations and examples explain clearly how to most easily reorganize or simplify a filing system.

The most efficient filing system saves you trouble, time, money, and space every day in the year. HOW TO FILE AND INDEX can give it to you. It works out in complete detail those changes which you have wanted to make. Follow this book and you will have no filing trouble.

MEMORIAL RESOLUTIONS
Adopted by the Board of Directors
OF THE

Columbian National Life Insurance Company.

At a meeting
held in Boston, Massachusetts
on October the eighteenth, nineteen thirty-five.

Henry A. Wyman

whose death occurred on September 26, 1935, was long an active and valued member of the Board of Directors of this Company.

Born in Skowhegan, Maine, February 3, 1861, the son of a noted country lawyer, he came to Boston after graduation from high school at the age of fourteen and started work in a wholesale house, and saved enough money to enter the Boston University Law School, graduating cum laude in 1885.

He became Assistant Attorney General in 1887 and Assistant United States District Attorney in 1891. In 1893 he started private practice and became prominent in the practice of the law relating to trusteeships and receiverships.

In 1919 Governor Calvin Coolidge appointed him Attorney General and at the time of the police strike, under his advice, Governor Coolidge made the famous statement "There is no right to strike against the public safety by anyone, anywhere, any time."

Mr. Wyman became a Director of The Columbian National Life Insurance Company on November 10, 1916 and had served the Company both as a Director and as a member of the Executive and Finance Committees continuously except during the period of his service as Attorney General up to the time of his death. He was ready and willing to give from his busy life all the time the officers asked of him, and his wisdom and good judgment were of inestimable benefit to the Company.

By this memorial, the Directors record their appreciation of his character, his abilities, and the accomplishments of his useful life, express their deep sorrow at his loss, and extend to his widow and family their sincere sympathy. It is ordered that this memorial be spread upon the records of the Board of Directors and that an engrossed copy thereof be sent to the bereaved family.

LEFT-HANDED CLUB

auful
aukward
countenance
counterfeit
disguise
disinfectant
disobedience
dispense
disburse
dispensary
exceptionally
exclusively
executed
intolerable
judicial
mysterious
pronunciation
propaganda
rhyme
rumor
soluble
sophomore

A spelling lesson by Helen Zidel a student in the public schools of Latrobe, Pa. Miss Laura B. Shallenberger supervisor of handwriting.

Mrs. Earline G. Thompson, teacher of handwriting in the Herronville School, Oklahoma City, Oklahoma has organized a Left-Handed Club in her school with a membership of twenty-seven. Each Monday afternoon a meeting is held. This consists of extra practice and some social activities. Its purpose is to create a psychological atmosphere to eliminate inferiority complexes in left-handed children. This idea is not only unique but it strikes us as being very practical. It is estimated that about 5 per cent of the pupils on the average are left-handed and there is no doubt but that this minority group is somewhat handicapped, and sometimes neglected during the regular lesson. We trust that the publication of this photograph may lead to the organization of many left-handed groups in various schools of America.

LETTERING BY WILLIAM G. MASER · STUDENT OF ARTHUR P. MYERS BALTIMORE

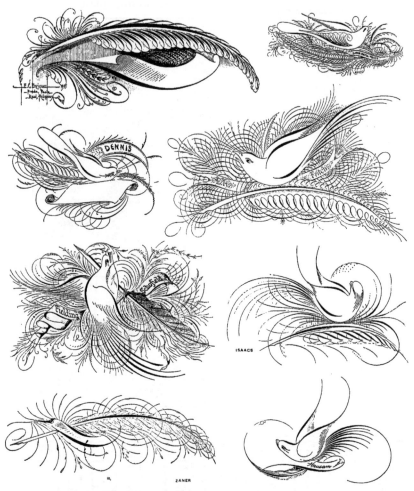

Eight of the masterpieces which appear in Mr. D. L. Stoddard's book, "Gems".
Mr. E. C. Enriquez is one of the finest penmen in the Philippine Islands, in fact, one of the finest living flourishers of today.
Dennis was recognized by many as one of the best flourishers of all times.
Fielding Schofield was one of the early fine flourishers. His work was very systematic.
Zaner was considered "The Prince of Flourishers."
Ames published a book on flourishing.
Fritch's work was very accurate and well balanced.
Isaacs was one of the pioneers in penmanship.
Hausam is still living and has enjoyed a long successful career.
All of the penmen whose work appears above have passed on with the exception of Mr. Hausam and Mr. Enriquez.

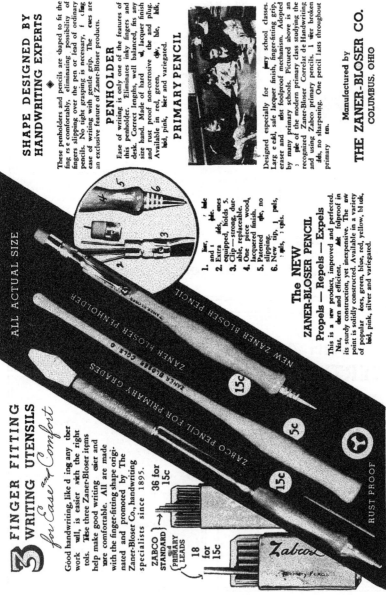

Lightning Source UK Ltd.
Milton Keynes UK
UKHW021143100119
335177UK00006B/473/P